WILD IN THE WILLAMETTE

Wild in the Willamette

EXPLORING THE MID-VALLEY'S PARKS, TRAILS, AND NATURAL AREAS

Edited by Lorraine Anderson
with Abby Phillips Metzger

OREGON STATE UNIVERSITY PRESS • CORVALLIS

Willamette River Basin map by Robert and Laura Peckyno. All other maps by Monica Drost.

Credits for drawings and writing borrowed from other sources and reproduced with permission in this book appear on page 301.

Every effort has been made to assure the accuracy of the information in this book, but changes inevitably occur over time. Corrections and updates are welcome and can be sent to info@greenbeltlandtrust.org.

All proceeds from the sale of this book will be donated to Greenbelt Land Trust.

The paper in this book meets the guidelines for permanence and durability of the Committee on Production Guidelines for Book Longevity of the Council on Library Resources and the minimum requirements of the American National Standard for Permanence of Paper for Printed Library Materials Z39.48-1984.

Cataloging-in-Publication data is available from the Library of Congress.

ISBN 978-0-87071-780-2 (original trade pbk. : alk. paper)

© 2015 Oregon State University Press

Printed in the United States of America

Oregon State University Press
121 The Valley Library
Corvallis OR 97331-4501
541-737-3166 • fax 541-737-3170
www.osupress.oregonstate.edu

Contents

Foreword: The Blessed Truth – KATHLEEN DEAN MOORE xi

How to Use This Book xiii

Welcome to Our Valley – C. A. ACHTERMAN, MD xix

A SENSE OF PLACE 1

Watersheds of the Mid-Willamette Valley – DAVID ECKERT 3

Looking Back and Ahead: Protecting the Valley's Natural Treasures –
    MICHAEL POPE 6

Story Mapping – ABBY PHILLIPS METZGER 9

Reinhabiting the Valley: A Field Guide to Being Here – CHARLES GOODRICH . . 13

Vision Begins: On Dixon Creek – JOHN R. CAMPBELL 18

PADDLING THE MID-WILLAMETTE RIVER 23

Connecting with Your Great Oregon River – TRAVIS WILLIAMS 25

McCartney Park to Peoria County Park 28

Peoria County Park to Michael's Landing 30

Michael's Landing to Bryant Park 31

Takena Landing to Buena Vista Park 31

Buena Vista Park to Independence Riverview Park 32

Independence Riverview Park to Keizer Rapids Park 32

Keizer Rapids Park to Wheatland Boat Ramp 34

Grand Island Access to Rogers Landing 35

MARYS RIVER WATERSHED 37

Imagining the Marys – LEE ANNA SHERMAN 39

Marys Peak 44

    Meadow Edge Loop Trail 46

    East Ridge Trail 47

    North Ridge Trail 48

Fitton Green Natural Area 49

Allen Throop Loop 50

Cardwell Hill Right-of-Way Trail 50

Bald Hill Natural Area and Bald Hill Farm 51

Mulkey Creek Trail. 53

Bald Hill Summit Loop 54

McDonald Forest 56

Homestead Loop 57

Dan's Trail to Dimple Hill. 59

Soap Creek Valley to McCulloch Peak Loop 60

Old Growth Trail and Quarry Loop. 61

Section 36 Loop / Powder House Trail 62

Jackson-Frazier Wetland 66

Willamette Park / Kendall Natural Area. 68

William L. Finley National Wildlife Refuge. 70

Mill Hill Loop. 71

Woodpecker Loop 72

Snag Boat Bend Unit, William L. Finley National Wildlife Refuge. 74

Biking the Marys Watershed 76

Biking McDonald Forest. 76

Philomath to Bellfountain County Park. 77

Paddling the Marys River. 79

CALAPOOIA RIVER WATERSHED 81

The Beginnings of the Kalapuya People – ESTHER STUTZMAN. 84

City of Albany Trails 86

Simpson Park Trail. 87

Talking Water Gardens 88

Takena Landing Trail 89

Thompson's Mills State Heritage Site. 91

McKercher County Park. 93

Tidbits Mountain Trail 94

Biking the Calapooia Watershed 96

River Valley Loop from Albany 96

Brownsville to Peoria Loop via Thompson's Mills. 97

Paddling the Calapooia River 99

McClun County Wayside to McKercher County Park. 100

McKercher County Park to Brownsville. 101

LUCKIAMUTE RIVER WATERSHED 103

Fort Hoskins Historic Park 106

Beazell Memorial Forest 108

Paul M. Dunn Forest. 110

E. E. Wilson Wildlife Area 113

Luckiamute Landing State Natural Area 116

Biking the Luckiamute Watershed 119

Corvallis to the Buena Vista Ferry. 119

Paddling the Luckiamute River 121

SOUTH SANTIAM RIVER WATERSHED 125

Salmon on the Santiam – HENRY HUGHES. 128

Cheadle Lake Park 134

Waterloo County Park 138

McDowell Creek Falls County Park. 140

Crabtree Lake Trail, Crabtree Valley. 142

Yellowbottom Recreation Site and Rhododendron Trail 145

River Bend County Park. 147

Cascadia State Park 149

Trout Creek to Rooster Rock, Menagerie Wilderness. 152

Chimney Peak Trail to the Middle Santiam River 154

Santiam Wagon Road, Mountain House to House Rock. 157

Biking the South Santiam Watershed. 159

Lebanon to Roaring River County Park. 159

Paddling the South Santiam River 160

Sweet Home to Waterloo Park 161

NORTH SANTIAM RIVER WATERSHED 163

The North Santiam Microcosm – JAMIE WYANT 166

The Fight for Opal Creek – CAROL SAVONEN 170

Opal Creek – JOHN DANIEL. 175

Kingston Prairie Preserve 177

John Neal Memorial County Park. 180

Shellburg Falls Recreation Area 182

Opal Creek Wilderness and Scenic Recreation Area 185

Opal Pool Loop. 187

Henline Falls Trail 188

Little North Santiam Trail 189

North Santiam State Recreation Area 191
Niagara County Park 192
South Breitenbush Gorge Trail 194
Stahlman Point Trail 197
Duffy Lake Trail, Mount Jefferson Wilderness 198
Biking the North Santiam Watershed 201
    Covered Bridge Loop from Stayton 201
Paddling the North Santiam River 202
    Packsaddle Park to Fishermen's Bend 203
    Fishermen's Bend to Mehama 204

MIDDLE WILLAMETTE WATERSHED 207
Birds of the Mid-Willamette Valley – DON BOUCHER and LISA MILLBANK 211
Ankeny National Wildlife Refuge 215
Willamette River Trail, Independence 218
Baskett Slough National Wildlife Refuge 220
Minto-Brown Island Park 223
Keizer Rapids Park 226
Willamette Mission State Park 228
Champoeg State Heritage Area 231
Biking the Middle Willamette Watershed 233
    Independence to Ankeny National Wildlife Refuge 233

YAMHILL RIVER WATERSHED 235
Following the Kalapuya Shadow Trails – LAURA McMASTERS 238
Niagara and Pheasant Creek Falls 242
Fort Yamhill State Heritage Area 244
Mill Creek County Parks 246
Deer Creek County Park 248
Erratic Rock State Natural Site 250
Miller Woods 252
South Yamhill Trail, Kiwanis Marine and Joe Dancer Parks 254
Biking the Yamhill Watershed 255
    Farmland Loop from Amity 255
Paddling the Yamhill River and Its Tributaries 256

PUDDING RIVER WATERSHED 259

Silver Falls State Park. 262

    Trail of Ten Falls. 262

    Buck Mountain Loop. 265

Silver Creek Walk, Silverton 266

Abbey Walk, Mount Angel Abbey 268

Abiqua Falls. 270

Butte Creek Falls 273

Molalla River State Park. 275

Biking the Pudding Watershed 277

    Farmland Loop from Silverton 277

Paddling the Pudding River. 278

    Lower Pudding to the Willamette. 278

Appendix A: Best Outings. 281

Appendix B: Who to Contact 285

Appendix C: Further Resources. 289

Acknowledgments. 293

Contributors. 295

Credits 301

Index 303

"In the Northwest we are never far from the lilt and swirl of living water. Whether to fish or swim or paddle, or only to stand and gaze, to glance as we cross a bridge, all of us are drawn to rivers, all of us happily submit to their spell. We need their familiar mystery. We need their fluent lives intermingling with our own."

John Daniel, from "A Place in the Rivered Land," *The Far Corner*

Foreword: The Blessed Truth

The Willamette Valley astonished us when we moved here three decades ago with our newborn daughter. Who could have imagined the abundance of rivers, each flowing through its own wildness? Understand: my husband and I came to Oregon from Cleveland, where we sometimes sat in a locked car at the edge of the Cuyahoga River to watch the oil slicks burn. These Oregon rivers were clean and green. They were gentle; a family could float these rivers. Float them we did, on silver mornings or golden afternoons, in inner tubes or canoes. There were islands—cobblestone islands waving with yellow poppies and heat, smelling of sweet cottonwoods and mud. A family could camp on these islands, and we did this too, beaching a canoe on an island's downstream tail and pitching a tent on a patch of sand in the willows. We tossed spinners for trout and cooked the little fish on a campfire of beaver-stick driftwood, like Huck Finn, sure that we were the luckiest people in the universe.

It wasn't just the rivers that thrilled us. It was the abundance of public land that was open to everybody, rich or poor or graduate students—refuges, parks, state forests, scenic rivers, greenbelts, tracts of national forest. Understand: where we came from, a public park was a small square of lawn with a cannon from the War of 1812, and farm ponds were posted with *No Trespassing* signs. But in these fern-tangled hills, we found we could walk in wildness for hours. We could get lost in it—lost, for example, in fog and moonlight on Marys Peak—and emerge at daybreak, scratched and grinning.

But here's the truly astonishing and blessed truth. The rivers are even cleaner and the forests even greener than they were when we first arrived. The wild riparian corridors are wilder, the rivers more at liberty to go their own ways. Most island beaches are still tracked only by geese and a beaver or two. Decades of volunteers in yellow slickers and muddy hats have cleared blackberries and planted native trees—more willows, more dogwoods, more Willamette Valley ponderosas. They have burned the prairies and restored the oak knolls. All of these places, and even the rarest and most precious of them—salmon waterfalls, rain-spangled forests, goose-graced islands, and meadowlark prairies—are free for the sharing.

And now, here is this supreme act of sharing: at the urging of dear Gail Achterman, the Willamette Valley's writers, hikers, bike riders, paddlers, conservationists, and naturalists have come together to make this book, which is an open invitation to the mid-valley's wild places. Their hope is that the people who visit these places, in person or in their imaginations, will come to love them. And loving them, the people will treat these places well and keep them from harm.

Kathleen Dean Moore
Corvallis, Oregon

How to Use This Book

This book aims to encourage residents of and visitors to the mid-Willamette Valley to get out and enjoy the vast natural treasures offered by this place. You'll find a wealth of ideas here about outings—hiking, biking, paddling—collected from more than three dozen local nature lovers. In addition, essays by some of the valley's finest writers get you thinking about larger questions regarding humans' relationship to the valley and its nonhuman life.

Wild in the Willamette is organized by watersheds. You probably usually orient yourself by cities and highways, but we invite you to orient yourself by rivers and their tributaries, a way of thinking that honors the natural contours of this place. The eight watersheds included stretch from midway between Corvallis and Eugene in the south to midway between Salem and Portland in the north and are held within the Willamette River Basin, the largest watershed in Oregon at nearly 11,500 square miles. (A companion book, *Wild in the City,* covers the northern reaches of the basin in the Portland area.)

At the heart of this book is the Willamette River, which flows from south to north to empty into the Columbia River and is the thirteenth largest river by volume in the United States. It is one of only fourteen rivers in the United States designated by the Environmental Protection Agency as an American Heritage River and is the only such river in the entire western United States. The field guide portion of this book begins with a paddle guide to the middle stretch of the river. Subsequent sections cover the watersheds of the major tributaries to this reach of the river, from south to north.

Human marks upon the land become evident to anyone who ventures off the beaten path and knows what to look for. The population of the mid-Willamette Valley is growing, and so are efforts to restore the landscape. We hope that as more people immerse themselves in nature in the valley, more people will come to care about the marks we leave.

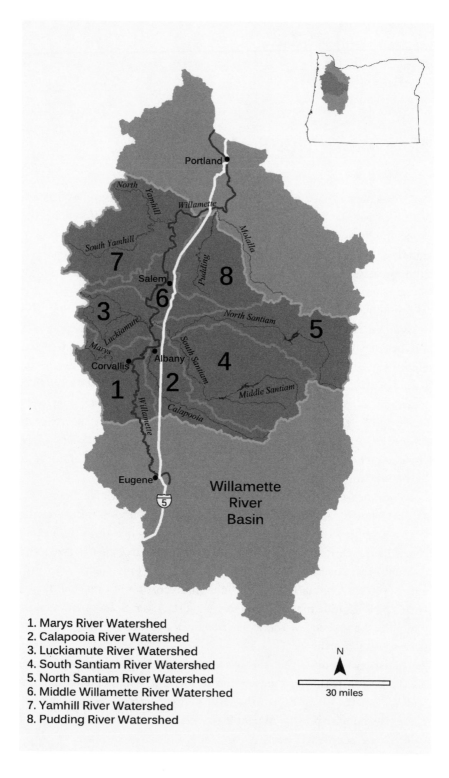

1. Marys River Watershed
2. Calapooia River Watershed
3. Luckiamute River Watershed
4. South Santiam River Watershed
5. North Santiam River Watershed
6. Middle Willamette River Watershed
7. Yamhill River Watershed
8. Pudding River Watershed

N

30 miles

The hikes in the book represent a range of difficulty levels, while most of the bike and paddle trips are accessible to beginners and advanced beginners. More advanced bicyclists and paddlers will find many resources in the mid-valley; some of them are listed in Appendix C.

ABOUT THE HIKE DESCRIPTIONS

The difficulty of each hike is rated using this scale:

- **EASY**: Generally level and short, with a smooth surface; 4 miles or less round-trip, less than 700 feet of elevation gain; suitable for families with small children and hikers looking for a less demanding outing.
- **EASY/MODERATE**: May have some ups and downs and/or a variable surface; 4 miles or less round-trip, less than 1,000 feet of elevation gain; suitable for families with active children age six and older and reasonably fit hikers.
- **MODERATE**: May have a rougher trail surface; 4–8 miles round-trip and 1,000–2,000 feet of elevation gain; generally suitable for fit adults.
- **DIFFICULT**: Significant climbs and/or challenging footing; 4–12 miles round-trip and 1,800–2,800 feet of elevation gain; suitable for very fit hikers who are looking for a good workout.

TRAIL ACCESS FOR THE ALTER-ABLED

Muddy ruts, a steep grade, or a fallen tree on a public path may pose an inconvenience for the able-bodied, but the alter-abled can be completely stymied by such obstacles. And it may be difficult for a nature lover needing a wheelchair to get accurate information about how accessible a trail really is. That friendly stick-figure-in-wheelchair icon is not always a reliable guide. The path may be wide, but is the surface so bumpy that it will rattle your teeth? The asphalt is in good shape, but would that hill require Hercules to push a manual chair up and also to prevent a racing descent?

See the "Best for the Alter-Abled" list in Appendix A for several outing ideas. In addition, the website at wheelchairwild.com documents some good places for alter-abled people to enjoy the outdoors. A wheelchair user describes assets as well as pitfalls of each place for people with varied mobility abilities and equipment. The site aims to include a range of information for people who can walk only short distances before needing a bench and for those using walkers, electric scooters, manual wheelchairs, and power chairs.

ABOUT THE BIKE RIDE DESCRIPTIONS

Round-trip mileage and total ascent are given for each bike ride. In general, bicycling 10 to 20 miles in two to three hours is within reach for beginners, and 21 to 30 miles in two to four hours for advanced beginners. Wear a helmet, carry water, and take rest stops off the road at 10-mile intervals. Warn other riders and drivers by using arm signals for left and right turns. Carry an extra tube, a tire pump, and tools for changing flats and minor repairs.

ABOUT THE PADDLE TRIP DESCRIPTIONS

Used in descriptions of paddle trips on the Willamette River, RM means river mile, indicating the number of miles upstream of the river's confluence with the Columbia River in Portland. The skill level of paddle trips is rated using this scale:

- **BEGINNING (CLASS 1)**: Moving water with a few riffles and small waves; few or no obstructions.
- **BEGINNING/INTERMEDIATE (CLASS 2)**: Easy rapids with waves up to 3 feet high and wide, clear channels that are obvious without scouting; some maneuvering required.
- **INTERMEDIATE (CLASS 3)**: Rapids with high, irregular waves often capable of swamping an open canoe; narrow passages that often require complex maneuvering; may require scouting from shore.
- **ADVANCED (CLASS 4)**: Long, difficult rapids with constricted passages, large waves, big holes, unpredictable currents, and dangerous obstructions requiring precise maneuvering to get through or around.
- **EXPERT (CLASS 5)**: Continuous, violent rapids with highly constricted passages and obstructions that pose significant hazard to life in the event of a mistake in maneuvering.

Paddle trip seasons are rated using these classifications:
- **YEAR-ROUND**: There is adequate water all year for boating.
- **RAINY SEASON**: Runnable levels are reached after several days of rain. Many of the rivers in western Oregon are in this group, with a season from about October to April.
- **DRY SEASON**: Runnable during the months from May through September.

The maps in this book are not intended for river navigation, and although more detailed maps can point you in the right direction, keep in mind that

SUSTAINABLE TRAVEL TO NATURAL AREAS

You've probably heard the old hiking adage "Take nothing but pictures; leave nothing but footprints." But what about the carbon footprints we blaze to and from the trail? Here are three options that can help you shrink yours:

Whether you explore the outdoors for relaxation, admiration, or fitness, you may find walking, running, or cycling to the trailhead a great way to extend the trek. You might discover scenic back roads and peaceful multiuse paths that connect your neighborhood to nearby recreation sites. Check with your municipality's parks or transportation offices for bike and pedestrian maps.

For longer day trips, carpooling is a great way to reduce your environmental impact and meet others with similar interests. Outdoors organizations like the Sierra Club arrange regular hikes, some of which include carpooling to and from the trailhead. DriveLessConnect.com is a centralized tool to find carpoolers throughout your region.

For farther or longer excursions, several shuttle, bus, and rail options can get you around, through, and beyond the Willamette Valley. After your hike, let someone else do the driving so you can relax, reflect, and arrange the next adventure. Search on Transit-Google Maps for assistance in finding mass transit lines and making connections between systems.

river conditions and routes can vary from season to season. It's always a good idea to scout take-outs and as much of the run as you can beforehand from the road. You can check river flows at the US Geological Survey website (waterdata.usgs.gov/or/nwis/rt) and at local and regional websites, some of which are listed in Appendix C.

Here are some other safety tips:

- *Always* wear a life jacket. No exceptions.
- Regardless of the length of your trip, always carry water.
- Take along sunscreen and a change of clothes in case of an unplanned swim or a freak summer rainstorm.
- Remember that rivers are ever changing and you are the one responsible for your safety. Always keep a watchful eye downstream and be on the lookout for hazards—such as logjams—not marked on the map.
- Watch out for strainers and sweepers—large woody obstructions such as tree roots or branches that are stationary in the current—and avoid

them at all costs. These can occur in the middle of the river (strainers) or sticking out from a bank (sweepers). If you make contact with them, they can stop you and your boat and hold you in place while the river sweeps past, which can be a deadly situation.

KEY TO MAP ICONS

 parking

 trailhead

 hand launch

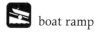 boat ramp

●●●●●●●●● trails and bike routes

▬▬▬▬▬▬▬▬ paved walkways

▲ summit

◮ campground

Welcome to Our Valley

Most Oregonians live in the Willamette Valley, but we have a limited knowledge of the place and the river that is its heart. This book is an attempt to connect residents of the mid-Willamette Valley in a new way to the place where we live. Through these chapters we hope you will learn more about this home of ours and begin a journey to know it better and explore it further.

This project grew out of the idea that in order to move into the future of our valley without destroying it, we need a basic understanding of what it is, how it works, and the ways in which humans have interacted with the landscape for millennia. When my sister, Gail Achterman, retired from her post as director of the Institute for Natural Resources at Oregon State University, she embarked on a new mission. In her journal she wrote, "I am pursuing two different but related callings: (1) deeply learn the Willamette Valley landscape, and (2) develop a practical action strategy for restoring the Willamette and a coalition to support it." She went on to state that political action will require compelling stories that can only come from an immersion in the landscape. Traveling the land slowly will allow connection to the place and to the people needed to build the coalition. As you read the chapters and visit the valley and its river in all of its variety, Gail would wish for you a similar calling.

Gail and I grew up in Oregon. Our father, who was raised in Eugene, developed a strong connection to this place and shared it with us. As young children we visited Celilo and saw the fishermen at the falls. We went dipnetting for smelt on the Sandy River in the evening when the runs were coming in. We hiked the trails around Champoeg State Heritage Area and learned its history. Our maternal grandmother, a graduate of Oregon Agricultural College (now OSU), told us stories of canoeing the Willamette and climbing Mount Hood as a young woman. She also took us to Abiqua Creek, where we learned to fish for crayfish with pieces of hot dog on a string and prepare them over a small open fire so we could eat them right there. When we were older we ventured to the Little North Fork of the Santiam and dared one another to jump from big rocks into the clear, cold water. Camping at Big Lake on Santiam Pass before there was much of a road and spending many weekends at Hoodoo Ski Bowl when it still had a wood frame chairlift were also part of our early years.

Gail delivered a speech to the Bright Lights Forum in April 2011 in which she began to publicly outline a conservation and development vision for the Willamette Valley. She cited demographic trends and asked how we thought we could deal with a greatly expanded population. She suggested that the *Willamette River Basin Atlas,* edited by David Hulse, Stan Gregory, and Joan Baker, provided an important body of data upon which we could build our plans. She also mentioned the public visioning process that preceded the mandating of statewide land-use planning by the Oregon legislature in the 1970s. She concluded with the idea that in order to continue to have the kind of place we love, we will need to make some fundamental changes.

She summarized by asking us to think about the following:

How are we going to save what we treasure with five million people living in the Willamette Valley by 2050?
How can we break through the inertia of habit to get people to pay attention to water and land use?
Is it possible to preserve what we love and the places that give our lives meaning?

She went on to quote a statement Governor Tom McCall made in 1972:

Today the future of the valley is in question. Will the valley fall prey to a now-familiar pattern of uncoordinated growth and urban sprawl, or can its people, working in a community, build a different future? Can they articulate their own ideas for the valley through a more responsive network of government? Can so vast a geographic area coordinate its growth under the common will of the people?

This book was envisioned by Gail as a teaching vehicle. She had started to work with the people who have now brought it to fruition, but her journey was cut short by pancreatic cancer in January 2012. She would want you to let these chapters tell you the river's story and show you how to get out and see the valley and its river. If you use this book as she intended, you will hike the trails, ride the back roads, float the streams, and then join the discussion about our Willamette Valley, think about its future, and take steps to make that future a reality. That is what Gail was trying to get us all to undertake.

C. A. Achterman, MD

A SENSE OF PLACE

Watersheds of the Mid-Willamette Valley
DAVID ECKERT

Searching for the highest source of Oak Creek in McDonald Forest, we stumbled up the streambed near McCulloch Peak. What we found deeply affected my perception of that watershed. Stuck in the mud near the peak on a steep slope in an alder grove valley was a small twig, dripping clear water from its protruding tip. Within a few feet, those drips magically combined into a tiny bubbling stream. What pure joy to find the pristine genesis of Oak Creek, my neighborhood stream!

Every neighborhood stream belongs to a watershed, defined as an area of land that sheds or drains rainwater runoff downhill to a specific low point, generally a tributary outlet to a larger river or a lake. Watershed drainage from both surface and groundwater carries the microscopic residue of everything it touches. Rocks, soil, live or dead plants and animals, microbes, fungi, herbicides, insecticides, fertilizers, roadway hydrocarbons, tire rubber, litter, and tens of thousands of human-made chemicals combine into a unique watershed soup flowing down the stream. As that water flows out of the watershed, it expresses the sum of the watershed's physical, chemical, biological, and cultural activity, a story embracing the region's heart and soul. And each time you enter a watershed, you become part of that story.

This book focuses on the major watersheds of the mid-Willamette Valley. Although each watershed is unique, watersheds have a number of features in common, including headwaters, outfall, ridges, and contours. Larger watersheds have many headwaters, such as springs and seeps. Oak Creek, a 13-square-mile watershed, has more than 125 ground-fed sources as its headwaters. The Willamette River watershed has many thousands of sources. Seeking these headwaters is a pilgrimage.

Watersheds drain to a single lowest-elevation outfall, generally into a larger stream or river. The Oak Creek watershed drains via Oak Creek into the Marys River. Watersheds have peripheral ridges that may be thousands of feet higher than the lowest point in the watershed. The highest ridges are often at the greatest distance from the outfall point. Ridges dividing watersheds in the lowlands are often imperceptible. Watershed contours—which result from a combination of earthquakes, erosion, and the significant ecological impacts of flora and fauna (especially humans)—drain water from the ridges toward the outfall. It is in this middle area between peripheral ridges and outfall where most watershed activity occurs.

Larger Willamette Basin watersheds depend on greater rainfall at higher elevations. Rain infiltrates during the rainy months and continues to be released into streams during dry months. The highest peak in the Oak Creek watershed averages 70 inches of rainfall annually, while the valley averages 40 inches. Changes in runoff patterns from climate change or human activity near ridgelines can impact lowland soil moisture during dry seasons.

Small watersheds nest within larger watersheds. Runoff from small watersheds can have a big effect on larger watersheds. Pollution, erosion, or flooding on any of its 125 small headwater tributary watersheds can impact Oak Creek; problems on Oak Creek can impact the Marys River; and problems on the Marys River can impact the Willamette River. So clear-cutting on McCulloch Peak impacts the Willamette River.

Three main forces of change affect watersheds: geological, climatic, and ecological. The peripheral ridges of the Willamette Valley rose from tectonic movements. The west-slope drainages are underlain by older geological formations of a sedimentary origin, whereas the east-slope drainages are commonly of a volcanic origin. This volcanic rock allows water to infiltrate deep into fissures rather than quickly running off downhill. Climatic changes have reshaped the valley as well. More than thirteen thousand years ago, large temperature swings created and melted huge ice dams on the Columbia River, resulting in multiple stages of biblically proportioned Missoula floods in the Willamette Valley. The valley floor was deeply scoured, and thick layers of rich sediment were deposited on top.

Since then, Willamette Valley watersheds have experienced major ecological changes, primarily from human intervention. In just the last two hundred years, humans have significantly altered the physical, chemical, and biological elements of every Willamette Valley watershed. In the early 1800s, European settlers killed off the beaver, resulting in significant loss of wetlands and wet prairie and the initiation of simplistic lowland stream channelization. Settlers stripped upland forests, resulting in immediate loss of the rich, thick forest topsoil by erosion. Farmers tilled under rich savanna soils, resulting in the loss of bottomland soils by erosion. Rainwater that had infiltrated into the formerly rich soil now quickly drained from the newly exposed hard clay. Landowners dug channels to drain marshlands to keep farms from flooding. Channels quickly incised to deep gorges that kept the streams from flooding and dropping rich sediment onto the surrounding land.

Stabilization measures and paving also changed the face of watersheds. Mills, dams, sluices, bridges, and stone abutments changed otherwise flexible streams into rigid pathways. Water drained faster and incised the channels more quickly. The lowland channels of Oak Creek were already 6 feet deep more than a hundred years ago. As human population grew in the 1900s, buildings, pavement, and storm drains reduced rainwater infiltration and increased the volume and velocity of runoff. That runoff also carried higher pollution levels to streams.

Legislation has also had an ecological impact on watersheds. The Clean Water Act (1972) and the Safe Drinking Water Act (1974) tasked the federal government with regulating the quality of our nation's waters. While the regulations have failed to meet the expected goals, legislation has reversed the downward spiral of our watersheds. Along Oak Creek, a dam has been removed, creek-side trees planted, litter removed, pollution reduced, and stream-bank land preserved as a direct result of legislation.

Now, when I hike in the Oak Creek watershed, I imagine that twig, dripping its clean drops of water—the genesis of Oak Creek—and I think about the stories that water could tell. As you explore the mid-Willamette Valley watersheds praised in this book, listen to the water's stories—stories that may grab your heart and your soul.

Note: David has posted "Oak Creek in Corvallis—Journey of an Ancient Stream" on YouTube (youtube.com/watch?v=oGofWeBIWBo).

Looking Back and Ahead
Protecting the Valley's Natural Treasures
MICHAEL POPE

In the autumn of 1987, Becca and I packed a U-Haul truck to the brim with household furniture, attached a trailer carrying our elderly Toyota Tercel to the back end, filled our Mazda pickup with plants, bicycles, and whatever else was left from our two-bedroom apartment, and headed south down I-5 from Seattle. I drove the truck with my nine-month-old son next to me in the cab. Becca drove the Mazda with our German shepherd and white Persian cat sitting next to her. We were going to Oregon to live in the Willamette Valley.

Throughout its history, the Willamette Valley has been a rich repository of natural resources created by volcanic flows and massive prehistoric floods. Ribbons of dark soil found in deeply incised banks along the Willamette River describe a violent Pleistocene epoch during which, after the repeated collapse of the ice dams containing Lake Missoula in Montana, enormous waves of water rolled into the Willamette Basin, depositing layer after layer of topsoil and clay scoured from the Washington Palouse. Spring snowmelt from the high Cascade meadows that flowed into the Santiam, McKenzie, and Middle Fork tributaries of the Willamette River plus seasonal rains in the Coast Range sometimes exceeding 200 inches a year fed periodic winter and spring floods and deposited alluvial soils in valley floodplains.

Humans have left footprints in the Willamette Valley for ten to twelve thousand years. Near the end of the Pleistocene, they may have hunted giant bison, mammoths, and giant sloths in the valley bottom grasslands along the Willamette River. Prehistoric humans in the Willamette Valley intensively managed their natural world. The Kalapuya people, as a matter of continuous stewardship, ignited local fires to maintain favorite foods such as tarweed, camas, biscuitroot, and yampah. They also burned prairies in late spring and fall to create lush meadows of succulent grasses—which today bear names such as blue wildrye, Roemer's fescue, and Lemmon's needle-grass—for elk and deer. In 1826 the great Scottish botanist-explorer David Douglas traveled for fifteen days through the Willamette Valley on his way to the Umpqua River and complained that there was "not a single blade of grass except on the margins of rivulets to be seen" because all was burned.

In the mid-1800s, the rich valley soils attracted farmers from Kentucky, Missouri, and other southeastern states. They arrived in the valley, built rough cabins, planted grains and vegetables in river-bottom soils, and grazed cattle, sheep, and goats in the upland grass-covered prairies and savannas. Coming from farming communities in the Southeast that clearly understood the impacts of floods, they built dikes and dams, installed revetments, diverted channels, and filled sloughs to restrain and control the wildness of the basin's rivers. Small communities such as the German settlement of Orleans across the Willamette River from Corvallis erupted along the banks and were occasionally swept away by floods. The steady stream of migrants increased exponentially beginning in the early 1900s, and large river cities including Portland, Salem, Corvallis, and Eugene collected along key reaches.

Today the vast prairies that early settlers and explorers described as oceans filled with waves of blue camas are mostly gone. Upland grass savannas with huge legacy oaks that were adult trees when Lewis and Clark paddled down the Columbia River are greatly diminished. The Willamette River's tributaries are constrained by numerous dams that regulate flows and keep the river from fully interacting with its broad floodplains. With abundant water, fertile soils, and a mild climate, the Willamette Valley is a destination for many who admire Oregon's unique streak of independence, ecological diversity, and plentiful farms. The valley holds 70 percent of Oregon's population, with an expected increase of 40 percent by 2050.

Since our fall migration to Oregon in 1987, we have mostly lived a few blocks from the Willamette River in Corvallis. Like many urban areas, and particularly river communities in Oregon, Corvallis has grown and sprawled. It has spread way beyond the lines originally platted by Joseph Avery in 1851 when Benton County's population barely exceeded eight hundred residents. The valley is a dramatically different landscape from what it was in the days of David Douglas and Joseph Avery. However, this biologically diverse and rich ecoregion retains many relics of its vast natural resource legacy. I can still walk under the huge limbs of three-hundred-year-old Oregon white oaks and encounter fields of purple camas in the spring. The Willamette River occasionally still expresses its remarkable exuberance, as in 1996 when it flowed into many of those historic remnant side channels and floodplains during a February flood.

Beginning with the conservation ethic of Governor Tom McCall and many others during the 1960s, a dynamic movement to protect the remaining natural resource heritage emerged in the Willamette Valley. The urgency of implementing these protections has increased given the expected future of many more people migrating to this region. Nearly 98 percent of all land in the valley is privately owned, so the task of protecting this remnant legacy is an intimidating one. It will require a unique confluence of partnerships between local and state governments, nonprofits, and private landowners.

The partnership work has already begun. From 2003 to 2013, nearly 4,000 acres of Willamette River floodplains were placed in permanent protections through the remarkable efforts of nonprofit land trusts, state and federal funding agencies such as the Bonneville Power Administration and the Oregon Watershed Enhancement Board, and foundations like the Meyer Memorial Trust. Watershed councils in many subbasins of the Willamette Valley are deeply engaged with landowners in their communities to plant ash, cottonwood, and valley pine along stream banks and to install in-stream fish passage devices. Local governments are creating and actively restoring natural areas. The future of the Willamette Valley's natural treasures is deeply intertwined with the ability to connect people to the land and the recognition that farming, conservation, and residential development can co-exist and be mutually beneficial.

The Kalapuya burned the prairies because they knew that fire was restorative and sustained prairies and savannas that offered a possibility of future foods and fiber for the tribe. They worked to create resources for the future health and well-being of their people. Similarly, the challenge for us today is to be the great forecasters of the future of our valley and work to create a natural resource legacy that we can leave for the people who will be living along our rivers and in our uplands. The cottonwood, oak, and ash saplings that Greenbelt Land Trust volunteers plant this winter in the wet clay river-bottom soils of the Willamette River should be towering forests by 2050 when many more people reside in this fertile valley. I would like the lands we protect and restore today to provide quiet back-channel sloughs with pond turtles sunning themselves on downed logs, open prairies graced by singing meadowlarks, and majestic white oak trees for Oregonians who inhabit our valley in 2050 and beyond.

Story Mapping
ABBY PHILLIPS METZGER

"The universe is made of stories, not of atoms," says poet Muriel Rukeyser. If she is right, then stories form complex narrative compounds that build our bones and skin, combining in odd and wondrous ways as we grow. Around campfires and dinner tables, between two friends, and in the tight circles of teenagers, people share the essence of their lives—the communion of experience fundamental to our existence.

Stories of the land fascinate me because they reveal the intricate tangle between humans and the places they live, the topography of both earth and storyteller. I wonder what tales rest in the soft mud by the Willamette's banks, what bits of narrative would waft up like molecules if I pressed my palms into the wet stones of a gravel bar. What does the Willamette River look like in story form, a great tome written by thousands of people, told over thousands of years?

One Kalapuya story tells of a man who lay down in an alder grove and "dreamed his farthest dream." He dreamed of his lands taken over by white men: "The white men came," the prophecy reads, " . . . and we knew we would enter their dream of the earth plowed black forever."

The Kalapuya prophecy was right. The white man came, and Oregon's story changed. There were unforeseen consequences of the earth plowed "black forever," stories of pollution, chemicals, dried up back channels, and fields stripped of their rich soil. It's easy to vilify the farmer, but there are also stories about those trying to put it back, and those who see domestication as an advancement and sacred responsibility.

Despite the common narrative of landowners exploiting the river, I searched out people invested in the river's health because I wanted to learn how the Willamette used to look, how it changed over the years, and how it might look in the future. Taken together, tales of our landscapes are like moving maps, shifting through time and showing us the world in its past, present, and possible forms. What follows is the story of one landowner among many who is helping to restore the Willamette's complexity. I share it in hopes that it helps redraw a map of the river, a place deeper than our current experiences can take us.

The surname Kenagy—an altered spelling of Swiss German *Gnaegi* or *Gnagy*—denotes someone who lives in or by his fields as opposed to in a village. Peter Kenagy honors his family name well. In his fields, which include a mile of riverfront land, he's grown native seed, a mix of vegetables, wheat, grass, and forest buffers to improve streamside vegetation. He's won awards for his innovative approach to improving soil quality, and sustainable agriculture groups have given him the nod for his early adoption of cover crops and strip tilling.

His father's family acquired the first 50 acres in the early 1930s and grew pole beans, filberts, and gooseberries. Over the years, the Kenagys added to their acreage. An area with looming fir trees originally owned by a man named Sloper fell into his family's hands, and thankfully so. Sloper had dreams of turning his property into a motorcycle racetrack or even an airstrip. Another piece of land with sloughs running across it used to be owned by the Nebergall Meat Packing Company. The company changed hands a couple times, then the Kenagys acquired the land in 1985.

Peter is calm and quiet in speech but restless in his movements. He gets up from the chair to look at something, then suggests we move into his garage. Then he sits down and stands up again—to look at geese in his field, to fetch an aerial photograph of his land, or to show me pictures. I suspect this is why he has been able to manage his land so well—he has the right level of energy for a daunting task.

We take a tour of his farm, and Peter details field by field how he got the land, his plan for it, and what he's growing. It's a lot of land for one person to keep track of. I keep having to re-affirm I know what he is talking about: "You mean the 50 acres your dad first acquired, right?" Throughout his property, Peter has planted trees—firs and cottonwoods along one of his sloughs, which had been cleared for firewood by a previous owner. The slough may not look like much, but Peter says a fish biologist surveyed juvenile chinook salmon in it. Peter would like to replace a small culvert with tide gates to allow high water to flow out unimpeded but retain continuous flow. This would improve fish habitat, Peter hopes. "Can you think of anything better than to have [chinook salmon] restored?" he asks, still-faced and unblinking.

Peter has also done a lot of restoration work down by the river, an area that had been heavily grazed by cattle. I sit on the back of a Honda four-wheeler as he shows me the work he's done over the years. We crisscross through black walnuts, ash, cottonwoods, through snowberry and Oregon grape. He shows me the invasives he battles too—not just blackberry and reed canary grass, but common tansy, false brome, and wild carrot. To him, invasive species are the biggest impediment to river restoration. He's also worried that agencies don't have the funds or a plan to manage all the lands acquired for restoration. "The reality is we as a society don't have the capacity to do all the restoration work that people think we need to do. We're putting the cart before the horse in some cases," he says.

The following week, Peter invites me to join two friends and him on a motorboat ride to see the Willamette's high flows. I am delighted at the chance, since I never float the river in the dead of winter with so much rain. We put in at Hyak Park near Albany and zip up and down the brown waters of the Willamette.

We pull into Frazier Slough, venture around Truax Island, stoop between willows and twigs to check the backwaters. We go down the Little Willamette and explore Bowers Rock State Park by foot. Trudging over wet blackberries with mean thorns, I follow behind these three men. They are looking for something, but what? Somehow, I can't keep up with the names and places they are talking about. The old Berger place. The abandoned gravel pit. Horseshoe Lake.

From the thick undergrowth, a small meadow yawns open. This clearing is the place they were looking for, I find out. Somehow, the meadow has no blackberries or big fir trees on it. Somehow, it has stayed open all these years. Has it ever been farmed? If no one is managing it, why is it not overgrown with trees and invasive shrubs? Was this once a gravel bar when the river flowed through here? Could it be untouched from indigenous burning practices? Could we have found a place preserved in the amber of time?

Without reaching a conclusion about the meadow, we slog back through the underbrush and back to the boat. The three men talk about who used to own what land, and when and why certain families left. They talk about fishing and exploring old sloughs that are now filled up with silt. It must be hard to see the places you once explored as a child disappear.

I strain to hear what they are saying, but many of their words are swallowed by the noise of motor and wind. I want to lean in and listen, but somehow it feels like eavesdropping on three friends. It doesn't feel right to learn the stories from a simple telling, to rob the men of a thing they earned through years of watching and running the river. Part of me wonders if some stories of a wilder Willamette will get lost like that—muffled by a cold wind, silenced by time, plugged up by silt, sealed shut by forgetting, until the stories lapse into the dim recesses of a thing long gone. Or will the stories keep rising up, under stones, in the brush, in the fields, and in the winter waters resting in a slough, like atoms sifting into the air?

Reinhabiting the Valley
A Field Guide to Being Here
CHARLES GOODRICH

Though I've only lived here in the neighborhood thirty-some years—
shorter than the life span of your average carp—I would like to say a word
in favor of making a long-term commitment to one's place. I want to speak
up for digging in, for putting down roots, for learning to alertly inhabit the
land. Wendell Berry says the commitment to place is a kind of marriage,
making a vow of allegiance to the land and its creatures. Gary Snyder calls
it *reinhabitation*, learning to live and think as if we are indigenous.

Reinhabitation means knowing, and caring about, our neighbors, human
and other-than-human. It means being aware of where our food, water, and
weather come from, and where our waste and refuse go. It might involve
plugging into any sort of community self-sufficiency. Gardening, carpen-
try, habitat restoration work. Homemade music, hand-dipped candles, the
venerable gift economy of potlucks. And it's not just hand-and-heart stuff.
There's intellectual labor to be done, figuring out how an ecologically aware
politics can forge alliances across regions, nations, and ethnic groups. Or
bringing the best scientific research to bear on our daunting environmental
problems, especially now that global warming has begun to hammer us
all. Reinhabitation makes daily life into a kind of no-fuss, every-moment-
counts spiritual practice, because paying attention creates empathy. If we
see more clearly what's going on in nature, we'll find ourselves caring more
and working harder to take care of our place.

One of the best ways to practice reinhabitation is to step outside our
doors, peer up at the sky, look around at the buildings, the trees, the pavement, sniff the air for stray fragrances, and start walking. Whether around
the block or across the country, taking a walk is an opportunity to fully
sense that we are not just *on* the planet but wholly within the embrace of
earthly ecology, breathing the locally sourced and recycled air, thinking

big thoughts and testing them against present experience, all the while scanning the ever-changing landscape, eavesdropping on the conversations of chickadees, feeling the earth rise under our feet to meet every stride.

So how about joining me now on a two-mile walk around my neighborhood?

1. GATHER AT THE RIVER

Let's meet at the Crystal Lake boat ramp parking lot. You'll see the Willamette River coursing past, wonderfully inviting to gaze at. Turn your back on it. Because that's what we did for our first century and a half here. We treated it as a roadway at best and a sewer at worst and seldom regarded its beauty or its bounty.

We'll come back at the end of our walk and face up to the river.

2. ASPHALT, POTLATCH

While we're standing here on the asphalt, let us recall that we are guests in the land of the native people, the Kalapuya, who had a potlatch ground near the confluence with the Marys River. They were decimated by our diseases, but plenty of Kalapuya people still live around here. Our gratitude to them for taking care of this place for so many centuries.

Okay, let's head down the trail.

3. YOUNG PONDEROSA PINE

The City of Corvallis bought this 120 acres of former farmland in 1995 because it needed more baseball and soccer fields. Some of us citizens and neighbors took part in the planning process and convinced the city to plant two-thirds of the land back to native trees: Oregon white oaks, bigleaf maple, black cottonwoods.

Note especially the ponderosa pine, a species more commonly associated with the drier east side of the Cascades. This subspecies, the valley ponderosa pine, was almost all harvested by earlier settlers. Only a few remained, but they now are being widely propagated. I planted this particular tree myself. It looks happy here, doesn't it? Give it another hundred years and its cinnamon-orange bark will be exquisitely beautiful.

4. BROKEN-TOPPED FIRS

In 1826 the Scottish botanist David Douglas prospected through the Willamette Valley, searching for new plant species to send back to England. He complained to his journal that all the extensive grasslands had been

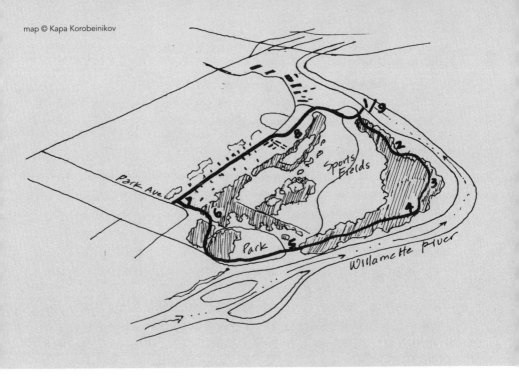

map © Kapa Korobeinikov

recently burned by the Kalapuya, a landscaping they performed every autumn to renew the grasses for the deer and elk that they hunted, and to make it easier for them to gather acorns and tarweed seeds. There was hardly a mouthful of grass for his horse, and he wasn't very happy about it. But he got on fairly well with the Kalapuya. They thought his obsession with collecting plants was a bit odd, but he didn't seem scornful or threatening, like so many other newcomers.

The Douglas-fir, *Pseudotsuga menziesii*, still carries his name. Tall, strong, straight-grained, and fast growing, Doug firs have fueled our woodstoves and our regional economy for more than a century. Look across the soccer fields: that's the cemetery up there on the bluff, bordered with craggy old broken-topped firs. It looks like a Chinese landscape painting, doesn't it? I want to be an old snag like that someday.

5. FLOODS AND VOLCANOES

These little ponds beside the trail are borrow pits from past gravel quarrying. Much of the concrete for our roads and buildings is made of stones dug up from old riverbeds. The rocks here are mostly volcanic basalt from lava that got slathered all over this part of the continent in eons past. And will again.

A lot of the deep soils of the valley were dumped here by immense floods at the end of the last ice age, just ten or twelve thousand years ago. It's pretty good soil for farming and gardening.

Eruptions and floods have given us some good stuff to work with here. I need to remember those stupendous catastrophes as the future gets rocky.

6. TASTING THE WILD

Time for a snack. Here, try a leaf of wood sorrel. It has a tart, lemony tang. Other plants we could sample along our way include miner's lettuce, chickweed, wild fennel, several wild and feral mints, maybe a few thimbleberries or salmonberries. In August the place will abound with ripe blackberries.

Eating the gifts of the land imports the material substance of the place into our bodies. Our muscles are made of local molecules.

It should also remind us to practice reciprocity. We could return the gift of wild foods with some words of gratitude, or by planting a tree, or by spreading some compost. (If anyone needs to take a leak in the bushes, that would suffice.) I sometimes whistle a little tune for whomever may be listening.

7. VEGETABLES AND ETHICS

This is the street where I live. You'll notice lots of small orchards and big gardens, plenty of chickens and ducks. And a lot of tall fences: the neighborhood deer population is on the rise. The deer are very beautiful and indiscriminately voracious. Or, no, that's not true: they discriminate in favor of roses, green beans, fruit trees, all the good stuff.

Other critters with whom we begrudgingly share our apples and cherries, our lettuce and broccoli, blueberries and rhubarb, peonies and petunias, include: skunks, raccoons, moles, bats, scrub jays, robins, screech owls, hummingbirds, yellow jackets, bumblebees, mosquitoes, garter snakes, box elder beetles, and gopher snakes. Our vegetable affluence brings more complicated relationships with our animal neighbors. Luckily, ethical dilemmas, no less than meat and potatoes, are the staff of life.

8. MARBLE ORCHARD

Here we are at Crystal Lake Cemetery. A pretty place. I always slow down, walking through here. Remembering the dead is good for whatever ails me.

The graves go back to pioneer times. Lots of kids buried here. Plenty of soldiers. A few African Americans. In the fall it's a good place to find shaggy mane mushrooms. If you look over the bluff, that's Crystal Lake, a muddy old slough of the river, named by some real estate shark, probably.

9. BACK TO THE RIVER

Okay, we've circled back to the river. Let's go down to the boat ramp and stick our toes in the water. This is the river Siddhartha sat beside, the one Heraclitus couldn't step into twice. It's the river at the center of all life.

Nah, it's just the Willamette. Eleventh longest river in the United States. Less polluted than it was forty years ago, but you still wouldn't want to drink it. Although you do, if you live here. We get a big share of our drinking water from it. Has to be treated, of course. Then we flush it down our toilets and send it off to Portland. Thank you, river of life.

Reinhabitation can be a dangerous practice because as we begin to see our place more clearly, we'll care more about it. We may experience a wider range of emotions: fear for the future in the face of global warming, anger about the industrial exploitation of our lands and rivers, or guilt over our own complicity in an economic system that doesn't know how to say "enough." But it's also sure to increase our chances of experiencing upstart wonder at the waddling progress of a newt, or a sighing delight at the first bite of a backyard tomato, or charged excitement at the swirling excesses of approaching storm clouds. And we might find ourselves energized by the fresh tenderness we feel toward the larger family we hadn't realized we were part of.

In one week this summer I met three people who were traveling around the Northwest looking for a place to resettle, from Arizona, Colorado, and New Mexico. Each of them described themselves as a "climate refugee." As climate change inundates coastal areas, parches more western landscapes to desert, tears up the country with storms, fires, floods, and droughts, the Willamette Valley is going to see a lot of in-migration. As a man who likes his solitude, who loves hiking and camping in relatively unpeopled landscapes, I expect that influx of humans is going to hurt. As a man who understands that that hurt is a function of my love for this place, I plan to do everything I can to welcome newcomers and share my love and lore with as many as I'm able.

I'll ask everyone I meet: Shall we try to make this place beautiful and abundant for a thousand years?

I'll say: In early spring, you can pick young stinging nettles here. They are delicious steamed, sprinkled with a little vinegar.

Vision Begins
On Dixon Creek
JOHN R. CAMPBELL

I'm standing on a pedestrian bridge over Dixon Creek, at Arthur Avenue in Corvallis, just steps from my front door. It's a fine September day under scattered clouds. The hawthorns are laden with berries. The blackberries are dry and mealy on their canes. Willows hint at autumn with a yellow tinge. Elm bark, black, is marvelously textured, riddled with woodpecker gouges. Below, the water is coppery green, feathering around a few basalt rocks. The creek bed is silty clay, marked only with a smattering of algae and some broken blue glass.

A simple scene. Ordinary. Certainly familiar to me, as I've stood here often in the six years I've lived on the creek. But I'm learning the quiet joy that such attendance can bring. After years of traveling to wild locales, seeking, in distance, an intimacy with nature, these days I find myself closer to home. I walk the streets of Corvallis as if I were experiencing wilderness, with that same quality of attention.

Here the old categories of wilderness and everyday experience begin to dissolve. Wild birds thrive in the urban riparian corridor. Warblers, wrens, chickadees, nuthatches, crows, jays, and grosbeaks move through. A mallard glides cautiously on the channelized water. A secretive green heron sweeps in. A Cooper's hawk plucks a sparrow from our feeder. A barred owl visits, hunting rodents and sleeping by day in the big sugar maple.

Among these fresh presences, categories can't hold. The creek reminds me to begin again, right where I am. After a lifetime spent learning how to see, I find myself tracing vision to its origins. What do I require? An instruction manual (*Vision for Beginners*)? Field glasses? A global positioning system? A field guide to the invisible?

Here's what I know.

1. VISION BEGINS IN THE UNSEEN

Zoom in. Microscopic scale. A menagerie of fanciful shapes in the water. A child's drawing come to life. Single-celled dots, or strands, of bacteria. Protozoa rimmed with hairlike pseudopodia. Wheel-like rotifers, transparent, with feathery appendages. Various worms, and bryozoa with their crowns of tentacles. Water fleas. Mites. And water bears, lumbering on their eight stumpy feet.

Zoom out a bit, to the macroinvertebrate scale. Mayfly larvae frequent the slower water, their flattened bodies keeping them from sinking into the muck. In the faster sections, caddis flies have assembled little houses to fix them against the current. There they extend a silky net to snare passing food. On the stream bottom, dragonfly naiads have burrowed up to their eyes, waiting for prey to come within reach.

At this scale, I'm privy to an intimacy. Yet I can't, from my ordinary perspective, actually see these wonders at all. They're down there, all right, but not readily accessible. (Of course I can always get out the rubber boots, the magnifying lens, the sampling jar, and the microscope.) But whether or not their images are immediate, these unseen organisms allow for the seen—allow dragonflies, crayfish, turtles, trout. They allow the seen either as larval forms or as food. They root my vision in the depths of invisibility, given only my awareness and some cursory knowledge.

Further, I've heard rumors of another stream flowing below the creek bed, where underground waters exchange nutrients and organisms with the visible water. Groundwater: another form of invisibility underlying— literally—the visible.

And there is no escaping it—I also witness invisibility in the form of absence. Where, I wonder, are the snails, the native crayfish, the freshwater clams on my stretch of Dixon Creek? Where is the woody debris, or the gravel on the creek bed? Where are the eddies, the quiet backwaters? Where are the salmon that, I'm told, spawned here back in the '60s? Or the legions of ducks that the neighborhood elders describe? As I straddle this altered and diminished stream, my vision begins to blur.

2. VISION HAS A HISTORY. A NATURAL HISTORY, AND A HUMAN HISTORY AS WELL

Dixon Creek originates in the hills of northwest Corvallis. Three main tributaries flow southeast and join just south of Walnut Boulevard. The creek, now mostly channelized, flows through town before draining into the Willamette River at the sewage treatment facility.

Seeking origins, I visit the creek's headwaters. But to trace Dixon Creek to some of its several springs requires maneuvering through streets of ritzy McMansions. There, on a weekday afternoon, the streets are empty of people. Deer stand around on the sidewalks, and a sign informs me that a corporation owns the remnant woods ("All rights reserved"). So following Dixon Creek to its beginnings means encountering the old suburban dream, wherein nature meets, and acquiesces to, human comfort and status.

I walk. Just off a sidewalk through a stream corridor, in among the formidable homes, I find the spot. Springs emit from nondescript banks amid the sound of hammers and power saws. Suddenly I'm fully in the grip of my own personal history: raised in the suburbs of Chicago, I left the Midwest as a young adult to seek western wildness. Now here I am, again wandering this staid American Dream. Again I seek the wildness it surely contains.

But let's go further back. Before European settlement, before the eradication of the beaver, Dixon Creek was more a series of wetlands than a well-defined stream. After settlement, farmers drained their fields and created a curvilinear creek. By the 1940s, Dixon Creek was a ribbon, abutted by farm fields, winding down to the Willamette River. Even in town, there were discernible open spaces fringing the creek. By the 1960s, as development increased, the creek was crowded and channelized. It was wrenched from a little bend in what is now my backyard and put right, made straight.

Now, here in town, the banks are either denuded or dense with invasive plants. Everywhere blackberry canes mantle over the water. Images of diminishment abound. At the same time, willows are planted to slow erosion. Community groups gather to help heal the creek. Schoolchildren study it. A poet or two might even sing its praises. Their songs are not elegies, for the creek is still among us.

3. VISION OBLITERATES BOUNDARIES AND SO OPENS TO THE WORLD

Sometimes I remove my glasses—I'm quite nearsighted—just for the sensation of blurring the world. (And then, putting them back on, the delight of delineation!)

I'm told that the blind, in those rare cases when they are provided sight surgically, must still *learn* to see. At first, they perceive blurs and patches of color. It's only when they learn categories, apply labels to the world, that they see edges and limits clearly, just like everyone else.

A SENSE OF PLACE

So underlying our habituated sight is a more homogenous vision. There's something to be said for that original perception. In such a vision, nature is received as a whole rather than an assemblage of types.

What we say, we see. And vice versa. We say "wild" and "domestic." We say "urban" and "rural." We say "nature" and "culture." We identify difference; we name species; we delineate terrains. These distinctions are necessary to us, and yet in maintaining them, we may lose sight of the essential fact that nature encompasses them all.

The altered creek alters the observer. Perhaps diminished nature diminishes those who experience it. And yet the creek enacts, in its impartial passage through wild patches and industrialized zones alike, our own longing for passage, for conduits, for connections and continuity.

The creek enacts, as well, the inevitability of change. It illustrates degradation, yes, but it also allows for our submerged memory of salmon, which will, one day, resurface in the form of actual fish.

Honestly, some days the creek appears to me as nothing more than a drainage ditch. And yet, what is that stirring at the bend where my line of sight vanishes, there at the border between the mundane and the mysterious? The creek quickens my vision. It creates pockets of intelligence—I mean contact and communication with the world.

These pockets are illuminations against an oil-stained backdrop. They are graceful figures where one expects only grids and right angles. They are tiny insights into a world so vast as to astound us. They intimate a day when we'll walk the streets of our ordinary towns amazed and dumbfounded at last.

PADDLING THE MID-WILLAMETTE RIVER

Since the earliest times, people have come to the Willamette River to fish and to paddle. Today there is a new wave of recreation along the river, from people fishing the riffles between Eugene and Corvallis to canoeists, drift boaters, and kayakers pitching their colorful tents along the shoreline. The heart of the Willamette River, the stretch from McCartney Park in Linn County downstream to Yamhill County, is replete with opportunities for paddling and exploring. You can find floodplain natural areas, rustic campsites, and bald eagles, osprey, kingfishers, river otters, beavers, deer, bobcats, coyotes, shorebirds, migratory songbirds, and even an elk or two along its length.

During much of the year the river is accessible to paddlers who have solid paddling basics, as well as those more advanced. This is not to say the river does not have ample hazards year-round—like any river, it truly does. At high flows, which usually occur January through March, the main stem of the river can become a brown mass of swirling water and should only be traveled by those with a significant level of experience. Eddy lines can be ferocious, and upwellings—those sudden surges of water from somewhere in the depths to the surface that result in a circular gurgling mass—can surround canoes.

The main thing to keep in mind if you're thinking of paddling the Willamette River is that it contains moving water, so it's not like paddling a lake. You should have the ability to maneuver in the current, and you should be alert to pieces of wood and other hazards. Also keep in mind the big difference between late summer flows and those of winter and spring. A trip that takes two

Osprey © M. L. Herring

hours during higher flows can take four hours during the late summer months. You can check river flows at the US Geological Survey website (waterdata. usgs.gov/or/nwis/rt) and at local and regional websites, some of which are listed in Appendix C.

Each segment of the river described here (by river mile, or RM, indicating the number of miles upstream of the river's confluence with the Columbia River in Portland) is suitable for a day trip. Two or more segments can be put together into a multiday trip. Campsites along the way are mentioned, as are side channels (channels connected to the main stem at both ends) and back channels (channels connected to the main stem at only one end). Side channels are more prone to large wood obstructions than the main stem Willamette, so if you doubt your ability to turn your boat around and head upstream, stick to the main channel. In most cases, camping along the Willamette requires you to bring everything in and take everything out—in other words, "leave no trace" camping.

LEAVE NO TRACE CAMPING

The seven principles of Leave No Trace camping, from the Leave No Trace Center for Outdoor Ethics, are as follows:

Plan ahead and prepare.
Travel and camp on durable surfaces.
Dispose of waste properly.
Leave what you find.
Minimize campfire impacts.
Respect wildlife.
Be considerate of other visitors.

Connecting with Your Great Oregon River
TRAVIS WILLIAMS

The Willamette River is a world unto itself. Just a few blocks from the busy streets of the cities and towns that dot its banks, the river swirls past, its backwaters teeming with wildlife, its side channels crisscrossed by deer, its islands thickly coated with willows and cottonwoods. Birds converse and beavers slap the surface of broad backwater pools with their tails. Shifting gravel bars create narrow channels that appear with the whims of the season, storms, and river dynamics. Giant snags bob in the water, and here and there whole black cottonwood trees have fallen into the river, where they create a rush of noise as the current pushes through the branches. Vast collections of large wood deposited by high spring currents can block entire channels. Every few years the river gets big enough to fill its historic floodplain and deposit trees in the middle of grass-seed fields.

Since 2000 I've explored the Willamette River Basin extensively, having a job that has allowed me to canoe much of the Willamette River and its tributaries during high flows and low. During my free time as well, I have made frequent trips with my children and friends along the river to explore, camp, and relax. A few years ago, one quiet spring morning as I was paddling my canoe somewhere near Peoria, I realized I could envision in detail each and every stretch of the Willamette—every bend, tributary confluence, island, quiet alcove, and backwater—from south of Eugene nearly 200 miles north to the Columbia River. In that moment, I was heartened by what this great river has and cognizant of what it still needs. While important issues remain to be addressed with regard to its health, from water quality to habitat restoration, the river can provide a top-notch natural experience for the hundreds of thousands of people who live nearby.

This riverine world of the Willamette has changed much in the last 150 years, with many of its banks hardened by riprap, its backwaters cut off from the main flow, and its channel simplified. The main story associated

ORIGIN OF THE NAME *WILLAMETTE*

While it seems no one can say for sure, the word *Willamette* probably comes from a Kalapuyan word—*Wal-lamt, Wallamet,* and *Whalamet* are just three of the spellings given in various sources. The word seems to be derived from the same root as *Walla Walla* and *Wallula,* meaning "running water." One authority gives its definition as "the long and beautiful river," another as "spillway," referring to the falls at Oregon City. In the mid-1800s there was heated debate (the "Will-Wall controversy"), reflecting social and political divisions, about whether to adopt the name *Willamette* or *Wallamet* for the river. *Willamette* was the word in favor in 1870 when Wallamet University changed its name to Willamette University, and it stuck.

with the Willamette River over the past few decades has been of the river's pollution and efforts to clean it up. Images of industrial effluents and municipal wastewater that had received the scantest of treatments being spewed into the river dominated the story for many decades. Significant improvements were made in the late 1960s and into the 1970s that resulted in a much cleaner river.

Since that time, new concerns have arisen related to pesticides, emerging contaminants (such as flame retardants), and the overall impact of runoff from the thousands of square miles of land that make up the Willamette River Basin. But a greater understanding of how the river's degraded habitat and the dams that block some of the major tributaries affect the ability of native species to survive has also taken root. Today, community-based efforts aim to restore habitat on many of the Willamette's tributaries, as well as its main stem. Projects to restore riverside vegetation, improve floodplain forests, and bring back historic channel complexity are all moving forward.

One of the final and most important pieces to enable the river to function naturally is to alter the dams on the Willamette's tributaries to allow fish passage. Willamette Riverkeeper sued the US Army Corps of Engineers in 2007 to get action on the issue. As a result, work that will enable juvenile fish to migrate downstream of the dams and adult fish to make it upstream of the dams is under way. Progress is slow, but incremental improvements are being made.

Meanwhile, the new Willamette story is about connection. With nearly 200 miles of flat and moving water, winding its way from south to north, the Willamette invites connection for those willing to take the time and make the effort. Connection can come in a short visit to your local natural area, a day paddle between Peoria and Corvallis, or a multiday trip between Corvallis and Salem.

Anchoring what can be explored along the mid-Willamette River are the public parks and natural areas of the pioneering Willamette Greenway program. Originally proposed by Governor Bob Straub and eventually created by the State of Oregon in 1972, the Greenway program started with a concept of a continuous band of parkland along both sides of the river, rivaling the long swath of the Oregon Coast and the expanse of the Oregon Cascade Range. But today, cities and agricultural lands still dominate along the Willamette, leaving sometimes razor-thin lines of cottonwoods separating the river from vast fields producing grass seed or other crops. Though the program has not reached its original goal, the Oregon Parks and Recreation Department (OPRD) manages more than 5,000 acres of parks along the Willamette as part of the Greenway program and continues its efforts to restore floodplain lands and to secure areas that are held privately through outright purchases from willing sellers or through conservation easements.

The Greenway natural areas provide ample opportunities to paddle a canoe or kayak into a secluded property to experience wildlife and to camp. In the mid-Willamette Valley, some standout properties for exploring and camping include Sam Daws Landing, Riverside Landing, Luckiamute Landing State Natural Area, American Bottom, and Tripp Island. These properties are generally quiet, attract a range of native wildlife, and are suitable for rustic camping. Typically, a Willamette Water Trail sign along the bank marks these Greenway campsites.

I remember a trip to Sam Daws Landing, a natural area about 15 miles upstream from Corvallis on both sides of the river. On the east side of the

WILLAMETTE RIVER WATER TRAIL

The Willamette River Water Trail project—established in 2005 in a cooperative effort between OPRD, Willamette Riverkeeper, and a host of partners stretching from Eugene to Portland—provides paddle access to the Willamette River and an abundance of information for the river traveler. The project has published two waterproof guides to the river—one for the upper reaches and one for the lower reaches, with the midpoint being the Buena Vista Ferry—and maintains a very detailed website at willamettewatertrail.org. The *Willamette River Recreation Guide* from OPRD (oregon.gov/osmb/library/docs/willametteriverguidepdf.pdf) is also a valuable companion to river travel.

river, the area encompasses approximately 350 acres of floodplain habitat, with another 50 or so on the west side. We explored the east side, finding a deep green expanse of willows transitioning to Oregon ash and cottonwood. Birds whisked through the underbrush as we worked our way through the property. We met a sliver of backwater with a wide muddy bank that tried to suck the sandals off our feet. In natural areas like these, I sometimes wonder if birds that are no longer found along the Willamette, like the yellow-billed cuckoo, might someday find their way back. Sam Daws is a great place to camp, with open sandy swatches between stretches of rounded river rock.

The opportunity is clear, and any time spent on the Willamette is well worth the effort. So grab that old canoe, put on your personal flotation device, stick your paddle in the water, and pull on it. Once you spend some time along the river, you will likely develop a connection to it that will last a lifetime.

McCARTNEY PARK TO PEORIA COUNTY PARK

RM 156.5 to 141 (15.5 miles). **Duration:** 5 or 6 hours. **Facilities:** Vault toilet and parking at put-in; portable toilets and parking at take-out.

McCartney Park makes a great place to start your riverine journey into the mid-Willamette Valley. As is typical of this stretch of river, the current is lively from the get-go.

Just a few miles from McCartney Park at RM 149, Norwood Island comes into view. This island, owned by Willamette Riverkeeper, has a back channel into which the Long Tom River empties. If you enter the back channel, look closely at the bottom and you may see something that looks like a large clam, the western pearlshell mussel.

Downstream from Norwood are two adjacent Greenway parks, Sam Daws Landing and Buckskin Mary Landing, between RM 146 and 145. These parks encompass a few hundred acres of Pacific willow–coated gravel bars and black cottonwood forest. Here the main channel broke through a peninsula a few years back, leaving Buckskin Mary an island. You will notice efforts to keep the west bank in place at one of the Stahlbush Island Farms properties. Take note of the backwater on the east side (river right), and the seasonal channel where during low-water months you will spot a few western pearlshell mussels.

Just downstream you will see a small, usually impassable channel on river left that traces its way around Hoacum Island. Hoacum Island

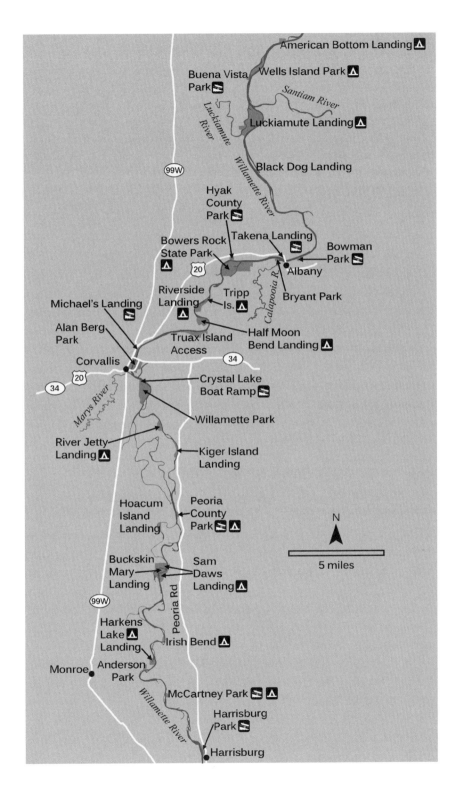

American Bottom Landing 🔺

Buena Vista Park 🚤

Wells Island Park 🔺

Santiam River

Luckiamute River

Luckiamute Landing 🔺

99W

Black Dog Landing

Willamette River

Hyak County Park 🚤

Bowers Rock State Park 🔺

Takena Landing 🚤

Bowman Park 🚤

20

Albany

Calapooia R.

Riverside Landing 🔺

Tripp Is. 🔺

Bryant Park

Michael's Landing 🚤

Alan Berg Park

Half Moon Bend Landing 🔺

Truax Island Access

Corvallis

34

20

34

Marys River

Crystal Lake Boat Ramp 🚤

Willamette Park

River Jetty Landing 🔺

Kiger Island Landing

Hoacum Island Landing

Peoria County Park 🚤🔺

N

5 miles

Buckskin Mary Landing

Sam Daws Landing 🔺

99W

Peoria Rd

Harkens Lake 🔺 Landing

Irish Bend 🔺

Monroe

Anderson Park

Willamette River

McCartney Park 🚤🔺

Harrisburg Park 🚤

Harrisburg

> **WESTERN PEARLSHELL MUSSELS**
>
> The Willamette River is home to several species of freshwater mussel; the western pearlshell and Oregon floater are the most common. Mussels stay in the same general area once mature and can be found in beds containing hundreds of individuals. The western pearlshell can live to be more than one hundred years old. More than other species, western pearlshells depend on cold, clear water, so they are a good indicator of river health over time. They also depend on native fish species, to which they attach themselves in larval form to be transported until they drop off to mature in the sediments on the river bottom.

Landing, a good-sized Greenway property, is on this channel. On river right, between RM 144 and 143, the Snagboat Bend Unit of Finley National Wildlife Refuge comes into view. Look for herons nesting in the black cottonwoods and western pond turtles sunning themselves on riverside logs along the sizeable back channel.

Just downstream of Snagboat, the channel around Hoacum Island rejoins the Willamette. As you round past a large gravel bar on river right, keep an eye out for the backwater alcove that you'll need to dart into to paddle a bit upstream to the boat ramp at Peoria County Park. A large patch of wapato can be found along the backwater leading to the ramp.

PEORIA COUNTY PARK TO MICHAEL'S LANDING

RM 141 to 131 (10 miles). **Duration:** 3 or 4 hours. **Facilities:** Portable toilets and parking at put-in; portable toilet and parking at take-out.

Once you paddle out into the main current from the backwater alcove at Peoria, you will quickly encounter, on river left, the opening to Clark Slough, which separates John Smith Island from land and is typically impassable. Shortly thereafter on river left you will see the opening to the 8-mile-long side channel that separates Kiger Island from John Smith. This channel has fast, shallow water and provides good views of local wildlife but can contain newly deposited logs and other wood.

The side channel rejoins the river at RM 134.5, where the Willamette Landing housing development is visible at river's edge. Soon the main water intake for the city of Corvallis comes into view on river left. After the river rounds a long left turn, Willamette Park comes into view, and after that the Crystal Lake Boat Ramp. Pass under the Highway 20/34 bridge and look for the take-out on river left.

MICHAEL'S LANDING TO BRYANT PARK

RM 131 to 120 (11 miles). **Duration:** 3 or 4 hours. **Facilities:** Portable toilet and parking at put-in; beach, gravel parking lot, and flush toilets at take-out.

This trip is great for newer paddlers who want to log only a few miles on relatively tranquil water, though there is current in a few places. Greenway properties on this stretch are Half Moon Bend, Riverside Landing, Tripp Island, and Bowers Rock, all of which offer rustic camping.

After about 3 miles of flat water that runs parallel to Highway 20, the river suddenly becomes quiet and the scenery opens up as you round a corner and Half Moon Bend comes into view on river left at RM 126. Soon after, Riverside Landing can be seen on river right. Just downstream of these two is Tripp Island, which has a small back channel worth investigating, though during the low-flow months you may have to jump out of your canoe or kayak and work it across a gravel bar or two. Tripp offers an abundance of agates.

The last few bucolic miles of this trip bring you past largely undeveloped Bowers Rock State Park from RM 123 to 121. Bryant Park in Albany soon comes into view on river right.

TAKENA LANDING TO BUENA VISTA PARK

RM 120 to 106.5 (13.5 miles) **Duration:** 4 or 5 hours. **Facilities:** Flush toilets and parking at put-in; vault toilet and parking at take-out.

In general, the water on this stretch is mellow, interspersed with a bit of current. Of note is Luckiamute Landing State Natural Area from RM 110 to l08 on river left, one of the largest Greenway properties along the river. Camping is available all along the gravel beach that extends for more than a mile. From late May to late October, firepits, picnic tables, and portable toilets are provided here. The Santiam River joins the Willamette

---

WAPATO

Wapato, also known as broadleaf arrowhead, is an aquatic plant native to the Willamette River. With a distinctive large arrow-shaped leaf, it can be found in backwater areas or where the current is slow. It grows up to 4 feet tall, putting up flower stalks with whorls of white three-petaled flowers in summer and dying back in winter. This species was harvested by native peoples, who used its edible tubers as a key source of carbohydrates.

---

on river right just downstream; watch the quick current here, which results in a few eddy lines and occasional pieces of wood.

Downstream you will see a large eroded bank on the left side of the river with trees perched high on top, and in the distance the Buena Vista Ferry comes into view. The boat ramp at Buena Vista Park is on river left just before the ferry landing.

BUENA VISTA PARK TO INDEPENDENCE RIVERVIEW PARK

RM 106.5 to 95.5 (11 miles). **Duration:** 3 or 4 hours. **Facilities:** Vault toilet and parking at put-in; flush toilets and parking at take-out.

This trip floats you into the hills south of Salem. As you start off, be sure to time your passage by the Buena Vista Ferry carefully and don't count on the pilot seeing you. Just downstream from the ferry, a side channel to the left goes around Wells Island Park. This channel has a quick current and wonderful scenery; if you take it, be wary of strainers—large woody obstructions that are stationary in the current—that occasionally appear.

American Bottom Landing at RM 104 is a campsite with a seasonal toilet, two picnic tables, and a fire ring. American Bottom is frequently occupied, so if you want to camp, have a backup plan, such as the Department of State Lands island just downstream at RM 103.5 or Sidney Access at RM 102 on river right (although this latter site has a steep and difficult bank). On river left, the Rogue Brewery hop farm and tasting room can be accessed from the river. Ankeny National Wildlife Refuge is on the right side of the river, so be alert for bird life.

In another few miles you'll see the bridge at Independence. After you pass under the bridge, make for the take-out on river left.

INDEPENDENCE RIVERVIEW PARK TO KEIZER RAPIDS PARK

RM 95.5 to 80 (15.5 miles). **Duration:** 5 or 6 hours. **Facilities:** Flush toilets and parking at put-in; vault toilets, parking, canoe and kayak storage rack at take-out.

This trip takes you past Salem, as well as a few riverside natural areas. Leaving Independence, the river is slow moving and bucolic, with a few gravel bars here and there to challenge your river navigation skills. At RM 89, Hayden Island, purchased for public access to honor the late Gail Achterman and acknowledge her deep interest in the Willamette River Greenway program and the river's health, has a few hundred acres

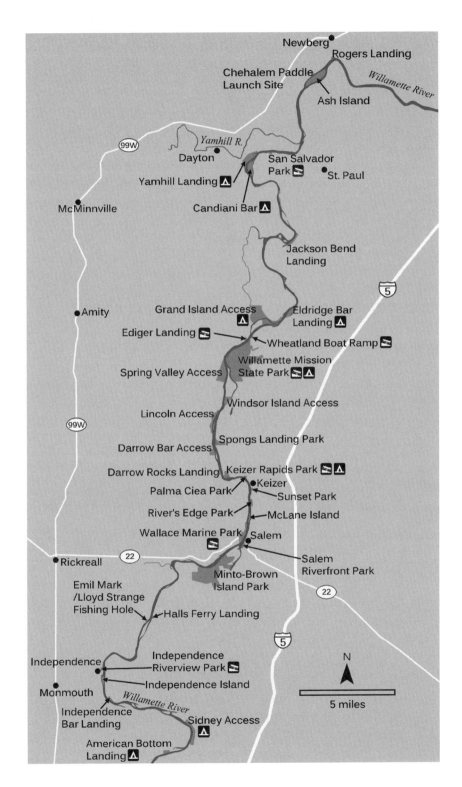

Newberg

Rogers Landing

Chehalem Paddle
Launch Site

Ash Island

Willamette River

99W

Yamhill R.

Dayton

San Salvador
Park

St. Paul

Yamhill Landing

McMinnville

Candiani Bar

Jackson Bend
Landing

5

Amity

Grand Island Access

Eldridge Bar
Landing

Ediger Landing

Wheatland Boat Ramp

Willamette Mission
State Park

Spring Valley Access

Windsor Island Access

Lincoln Access

99W

Spongs Landing Park

Darrow Bar Access

Darrow Rocks Landing

Keizer Rapids Park

Palma Ciea Park

Keizer

Sunset Park

River's Edge Park

McLane Island

Wallace Marine Park

Salem

22

Rickreall

Salem
Riverfront Park

Emil Mark
/Lloyd Strange
Fishing Hole

Minto-Brown
Island Park

22

Halls Ferry Landing

5

Independence

Independence
Riverview Park

N

Independence Island

Monmouth

Willamette River

Independence
Bar Landing

Sidney Access

5 miles

American Bottom
Landing

of floodplain forest that supports a range of native species. This makes a great campsite.

Before you reach downtown Salem, you will pass Minto-Brown Island Park between RM 86.5 and 85 on river right. In downtown Salem, a good stopping point is Wallace Marine Park at RM 84 on river left. Go downstream of the boat ramp to find a large gravel bar area that works well for canoes and kayaks. There are restrooms at the park.

As you pass Wallace Marine Park, McLane Island comes into view. It's fun to catch the current of the left channel as you pass this island; a small beach along this channel can be used for camping. You will paddle by suburban homes most of the final miles to the boat ramp on river right at Keizer Rapids Park. Just past the boat ramp is a boat-in campsite in the park.

KEIZER RAPIDS PARK TO WHEATLAND BOAT RAMP

RM 80 to RM 72 (8 miles). **Duration:** 2 or 3 hours. **Facilities:** Vault toilets, parking, canoe and kayak storage rack at put-in; vault toilets and parking for a fee at take-out.

When you get on the river at Keizer Rapids Park, you leave the suburbs of Keizer and enter a quieter, more scenic rural area. As you make your way through the riffle that gives the park its name, watch out for a couple

Dragonfly watching © Wendy C. Thompson

of sharp eddy lines on the left side of the main current. You will see a few rocks on river left, and Darrow Rocks Landing soon comes into view.

Darrow Bar is next, with a campsite at the south end of the island on the main channel side. If you take the side channel to the left of the island, watch for old pilings and make your way through them carefully. After Darrow Bar, Spongs Landing Park is on the right, and Lincoln Access on the left. There appears to be an island here, but the backwater is usually impassable.

As you pass Windsor Island you may hear the operations of Windsor Island Gravel, a fairly large operation, on river right. There is a large gravel bar in this area, so watch for the right spot to pass over it. Almost as soon as you pass this gravel bar, you will see the backwater that leads up Windsor Slough, which marks the start of Willamette Mission State Park.

As you round the bend, you will see the park's large gravel beach. At the park's north end you will pass the landings for the Wheatland Ferry; pass cautiously and don't expect the ferry pilot to see you. The take-out is soon after on river right.

If you continue on this stretch, take the side channel that travels around Wheatland Bar, an island that's more than 1.5 miles long and offers rustic camping. Extending off this side channel is Lambert Slough, a secondary side channel that weaves 10 miles through the floodplain and rejoins the Willamette at RM 65 to create Grand Island.

GRAND ISLAND ACCESS TO ROGERS LANDING

RM 70 to 51 (19 miles). **Duration:** 6 to 7 hours. **Facilities:** Portable toilet and parking at put-in; flush toilets and parking at take-out.

This northernmost rural stretch of the river weaves slowly past floodplain forests, farms, and multiple campsites. Leaving Grand Island on the back channel of Wheatland Bar, you will see a campsite on river right before you take five paddle strokes. This site offers a good view of the back channel, and at night you might see nighthawks or hear the slap of a beaver's tail somewhere up the channel.

As you head downstream, Eldridge Bar Landing immediately comes into view; this site can also be used for rustic camping. At RM 65 you will see Lambert Slough enter the main river again. Around the bend at RM 62 is Five Island. This 0.5-mile-long island has a scenic side channel with a good campsite just as you enter the channel, and a wide gravel beach on the main stem side.

In the next few miles, the river slows and becomes wider. Candiani Bar, from RM 59 to 58, is a large island with good camping on the upper end and a small side channel that can be taken at moderate flows. Keep an eye out for bald eagles in this stretch. Soon the Yamhill River comes into view on river left, emptying its sediment-rich brown waters into the Willamette's green. The open expanse after this confluence can have winds and whitecaps at times. Ash Island comes into view at RM 52. You can take the side channel by making your way through or around a series of pilings. About halfway down the channel you will encounter the Chehalem Paddle Launch, developed in 2012 as part of a community effort to create river access.

As you reach the end of Ash Island, in the distance you can see the pilings for the dock structure at Rogers Landing. Here you can take out on the dock or use the boat ramp. In summer, be prepared for significant powerboat traffic in this area, as well as people using the ramp to launch their craft.

MARYS RIVER WATERSHED

T he Marys River is perhaps best known to urban residents
of Benton County as the swirling brown watercourse they
cross when traveling Highway 99W between downtown and
south Corvallis. Locals may take a dip in the Marys at Avery Park in
Corvallis or Marys River Park in Philomath when steamy summer
weather drives them to it, but it's not really known as a swimming
river. In fact, although the river runs right through the heart of
both communities, unless it's spilling over its banks in a rare winter
flood, people often seem to forget it's there.

The watershed fans out from Marys Peak, the highest point in the
Coast Range at 4,097 feet. It drains 301 square miles on the east slope
of the range, gathering up the flow from half a dozen major subbasins
and funneling it all into the river's main stem. In the river's upper
reaches, the East and West forks come together near the tiny town
of Summit, and 40 rambling miles after that—having swallowed up
the waters of the TumTum River, Woods Creek, Rock Creek, Greasy
Creek, Oak Creek, Beaver Creek, Muddy Creek, and a thousand lesser
tributaries—a mature Marys loses itself in the powerful current of
the Willamette River in downtown Corvallis at elevation 207 feet.

The Marys River presents different aspects throughout the watershed, from leaping mountain streams to broad, sluggish meanders
down in the flats. Some two-thirds of the basin is forested, and timber
production is a major economic activity. Agriculture predominates in
the lower parts of the watershed, accounting for nearly a quarter of all
land use in the basin. Philomath pulls most of its municipal water supply from the Marys, and Corvallis fills about 30 percent of its needs
from the Rock Creek system in the upper part of the watershed.

Although 84 percent of the watershed is in private ownership,
a variety of recreational areas are open to the public. The private

McDonald Forest, owned by the OSU College of Forestry, offers public access to trails. Federal lands include Marys Peak and William L. Finley National Wildlife Refuge; Benton County parks include Fitton Green Natural Area and Jackson-Frazier Wetland; and City of Corvallis natural areas include Bald Hill and Kendall.

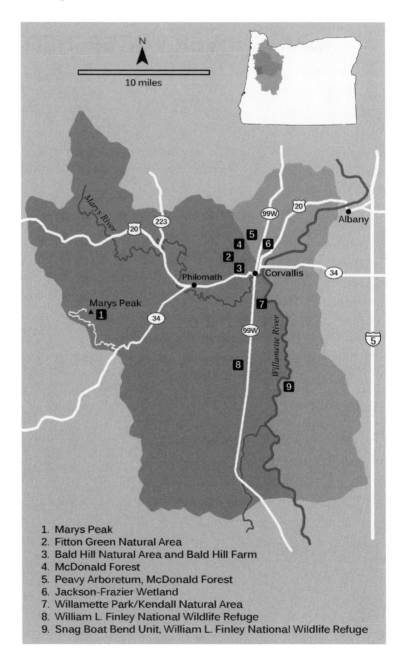

1. Marys Peak
2. Fitton Green Natural Area
3. Bald Hill Natural Area and Bald Hill Farm
4. McDonald Forest
5. Peavy Arboretum, McDonald Forest
6. Jackson-Frazier Wetland
7. Willamette Park/Kendall Natural Area
8. William L. Finley National Wildlife Refuge
9. Snag Boat Bend Unit, William L. Finley National Wildlife Refuge

Imagining the Marys

LEE ANNA SHERMAN

Its source is as murky as a *Masterpiece* mystery. Its namesake is as muddy as runoff from a flood. As it tumbles out of the Coast Range toward the Willamette, it intersects Highway 20 once, twice, three times. You see the signs as you cross each bridge: Marys River. From the car window you glance down, maybe catch a glint of watery sunlight. Only that.

I've lived in its watershed the better part of a decade, but I don't yet know this river named Marys. The main stem mostly hides, cutting through private property in heavy stands of fir. Its source is ambiguous, its namesake forgotten. The Marys seems more idea than entity, more aura than actuality, more rumor than comfy hometown waterway. Like something perceived out of the corner of an eye, the Marys exists for me just out of sight—a vibration. Or an echo.

How can you know a river?

Can you know it by its headwaters, the high, hidden place where it begins? What if that place is not a single place but a convergence, a coming together of springs and rivulets from many places? What if those headwaters have changed direction over the eons, gushing first from a mountain range 200 miles to the east, flowing westward to an Oligocene sea where the ancient whale *Aetiocetus* swam, while deep beneath, tectonic plates were diving, one under the other, heaving and pushing inland, raising the earth in folds until the land tipped and the river flowed backward?

If you ask a local expert where the headwaters are, she'll say, "Well, that depends." One expert will say the Marys begins near the hamlet of Summit in a secret place too overgrown to be seen. Another expert will say it starts on the north flank of the Coast Range's highest point, Marys Peak, where Greasy Creek and the TumTum River begin as trickles and embrace the peak as they journey downhill.

Both experts are right. "Headwaters" is a misleading idea when it comes to the Marys. When I ask Xanthippe Augerot, executive director of the Marys River Watershed Council, to sort it out for me, she apologizes for getting wonky even as she simplifies. "The upper Marys, which flows through Summit, is only one of many tributaries to the Marys River. We, as humans, have a compulsion to call one of these tributaries the main stem or origin. But in fact, the sources of the upper Marys, Greasy Creek, and the TumTum River all are headwaters of the Marys River."

The history of its naming is uncertain, too. "The story has a few holes," admits Jessica McDonald of the Greenbelt Land Trust. Make that "stories," plural. The European versions start from nineteenth-century French fur trappers calling it the Mouse River or Mice River—*Rivière des Souris*—possibly because Marys Peak was then called Mouse Mountain, "a translation of an Indian name," according to *Oregon Geographic Names*. Eventually, both the peak and the river became known as Marys. But exactly which Mary was the true namesake remains unconfirmed. The stories suggest various Marys, one the sister of a convicted murderer named Adam Wimple; another the daughter of John Lloyd, a nineteenth-century settler in Benton County; a third the Virgin Mary herself. And, of course, the First People of the watershed—the Siuslaw, the Kalapuya—bestowed names of their own, original names, generations before the first white trappers arrived in pursuit of pelts.

Can you know a river by its fact sheet, by statistics dutifully compiled to describe it in feet and miles and degrees Fahrenheit? Or by a topo map squiggled with colored lines?

A map—though two-dimensional and lacking the scents of mosses or the songs of larks—is a useful way to begin meeting a river, to see it as if from above, the way it tracks across the landscape. The Marys River watershed shows itself as the circulatory system of Benton County, a webbed network of veins bleeding from the peaks, seeping through the conifer forests, the oak savanna, the remnant prairie, nourishing the draws and valleys, feeding the wetlands. As Augerot notes, a watershed is like a tree. The main stem is the trunk, the creeks and rivulets, rills and springs branch up the hillsides, getting finer and smaller, like twigs. Like capillaries.

Can you know a river by its tributaries, the streams and creeks that join it as it gathers momentum toward the valley floor, each bearing its own story within its rocks and stoneflies and trout?

On the map, you see the Marys wend downhill, gather the waters of Woods Creek, Rock Creek, Greasy Creek, Muddy Creek—subbasins that are watersheds unto themselves. Tributaries flowing into tributaries, small watersheds flowing into big watersheds. Down it flows through the community of Wren before it angles toward the town of Philomath, makes a brief public appearance, and then heads southeast through farmlands and pastures. Finally, it picks up Muddy Creek, which meets the Marys just south of Corvallis after passing through Finley Wildlife Refuge, one of the last wintering grounds for the endangered dusky Canada goose.

Can you know a river by its confluence, the place where it pushes into a bigger river, swirling in riffles and eddies as two waters become one, where it ceases to exist as itself?

From the meeting of the Muddy and the Marys, it's a short race to the Willamette. To see the confluence, you have to go to Shawala Point on the edge of downtown Corvallis, walk under the freeway overpass, and find a little dirt path that takes you to an asphalt platform. You have to lean out and crane your neck around the underbrush to see the Marys meet the Willamette, two waters converging in churn and backwash before running seaward together. You can also see it from the footbridge just to the south of downtown.

Can you know a river by its wildlife, by the water-born and waterborne, the finned fish and the seven-gilled filter feeders, the diving birds and the bottom dwellers, the aquatic insects and the web-footed mammals? Can you know it by its people, the tribes and bands that long ago were acquainted with every bend and stone? The white settlers and farmers who raised families beside its waters, grazed cattle, grew crops, caught fish, paused to watch a pond turtle paddle or to hear a screech owl call, thanked God for this place? The concerned landowners who plant native wildflowers to save the endangered Fender's blue butterfly and then hover anxiously over their tender meadows like the parents of a newborn?

Old-timers remember when cutthroat trout as long as your forearm swam in the Marys. But after a century and a half of riverside human enterprise—roads, culverts, flumes, effluents, crops, livestock, tractors, axes, chainsaws, chemicals, clear-cuts—the cutthroat had nearly disappeared by the 1980s. Rumors of a federal endangered species listing were afoot. A listing would mean new rules and restrictions for landowners. So they banded together to head it off. That meant fixing the river. That meant scientists conducting temperature surveys and rapid bio-assessments. It meant biologists snorkeling the cold streams, counting cutthroat; volunteers planting ninebark, willow, and vine maple; backhoes hauling in conifer logs, angling them across the streams like pickup sticks to mimic blowdown; school kids wresting invasive knotweed from remnant wetlands. It meant trying to undo 150 years of alterations, to bring back the wildness, the clear, cold waters brimming with cutthroat trout and speckled dace and Oregon chub and Pacific lamprey.

River ecologist, river historian, and river guide Patricia Benner calls what's left of the long-ago Marys "the remnants of the remnants." She talks about the dam that once blocked the river's mouth, a log pond for the downed trees taken off Greasy Creek (named for the greased flume where logs rode downhill to the main stem). She talks about the floodplain, the flat places beyond the banks where, once upon a time, high flows escaped the channel, spread out and braided the river, gave refuge to fish, a place to rest and feed. "The floodplain was like an all-you-can-eat Abby's for fish—worms drowning, beetles swimming for their lives." She talks about the removal of woody debris (what Mark Twain called "the banishment of snags"), the natural detritus and blowdown that slowed the river's rampage, collected gravels, formed pools, created habitat for aquatic life but got in the way of logs rafting downriver to mills and other river traffic. She recalls the industry of beavers, their dams and ponds forming quiet waysides for cutthroat.

It was Twain, Benner tells me, who wrote about the futile efforts to "tame that lawless stream." He was talking about the Mississippi, of course. But the very same efforts to rein in rivers (to "curb or confine," to make them "obey") were happening everywhere in Twain's time. He watched his beloved Mississippi become a highway for commerce where once it had been a phenomenon of nature. But as a onetime riverboat pilot he knew that given enough time, the river would "tear down, dance over, and laugh at" human efforts to "fetter, handcuff, and boss" it.

Left alone and given enough time, the Marys will return to its wildness. But to step out of the way, to wait for nature to repair and restore, is to shrug off our complicity as invasive knotweed chokes native vegetation and Pacific lamprey larvae burrow blindly into contaminated sediments and "nuisance beavers" are relocated with traps and tracked with radio tags. So the return to wildness depends on us, the descendants of the tamers. It will happen one riparian seedling at a time. One patch of knotweed eradicated, one riffle engineered, one fish-blocking culvert removed.

"Can you go back?" Benner asks rhetorically, thinking about it for a minute. "Yeah. You can go back. But you have to allow the stream to do its natural thing. You have to allow disturbance. A tree falls, leave it. A beaver builds a dam, leave it. A flood comes, let it spill onto the floodplain. Flooding is as important to a river as fire is to a forest."

PACIFIC LAMPREY

Oregon filmmaker Jeremy Monroe calls Pacific lamprey "the lost fish" in his documentary by the same name. The jawless species—which evolved in the early Paleozoic and plied the primordial seas 250 million years before dinosaurs lumbered onto the Earth—has survived four mass extinctions and is found in the Marys River today. In the river's hidden pools, 3-to-4-inch-long lamprey larvae (nicknamed "river worms") forage invisibly in fine sediments until it's time for their metamorphosis. Then they ride the river currents to sea, expand in size five hundred times, and hitchhike on bigger fish before coming home to build their nests on the pebbly riverbed. They lay one hundred thousand eggs and leave behind carcasses that will feed raccoons, bobcats, worms, and bacteria.

The lamprey is threatened by dams on the Columbia and by the lasting effects of commercial overfishing in the mid-1900s and rotenone poisonings aimed at "nongame" fish in the 1970s and 1980s. Scientists with the Columbia Plateau tribes and Oregon State University are now monitoring lamprey numbers in the Marys in hopes that their slide to extinction can be halted.

Abruptly, she stops talking. "I had a dream about this the other night— that's so bizarre." She trails off as she sinks into her thoughts, her just-remembered dream. When she comes back, she says: "The thing is, a river is a package of many, many parts. There are just a whole lot of variables that make up a river."

Yet in the end, those variables, so infinitely tangled, can't define a river, not even if you could catalog them all. Maybe you can know a river, finally, only in your imagination. Or in your dreams.

On the highest peak in the Coast Range, this recreation area is cloaked with old-growth Douglas- and noble fir forests and graced with wildflower meadows and rock gardens.

To get there: From Corvallis, take Hwy 20/34 west through Philomath and stay on Hwy 34 for 8.9 miles past the 20/34 split. Turn right onto Marys Peak Rd. Drive 9.5 miles to reach Observation Point at the end of the road. Most of the trailheads are on this road. The trailhead for the North Ridge Trail is on Woods Creek Rd off of Hwy 20; see the trail description for directions.

Marys Peak, the highest point (at 4,097 feet) in Oregon's Coast Range, is a prominent Willamette Valley landmark west of Corvallis. The trail to the summit from the parking lot at the end of Marys Peak Road is short and relatively easy; from the summit, on a clear day, you can take in the Pacific Ocean to the west and the high peaks of the

ACTIVITIES: Hiking, camping (in the campground only), picnicking, skiing, snowshoeing, sledding, watching sunsets, stargazing; biking allowed on the North Ridge, East Ridge, and Tie Trails May 15 to October 15. **FACILITIES:** Picnic tables and restrooms at Conner's Camp, Marys Peak Campground, and Observation Point; campground (six first-come, first-served sites with no potable water, open mid-May to end of September). **FEES AND REGULATIONS:** Fee for camping. Northwest Forest Pass or day-use fee required for parking at Conner's Camp, Marys Peak Campground, and Observation Point. Dogs allowed on leash. No ATVs, ORVs, or horses allowed. **BEST MONTHS:** April through October. Expect snow at higher elevations from mid-November to April. The road to the top is not maintained for winter travel. **MANAGING AGENCY:** US Forest Service, Siuslaw Ranger District.

Cascades, from Mount Rainier far to the north to Mount McLoughlin in the south near Crater Lake, as well as Jefferson, Washington, and the Three Sisters to the east. In 1989 the Siuslaw National Forest designated 924 acres at the peak's higher elevations as the Marys Peak Scenic Botanical Special Interest Area to acknowledge its scenic, botanic, and recreational values. The almost pure noble fir forest at the summit is the largest stand of this species in the Coast Range.

For the native Kalapuya people, Marys Peak was a sacred place for spirit quests as well as for hunting and farming. When European settlers arrived in the late 1800s, they drove cattle, sheep, and goats to the peak's meadows in the summertime to forage. Since 1906, the City of Corvallis has used water from the Rock Creek watershed on the eastern side of Marys Peak to supplement its municipal water supply. The peak has also supported a fire lookout (from 1942 to the early 1960s), an Air Force radar station (from its completion in 1959 until a winter storm blew away

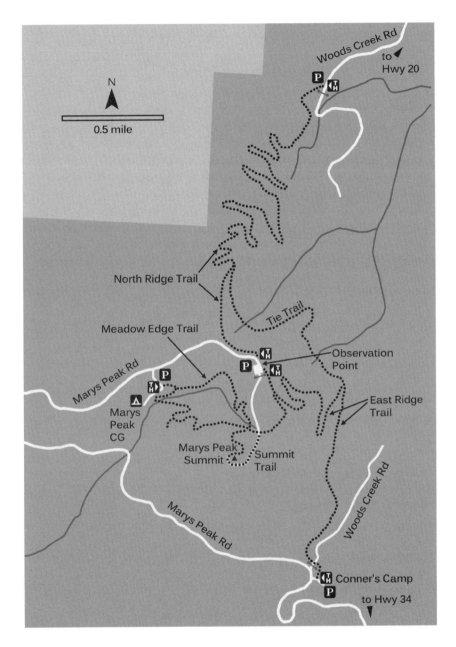

North Ridge Trail

Meadow Edge Trail

Marys Peak Rd

Marys
Peak
CG

Marys Peak
Summit

Summit
Trail

Tie Trail

Observation
Point

East Ridge
Trail

Woods Creek Rd

to ◄
Hwy 20

N

0.5 mile

Marys Peak Rd

Woods Creek Rd

Conner's Camp

to Hwy 34

the antenna shortly thereafter), and a ski tow (operated by the Helonskis Ski Club from 1942 to 1952 but abandoned because of the unpredictability of the snowpack).

Five trails provide varying degrees of challenge for hikers and bikers (though bikes are not allowed on the Meadow Edge or Summit Trails). These can be combined in various ways to satisfy everyone, from those

WILDFLOWERS OF MARYS PEAK

Bright yellow glacier lilies dot the meadows at the top of the peak in late spring just after the snow melts. Tiger lilies color the meadows orange in the summer. Oregon iris intermingles with wild strawberry. The summit rock garden contains lupine, Indian paintbrush, and spreading phlox; bleeding hearts and calypso orchids grace the moist woodlands. Botanizers love Marys Peak for its wildflowers. Determining the best time of year to plan a wildflower walk can be difficult, since the weather varies greatly from year to year and peak flowering periods can shift by a month or more. In general, though, from early May to late June is a good time to walk the trails and view early spring wildflowers. From mid to late June through July, the meadows around the top of the peak are sure to be spectacular. The book *Wildflowers of Marys Peak Meadows* by Steven Carpenter (maryspeakwildflowers.com) is a great resource for wildflower identification and timing.

looking for a simple family outing to hardcore peak baggers. Just remember that the weather atop Marys Peak can be much cooler, windier, and wetter than in the Willamette Valley, even in summer, and dress accordingly. To enjoy winter sports on Marys Peak when there's snow (not every winter), drive in as far as you can on the road or park at Conner's Camp and walk, ski, or snowshoe in by way of the road or the East Ridge Trail.

MEADOW EDGE LOOP TRAIL

A short hike from Marys Peak Campground loops through an old-growth noble fir forest and breaks into the open for views, with the option to continue to the summit.

Difficulty and length: Easy, 1.8 miles round-trip with 460 feet elevation gain; 2.3 miles round-trip with 567 feet elevation gain if you go to the summit. **To get there**: Drive 8.8 miles up Marys Peak Rd from Hwy 34 and turn right onto the Marys Peak Campground access road. Then take the left fork to the day-use parking area.

This uncrowded trail provides a wonderful half-day excursion from Corvallis, especially when coupled with a picnic on the summit. The basic loop trail forks at a kiosk 400 feet after it leaves the parking area. Interpretive brochures available at the kiosk align with numbered posts along the trail. Take the right fork and descend 0.25 mile to a bridge over Parker Creek. From here, the trail ascends by switchbacks for 0.9 mile to a junction with the Summit Trail, breaking from the forest into the open after 0.75 mile for views to the southwest (look for Grass Mountain on the left and long, flat Table Mountain on the right). At the junction kiosk, you can continue upward to the summit or loop back to the starting point.

If you continue upward, the trail leads out into the peak's upper meadow. Options from here include returning to the Meadow Edge Loop Trail the same way you came or walking down the access road to the Summit Trail crossing. In summer, descending via the access road allows for a survey of the plants in the south-facing rock garden. At the Summit Trail crossing, go left and enter the woods. Bear right at the next junction to get back to the Meadow Edge Loop Trail, and turn right onto that trail to complete the loop back to the trailhead.

Calypso orchid © Wendy C. Thompson

EAST RIDGE TRAIL

A well-trodden route from Conner's Camp to Observation Point climbs steadily through an old-growth Douglas-fir forest and finally traverses a stand of mature noble fir.

Difficulty and length: Moderate, 4.9 miles round-trip with 1,200 feet elevation gain. **To get there:** Drive 5.5 miles up Marys Peak Rd from Hwy 34 to a paved parking lot on the right.

The East Ridge Trail is a popular way to reach the peak in all seasons. Blue diamonds on the trees guide snowshoers and cross-country skiers when the trail lies under snow. In some winters it may also be a passable foot route to the summit. From the trailhead at the northwest corner of the parking lot, the trail dips into the woods and soon crosses the gated Woods Creek Road. It then steadily ascends for 2.2 miles to Observation Point.

The first mile to the Tie Trail junction passes through stands of old-growth Douglas-fir carpeted with woodland wildflowers. Bear left and continue uphill from here to stay on the East Ridge Trail instead of going straight ahead onto the Tie Trail. For the next 1.2 miles to the upper parking area, the trail is fringed with Douglas-fir, then vine maples, and finally noble fir trees. Just before the end of the East Ridge Trail, you reach a junction with the Summit Trail. Continue straight ahead on the trail to Observation Point.

Options: If the weather is good, you can take the sharp left turn onto the Summit Trail to make the 1.4-mile loop that climbs 385 feet to the summit, breaking out of the woods into the open meadows. From Observation Point, you can return on the East Ridge Trail or add another half mile by looping back by way of the North Ridge and Tie Trails.

NORTH RIDGE TRAIL

The longest and steepest but least crowded route to Observation Point climbs steadily through a Douglas-fir forest from a trailhead on Woods Creek Road.

Difficulty and length: Difficult, 8.4 miles round-trip with 2,165 feet elevation gain. **To get there:** From Corvallis, drive west on Hwy 20/34 through Philomath and stay on Hwy 20 for 1.7 miles past the 20/34 split. Turn left onto Woods Creek Rd. The paved road becomes gravel after 2 miles. From that point, continue another 5.5 miles to a gravel parking area on the left just before a gate.

Walk past the gate on the road to the marked start of the trail on the right. The trail begins climbing through the woods and does not stop its ascent until you reach the top. After you've been walking for 0.5 mile, the trail enters a series of long switchbacks that lasts for 3 miles. At the junction with the Tie Trail, where a bench has thoughtfully been provided, bear right to continue on the North Ridge Trail. The grade relents a bit and soon parallels Marys Peak Road before you reach Observation Point.

Options: If you haven't had enough climbing yet and would like an even better view, you can continue on the 1.4-mile round-trip Summit Trail, which gains 385 feet in elevation. You can make a longer loop, adding about 2 miles to your trip, by returning via the East Ridge Trail and the Tie Trail.

FITTON GREEN NATURAL AREA

This lofty park just west of Bald Hill in Corvallis affords views of the Willamette Valley, the Cascades, and the Coast Range from trails through restored oak savanna.

This 308-acre gem, open to the public since 2003, was acquired with funds provided by Charles and Elsie (maiden name Fitton) Ross, Benton County, and Greenbelt Land Trust. The rare upland prairie with oak groves and grasslands at the top of Fitton Green was used for grazing and was intensively logged before it was acquired as parkland. Ongoing restoration efforts aim to make the habitat attractive to the endangered Taylor's checkerspot butterfly. Habitat in lower areas of the park includes mixed Douglas-fir and hardwood forest and a riparian forest along the stream paralleling Cardwell Hill Drive.

ACTIVITIES: Hiking, biking, horseback riding. **FACILITIES:** Dog waste stations. No toilets. **FEES AND REGULATIONS:** No fee. Dogs allowed on leash. Allen Throop Trail closed to bikes and horses November 1 to April 15. **BEST MONTHS:** April through June, September through November; sparse shade in summer and muddy patches in winter and spring. **MANAGING AGENCY:** Benton County Natural Areas and Parks Department.

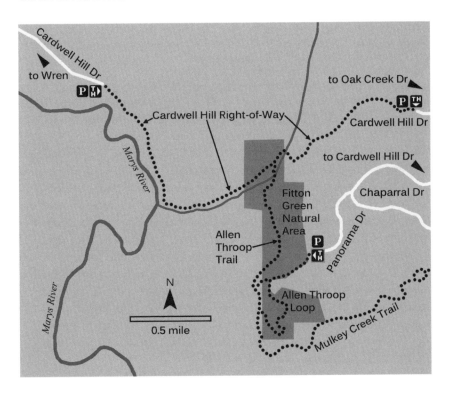

ALLEN THROOP LOOP

A pleasant trail circling the high point of Fitton Green offers expansive vistas without demanding a lot of walking uphill.

Difficulty and length: Easy, 1.3 miles round-trip with 185 feet elevation gain. **To get there:** From downtown Corvallis, take Harrison Blvd west and cross 53rd St, where the road becomes Oak Creek Dr. From the intersection, go 1.9 miles and continue straight onto Cardwell Hill Dr. Turn left onto Chinook Dr and go 0.5 mile to a T junction at the top of the hill. Turn right onto Chaparral Dr and follow the brown county park signs for 1.1 miles to the trailhead parking area on Panorama Dr.

From the kiosk, walk on a grassy road to the first junction and bear left to reach the panoramic viewpoint. The natural area is surrounded by privately owned lands, so please respect "No Trespassing" signs. A strategically placed bench lets you rest and take in the views. From here, the trail descends gently through an upland meadow and eventually connects back to the road you started on. For a longer jaunt, turn left at the signed junction to take the Allen Throop Trail downhill on a grassy road for a mile, following the Evacuation Route signs, to reach the Cardwell Hill Right-of-Way Trail.

CARDWELL HILL RIGHT-OF-WAY TRAIL

This broad up-and-down trail, which passes through Fitton Green Natural Area, follows an old roadbed along the Marys River and a tributary creek.

Difficulty and length: Moderate, 5.5 miles round-trip with 560 feet elevation gain. **To get there:** Parking lots are located at the east and west ends of the trail. East lot: From downtown Corvallis, take Harrison Blvd west and cross 53rd St, where the road becomes Oak Creek Dr. From the intersection, go 1.9 miles and continue straight onto Cardwell Hill Dr for 0.9 mile to the parking area. West lot: Take Hwy 20 west from Corvallis, go north on Hwy 223 (Kings Valley Hwy), then go east on Cardwell Hill Dr for 1.7 miles to the parking area.

Cardwell Hill Right-of-Way Trail follows a road once used to carry supplies and troops from the Willamette River waterfront in Corvallis to Fort Hoskins, along with local traffic. Although it isn't open to through traffic anymore, it's still used by local landowners, so you may encounter an occasional vehicle. Starting from the west end of the trail, the path is rolling and open with little shade. Pass through a gate at about mile 0.4 and encounter the first of a series of educational signboards about oak conservation forestry. Follow along the Marys River for a brief stretch and then wind upward through a mixed Douglas-fir and hardwood forest. At about mile 1.7, the Allen Throop Trail intersects the road. Once you reach the top of the hill, the last quarter mile is a steady downhill on loose gravel.

A unique conservation area on the far west edge of Corvallis offers trails to the summit of Bald Hill along with several miles of dirt, gravel, and paved paths.

To get there: There are three access points. From Corvallis, follow Harrison Boulevard west to 53rd St, where it becomes Oak Creek Dr. For access from the north, follow Oak Creek Dr for approximately 0.7 mile to the parking area on the left. For access from the east, turn left onto 53rd St from Harrison and then turn right into the Benton County Fairgrounds. There is unlimited parking at the west end of the fairgrounds lot; access to the natural area is by way of the Midge Cramer Path. For access from the south, turn left onto 53rd St from Harrison and turn right onto Reservoir Rd, then go 0.9 mile to the small gravel parking lot with kiosk on the right.

ACTIVITIES: Hiking, jogging, skating, dog walking, bird-watching year-round; horseback riding and biking allowed April 15 to October 31. **FACILITIES:** Restored barn (to reserve, call 541-766-6918); portable toilet and off-leash dog area near the barn. **FEES AND REGULATIONS:** No fee. Open 6:30 a.m.–10 p.m. Dogs allowed on leash, and off leash under voice control in designated area. Best months: Year-round, though paths to the summit are best walked in summer and fall to avoid mud. **MANAGING AGENCY:** Corvallis Parks and Recreation (Bald Hill Natural Area), Greenbelt Land Trust (Bald Hill Farm).

Bald Hill isn't completely bald anymore, as oaks and Douglas-firs have crept up all but the west side, but the view from the top to the south and west is still worth the hike up. The hill, once known as Old Baldy, is the centerpiece of the 284-acre Bald Hill Natural Area, encompassing a diverse mixture of fields, meadows, Douglas-fir/bigleaf maple forest, oak woodlands, and patches of remnant oak savanna. Wildflowers decorate the meadows and woods in spring; *Wildflowers of Bald Hill Meadows*

TAYLOR'S CHECKERSPOT BUTTERFLY

The orange, black, and white–checked Taylor's checkerspot butterfly is a prairie species that was once plentiful in the grasslands of the Willamette Valley, along with the Puget Sound area and south Vancouver Island. In Oregon, the species was collected or observed at fourteen different sites in the twentieth century. By October 2013, when it was listed as endangered under the federal Endangered Species Act, the butterfly had been reduced to one site in Oregon on Weyerhaeuser land near Fitton Green. The species depends on open grasslands and grassy oak woodland sites where food plants for larvae and nectar sources for adults are available.

by Steven Carpenter is a useful guidebook. A moderately level, 10-foot-wide asphalt path runs for 1.3 miles along the base of the hill and provides access to several miles of dirt and gravel foot trails that circle and climb to the summit of the hill, as well as connect to the Mulkey Creek Trail and Fitton Green Natural Area.

Public access to this very popular spot began in 1985, when the Coon family donated 60 acres and an old barn to the City of Corvallis. The newly formed Greenbelt Land Trust purchased the top of Bald Hill in 1990 and deeded 41 acres to the City of Corvallis in 1993. Greenbelt Land Trust purchased the adjacent 587-acre Bald Hill Farm in 2013. A piece of land connecting Bald Hill Farm and Fitton Green Natural Area will eventually be open to public access as well.

The Bald Hill property was actively managed with controlled burning by the Kalapuya for thousands of years. It was traversed in the early 1800s by Hudson's Bay Company fur traders and later by settlers arriving on the Oregon and Applegate Trails; the latter skirted the foothills of the Coast Range and Bald Hill. Brothers Johnson and Luke Mulkey staked out much of what is now Bald Hill Natural Area under the Donation Land Claim Act of 1850, passed by the US Congress to promote homestead settlements in the Oregon Territory, which granted 320 acres free of charge to every

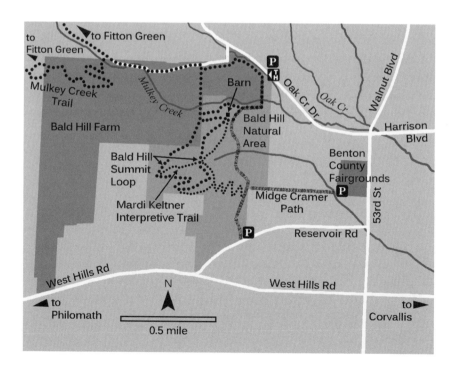

MARYS RIVER WATERSHED

POISON OAK

"Leaflets three, let it be" describes the western poison oak (*Toxico-dendron diversilobum*) that lines so many trails in the Willamette Valley and gives so many people a nasty rash. The plant, which can grow as a shrub or a woody vine, can be identified by its glossy lobed leaflets attached to the stem in groups of three. The leaves vary in size and color, from bright green in spring to yellowish-green or pinkish in summer to blazing red, orange, yellow, and maroon in fall. Throughout the spring, the plant bears pale yellow-green flowers in clusters near small greenish-white berries. Poison oak is easy to miss in the winter when its stems are bare.

Contact dermatitis results from an allergy to a chemical called urushiol that the leaf exudes when its tissue is damaged. Immediately washing with a solvent like Tecnu is essential to avoid an allergic reaction in those who are sensitive to the plant. It's a good idea to wear long pants and long sleeves if there's any possibility you're going to be stepping on or brushing past poison oak on the trail. Most mammals other than humans are able to contact and even eat poison oak without any reaction at all; the plant provides food and nesting places for many kinds of birds.

Poison oak © Wendy C. Thompson

unmarried white male over eighteen and 640 acres to every married couple (the act expired in 1855).

MULKEY CREEK TRAIL

This hike starts in open pasture with views of Bald Hill and Marys Peak before entering the forest, climbing Mulkey Ridge, and ending in a short loop around a false summit, with the option to press on to Fitton Green.

Difficulty and length: Moderate, 4.3 miles round-trip with 580 feet elevation gain (8 miles round-trip with 800 feet elevation gain with the Fitton Green option). **Regulations:** The route beyond mile 1.3 is closed to horses and bicycles October 31 to April 15. Dogs allowed off leash but must be under voice control because livestock graze next to the route.

From the Oak Creek parking lot, cross the paved bridge over Oak Creek and immediately turn right onto the gravel path. The path skirts a large oak-dotted pasture and follows blackberry-edged Oak Creek for a quarter mile. In spring, bluebirds and violet-green swallows nest in boxes along the fence.

At the junction with the access road for Bald Hill Farm, turn left and follow the path as it goes first south, then west and up the gentle grade marking the beginning of the ridge. In another quarter mile, pass a trail junction to the left that leads to Bald Hill and continue straight up the hill on the gravel road. This road is open to Bald Hill Farm traffic, so be aware of the possibility of passing vehicles. Just before reaching its end, pass a private drive to the left and look downhill to see the approximate site of Johnson Mulkey's original homestead.

Pass a second private drive to the left and bear right onto a gravel path into the trees that soon parallels Mulkey Creek. After a quarter mile of gentle ups and downs, where the path splits at a trail map on a post, go downhill to the left to continue along the Mulkey Creek Trail. The other fork continues straight west and reaches Wynoochee Drive, one way to reach Fitton Green on foot from Bald Hill.

Soon you cross Mulkey Creek on a footbridge and traverse the ravine above the creek via two long switchbacks. At the top of the grade, the path curves, continues gently upward, and twists around the headwaters of the tributaries of Mulkey Creek before splitting to make a small loop around a wooded false summit at elevation 870 feet.

Options: Extend your walk by continuing west from the far point of the loop. The path undulates along the side of the ridge through mixed hardwood and Douglas-fir forest and small meadows for another couple of miles before reaching the Allen Throop Loop at Fitton Green.

BALD HILL SUMMIT LOOP

One of several routes for reaching the summit travels past open pasture before climbing Bald Hill from the west, traversing upland meadow and oak woodland with views of Mulkey Ridge.

Difficulty and length: Moderate, 3 miles round-trip with 440 feet elevation gain. **Regulations:** Trail closed to horses and bicycles October 31 to April 15.

This hike starts at the Oak Creek parking lot and follows the same route as the Mulkey Creek Trail for the first half mile. Turn left off the Bald Hill Farm access road at the trail junction marked with a trail map on a post. The path cuts between two large pastures, enters an ash swale with scattered feral plums, and crosses several fingers of Mulkey Creek before reaching a junction. The grass path to the left leads to the off-leash dog area, and the gravel path to the left leads back to the paved multiuse path and the barn. Take the gravel path to the right and begin to climb around the northwestern foot of Bald Hill.

A half mile past the junction, the path turns sharply to the left and begins to climb to the summit. After you pass a bench with a view of Mulkey Ridge and McCulloch Peak to the north, you come to another junction. The Mardi

GREAT HORNED OWLS

The numerous large oaks at the northwestern foot of Bald Hill offer many hollows for wildlife, including a pair of great horned owls that has nested here for many years; listen for their deep territorial hoots and food-begging screams late fall through spring. These large owls—with obvious ear tufts, yellow or orange eyes, and wingspans of a yard or more—haunt many open habitats, particularly mixed woodlands and open fields. They are typically nocturnal hunters that prey mostly on mammals and birds, including rabbits, skunks, squirrels, mice, coots, ducks, and hawks. The females lay eggs as early as February, choosing a new nest site each year. In the daylight, mobbing songbirds, crows, or ravens may reveal a roost site.

Keltner Interpretive Trail, open to hiking only, goes off to the left along the north slope of Bald Hill. Continue straight along the steady grade through a forest of oaks, chokecherry, and hazelnut. Nearing the summit, the path takes a hard switchback to the right, then curves to the left to break out into open meadow on the west slope of Bald Hill, with views west to Marys Peak and north to Mulkey Ridge and the Oak Creek watershed.

The true summit is some 100 yards farther to the east; you can go this way when the trail is dry (see next paragraph), but the better option to avoid mud in wet weather is to take the path heading south of the bench. This path travels below the true summit around the south and east slopes of the hill. After a quarter mile, you reach a junction. The path to the right descends by switchbacks a little more than half a mile to the multiuse path near the Reservoir Rd parking area. Take the left fork and descend to the north around the slope of the hill. You will soon cross the old road from the summit, intersect with the other end of the Mardi Keltner Trail, and continue downward through oak woods. Watch for a stand of magnificent old madrones before reaching the barn. Go right on the gravel path and then left when you reach the multiuse path to walk the final third of a mile back to the parking lot.

If you choose to go over the summit, elevation 755 feet, follow the path past thickets of wild rose to catch views of the southern Willamette Valley and Cascades. The path turns into an old road that runs northeast down Bald Hill and comes out near the barn just east of the other trail.

McDONALD FOREST

A spacious research and education forest north of Corvallis offers a variety of trails and gravel roads for hikers, runners, bicyclists, and equestrians to enjoy.

The McDonald-Dunn Research Forest north of Corvallis belongs to Oregon State University, which uses the 11,250-acre forest extensively for research and instruction, and also generously opens its trails and forest roads to public recreation. A free Visitor Guide and Map is available at most information kiosks and online from the College of Forestry (cf.forestry.oregonstate.edu/ visitor-map-and-guide). Visitors should keep in mind, however, that this is a working forest, and passenger vehicles, construction equipment, and log trucks might be driving on the forest roads at any hour every day of the week.

ACTIVITIES: Hiking, running, dog walking, biking, horseback riding. **FACILITIES:** Portable toilets at trailheads. **FEES AND REGULATIONS:** No fee. Open dawn to dusk. Dogs allowed off leash. No motorized vehicles. Horses and bicycles generally okay, although some trails are for hikers only and some trails are closed to bicycles and horses during the winter season. Please stay on official trails and roads. **BEST MONTHS:** Year-round, with only localized muddy spots in the rainy season. **MANAGING AGENCY:** Oregon State University College of Forestry.

Acquisition of McDonald Forest lands began in 1926, spearheaded by Dean George Peavy and T. J. Starker. Much of the money to finance the acquisition was donated by Mary McDonald, a wealthy businesswoman whose late husband had owned timberland in northern California and southern Oregon. The McDonalds were childless, and Mary wanted to help the youth of the future learn more about agriculture and forestry.

The 7,250-acre McDonald Forest is included here in the Marys River watershed, and the 4,000-acre Dunn Forest is included in the Luckiamute watershed. You can access McDonald Forest from a number of different

HESTHAVN NATURE CENTER

The Audubon Society of Corvallis owns and runs the Hesthavn Nature Center at 8590 NW Oak Creek Drive just before the McDonald Forest trailhead at the end of the road. Since Corvallis mayor Helen Berg donated the 5.67-acre parcel of land with horse pasture and barn in 1993, volunteers have restored native vegetation and the barn has been renovated to house a museum of wildlife specimens. It's a great place to bring children to picnic, walk the nature trail, and play in Oak Creek. For info: audubon.corvallis.or.us/hesthavn.shtml.

points. From Oak Creek Drive, the Homestead Loop is a pleasant introduction to the trail system of the southwestern portion of the forest. From Lester Avenue through Chip Ross Park, Dan's Trail gives you a panoramic view from Dimple Hill. From the Lewisburg Saddle on Sulphur Springs Road, the Old Growth Trail and the Vineyard Mountain Loop are popular outings. Peavy Arboretum in the northeast part of the forest is laced with trails, including the Section 36 Loop / Powder House Trail and the Calloway Creek Trail.

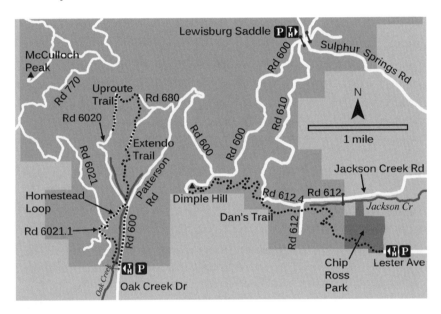

HOMESTEAD LOOP

This pleasant, shaded walk on trail and forest roads offers many access points to Oak Creek and lots of options for longer walks.

Difficulty and length: Easy, 1.6 miles round-trip with 110 feet elevation gain. **To get there**: From Corvallis, take Harrison Blvd west to 53rd St, where it becomes Oak Creek Dr. Follow Oak Creek Dr for 3 miles (making a right turn where it splits off from Cardwell Hill Dr) to its terminus at the McDonald Forest gate just past the Oak Creek Laboratory of Biology sign. Park along the road.

This walk, part of which is on the Homestead Trail and the rest of which is on forest roads, loops through the original donation land claim of Robert and Maria Biddle; the settlement history is evident from the many feral apple, plum, and pear trees that can be seen along this section of Oak Creek. The gravel Homestead Trail leaves the parking lot downhill to the left of the signboard in the midst of a complex of buildings that constitute the Oak Creek Laboratory of Biology, an OSU Fisheries and Wildlife research facility that thrived here from the 1950s to the 1980s. The trail soon crosses Oak Creek on a substantial bridge.

The path then continues along the edge of floodplain forest and blackberry thickets. Turning away from the creek, the path heads uphill and climbs steadily. This part of the loop is often slightly muddy as a result of hillside springs, making it a good place to find banana slugs. At the top of this grade, the Homestead Trail ends where you turn right onto an unnumbered gravel road. Following the road, look for wild columbine and iris in season, and listen for the pileated woodpecker family that has held a territory in this section of forest for many years.

To continue the loop, turn right at the next road intersection (onto Rd 6021.1) and follow the road as it dips down before climbing another short uphill stretch to a junction with Rd 6021. The left fork ascends the ridge and eventually McCulloch Peak. Stay right and continue downhill on Rd 6021 for another third of a mile to the next road intersection. Go right on Rd 6020 (you would go left here to reach the Extendo and Uproute Trails; see Options below), cross Oak Creek once again, and almost immediately go right again (onto Rd 600). Continue south past an orchard of old fruit trees on the left and riparian forest on the right. A nice variety of warblers, Swainson's thrushes,

BANANA SLUGS

Few people forget their first encounter with a banana slug. These slugs are among the largest in the world and play an important role in forest ecosystems by recycling nutrients, transporting spores and seeds, and selectively grazing understory plants. Banana slugs are also noteworthy for their many variations in color and spots. They are long-lived, reaching ages of six years or more in the wild. Banana slugs have well-defined home ranges and return to the same shelters over time.

Slime is very important to slugs for both locomotion and defense. They can change the chemistry and thus the stickiness of their mucus to suit their needs. Slugs use thin mucus to crawl across the forest floor, but they can create cords of thick slime for rappelling down from shrubs. A particularly sticky mucus is used for defense. Despite the slime, many animals—including large ground beetles, Pacific giant salamanders, garter snakes, various birds, and some mammals, such as raccoons—prey on banana slugs.

Banana slugs are very sensitive to moisture and temperature, so it is always best to enjoy them in their forest home rather than take them into captivity. If you find a slug in the middle of a trail on a day when many humans are also out and about, you can help by moving it to the edge of the trail. Slime comes off like superglue—just scrub your hands together or against your jeans and it will eventually roll off.

and other birds can be heard singing along this section in the spring. This final half-mile stretch is a pleasant rolling road walk back to the forest gate with several access points to the creek.

Options: The 1.4-mile Extendo Trail, which is steep in places and well worn by mountain bikers (who are not allowed on the trail from November 1 to April 15), takes off from Rd 6020 and climbs to Rd 680, where the gravel 0.7-mile Uproute Trail (open to horses and bicycles year-round) connects with it and leads back down to the top of Rd 6020.

DAN'S TRAIL TO DIMPLE HILL

A well-maintained trail meanders through Douglas-fir forest and climbs gradually to spectacular views of Marys Peak, the Willamette Valley, and the Cascades.

Difficulty and length: Moderate, 7.3 miles round-trip with 1,400 feet elevation gain. **To get there**: From Corvallis, take Highland Dr north, cross Walnut Blvd, and turn left onto Lester Ave at the sign to Chip Ross Park. Go 0.8 mile to the end of the road at the gravel parking area for Chip Ross Park.

Take the trail at the west end of the parking area for 0.5 mile and go left at the four-way junction to reach the Dan's Trail kiosk. Dan's Trail, which is open year-round to hikers, mountain bikers, and horseback riders. is divided into three parts. Lower Dan's Trail (0.8 mile) begins at the kiosk and heads northwest, descending through a lush forest where wildflowers abound in early summer. Stay left at the junction at mile 1.1 and reach Rd 612 shortly.

Middle Dan's Trail starts at Rd 612, goes 0.5 mile through an old orchard, and crosses a wooden bridge spanning Jackson Creek. Soon after the bridge you come to Rd 612.4. Just before the road, go left onto the marked Upper Dan's Trail. This section of the trail (1.8 miles) climbs gradually through a

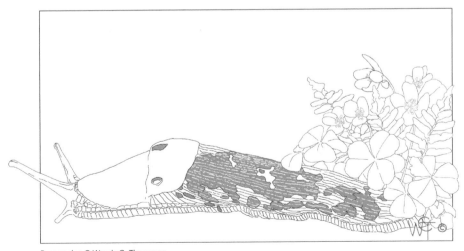

Banana slug © Wendy C. Thompson

parklike forest of mature Douglas-fir with an understory of sword fern and false brome, an invasive grass. Switchbacks lead you up to the summit of Dimple Hill (1,495 feet).

Options: You can either return to Chip Ross Park the way you came, or link to other roads or trails in McDonald Forest. The road descending from the Dimple Hill summit intersects Rd 600, which can take you to the Lewisburg Saddle (about 2 miles) or the Oak Creek entrance (about 3 miles).

SOAP CREEK VALLEY TO McCULLOCH PEAK LOOP

A long climb on gravel forest roads with occasional steep but short uphill grades offers views of the Cascades and places you atop the highest point in McDonald Forest, 2,155-foot McCulloch Peak.

Difficulty and length: Moderate, 7.8 miles round-trip with 1,500+ feet elevation gain. **To get there**: From Corvallis, take Hwy 99W north about 2 miles and turn left onto Lewisburg Rd. Drive 1.4 miles and go right onto Sulphur Springs Rd. Drive 3.3 miles, passing a right turn onto Soap Creek Rd and continuing on Sulphur Springs Rd when it turns to gravel. Park at the wide spot in the road on the left just before the Rd 700 gate.

This hike starts in the Soap Creek (Luckiamute) watershed and peaks out through the Oak Creek (Marys) watershed. Follow Rd 700, which crosses and then parallels Soap Creek at the outset. At nearly mile 0.9, a fork presents alternate paths to McCulloch Peak: you can go left on Rd 700 for 2.4 miles or right on Rd 760 for 3.7 miles. Choose the longer route, which takes you along the edges of the forest and provides additional views of valleys, ridges, and ranges as you traverse the northern basin of Soap Creek.

At about mile 1.5, your elevation affords you a first view east toward the Cascades. Over the next mile expect more climbing, broken by a downhill

FALSE BROME

False brome (*Brachypodium sylvaticum*), a perennial grass species native to Europe, Asia, and North Africa, is invading western Oregon and California. First reported in North America in 1939 near Eugene, false brome has spread quickly throughout the Willamette Valley and surrounding foothills. In many places in McDonald Forest, such as along Upper Dan's Trail, it dominates the understory to the exclusion of native flora.

False brome has remarkably broad ecological tolerance, thriving in both sun and shade. It reproduces by seeds that lodge in animal fur, footwear, and mud on bike tires. It is therefore important to clean shoes, socks, bikes, horse hooves, and dog fur to prevent the seeds from being dispersed to other locations. For info: appliedeco.org/invasive-species-resources/FBWG.

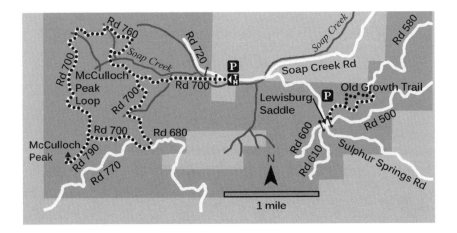

stretch, as you traverse a ridge. Around mile 2.7, at an open area to your left, the Three Sisters in central Oregon come into view just as Rd 760 becomes Rd 700. You're at McDonald Forest's northwest corner here. Continue on Rd 700 as you round a bend and look to your right into a cutover portion of Starker Forests.

Soon after, a steep climb curves sharply right. At mile 3.2, a clearing on the left offers an open view of snowcapped Cascade peaks including Mount Jefferson and Mount Hood. At a prominent intersection at mile 4.0, stay right toward McCulloch Peak on Rd 790. At mile 4.5, the trail ends at a bench. While you rest, gaze straight ahead to find Bald Hill and pan left to Dimple Hill and South Sister alongside her two siblings.

To complete the loop, head back to the intersection and make a right on Rd 700 toward Oak Creek. The road parallels a ridge dividing the Oak Creek and Soap Creek watersheds. Continue downhill on Rd 700 at all intersections to return to where your trek began.

OLD GROWTH TRAIL AND QUARRY LOOP

This short loop hike descends into an old-growth Douglas-fir forest and returns by a water-filled quarry populated by rough-skinned newts.

Difficulty and length: Easy/moderate, 1.6 miles round-trip with 300 feet elevation gain. **To get there:** From Corvallis, take Hwy 99W north about 2 miles and turn left onto Lewisburg Rd. Drive 1.4 miles and go right onto Sulphur Springs Rd for 1.4 miles to Lewisburg Saddle at the crest of the hill. Park in the lot on the right.

From the parking area, go through the gate to the northeast and take the lower road (580 or William A. Davies Rd) for 0.3 mile until you come to the marked trailhead for the Old Growth Trail on the left just past a wide spot in the road. As the trail switchbacks down from the road to the stream below, you see huge big-leaf maples and Douglas-firs more than two hundred years old, ancient giants that escaped logging and bear the scars of forest fires. The trail crosses two bridges and ascends by steps back up to Rd 580. When you reach the road, take a look at the Jory soil exposed by the roadcut.

Go right on Rd 580 for about 0.25 mile and take a slight detour to your left to observe an old quarry now partially filled with water. If you look carefully, you may see rough-skinned newts swimming in the water where they mate and lay eggs. On the rocky outcrop to your left, close to the trail, note the rounded upper outline of pillow basalt that was extruded through the ocean floor before it was uplifted hundreds of thousands of years ago. Continue on the road another 0.5 mile to return to the parking lot.

Options: Before reaching the Old Growth Trail on Rd 580 you can take the marked New Growth Trail, which links up with the Old Growth, if you want to see the difference between a managed site and an old-growth stand. After walking the Old Growth Trail, you can go left on Rd 580 and then right on Rd 500 (Nettleton Road) to complete the 6.5-mile moderately difficult Vineyard Mountain Loop, which offers northward-facing views of the Soap Creek Valley and Dunn Forest in logged sections. At the northeastern end of the loop, you can access the Section 36 Loop / Powder House Trail.

SECTION 36 LOOP / POWDER HOUSE TRAIL

This wooded hikers-only trail in the northeastern corner of McDonald Forest passes historic buildings, a small lake, a patch of dense old-growth forest, and forestry experiments in progress.

Difficulty and length: Easy/moderate, 3.9 miles round-trip with 840 feet elevation gain. **To get there**: From Corvallis, take Hwy 99W north for 5 miles to Arboretum Rd. Turn left and continue 0.8 mile to a sign for Peavy

Arboretum. Turn left and continue to fork left until you reach a small gravel parking area on the right just before an orange gate.

Walk past the orange gate and up gravel Rd 500 for 0.25 mile to the large brown Forestry Club Cabin, one of the more cherished buildings in Peavy Arboretum. The cabin was built with student labor and the first club meeting was held here in December 1925. That cabin burned to the ground in February 1949 after a fraternity dance but was quickly rebuilt by another student crew. Turn left just before the cabin to arrive shortly at a signed junction, the start of the Section 36 Loop. Go right to follow the loop counterclockwise.

You soon reach Cronemiller Lake, not a lake for swimming or fishing but a peaceful haven where you can watch ducks and kingfishers. It was created by a Civilian Conservation Corps crew in 1937 by damming Calloway Creek. The lake was used to water seedlings in the Oregon Forest Nursery, which were then planted in Coast Range forests devastated by the Tillamook Burn. The lake still irrigates the nursery, used for research purposes by the OSU College of Forestry. At the north end of the lake is a small outdoor arena where the OSU Logging Sports Team has tree-climbing and ax-throwing competitions. The log-rolling and limber pole events take place in the lake.

Bear left when you reach the lake to stay on the Section 36 Loop. Skirt the lake and ascend past a wolf tree and through a silent stretch of old growth for 0.8 mile. When the trail splits, take the fork to the right marked Powder House Trail. Pass another wolf tree, cross a bridge, and ascend another quarter mile to Rd 560. Here you see the cap house built in 1937 by CCC workers to store blasting caps for igniting dynamite (stored in a separate powder

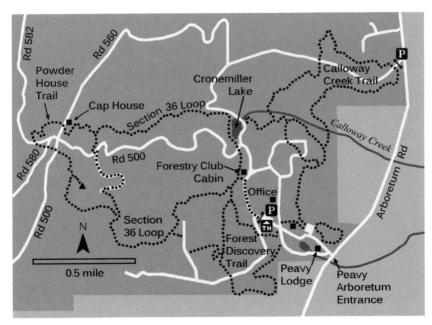

house, of which only the foundation remains) for stump removal and road clearing. Cross the road and continue on the marked Powder House Trail. You soon come to a site that's been harvested, leaving stumps and open views to the west across the Soap Creek Valley and Dunn Forest.

Descend this denuded hillside and when you come to a fork, bear right to soon reach Rd 582 below. Following the markers for the Powder House Trail, cross this road and then two more (580 and 500). Wind toward the top of Peavy Peak (about 1,280 feet in elevation) and when you reach a junction, go left if you want to take a short spur to the top. Otherwise, go right and stick to the marked Section 36 Loop at all spurs to complete the loop. On this return

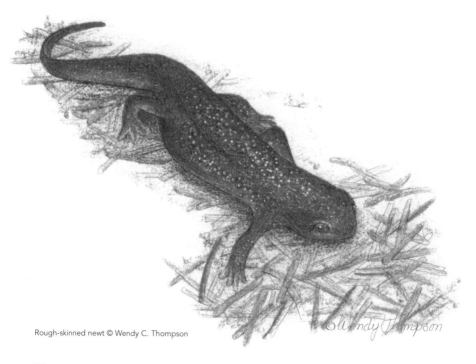

Rough-skinned newt © Wendy C. Thompson

leg, you'll see signs marking several experiments being conducted by the university, including a study of ponderosa pines from ten different locations that goes back to 1928. Keep descending until you reach the Forestry Club Cabin and retrace your steps to the start of the hike.

Options: To extend the Section 36 Loop with a side trip to see the exotic trees planted in the arboretum, take a right turn onto the 1.3-mile Forest Discovery Trail loop just before you reach the Forestry Club Cabin. You can also access the Calloway Creek Trail, a pleasant wooded 2.4-mile loop with 150 feet of elevation gain, by taking the gravel road along the east shore of Cronemiller Lake and turning onto a well-marked quarter-mile tie trail to the right.

JACKSON-FRAZIER WETLAND

A wetland at the northern edge of Corvallis offers a meandering wooden boardwalk with views of native plants as well as birds and wildlife.

To get there: From Hwy 20 or Hwy 99W in north Corvallis, turn onto Conifer Blvd and follow the signs, turning north onto Lancaster St. Drive 0.3 mile to the cul-de-sac at the end of the street, which is also the west entrance and parking area for the wetland.

The 144-acre Jackson-Frazier Wetland is close enough to sites in the Marys River watershed to be grouped with them, but it's actually in a different watershed. Also within the Corvallis area, but in the Marys River drainage, are two smaller public wetlands: Dunawi Creek at Sunset Park (4557 SW Country Club Drive) and Marys River Natural Area off of SW Brooklane Drive.

ACTIVITIES: Walking, bird-watching. FACILITIES: ADA boardwalk, dog cleanup bags. FEES AND REGULATIONS: No fee. Bikes, rollerblades, and skateboards prohibited. Dogs allowed on leash. There are no posted limits on visiting hours, but the area is unlit after dark. BEST MONTHS: Year-round, though the boardwalk is dangerously slick in freezing temperatures and the entry sidewalk can be flooded after heavy rain. MANAGING AGENCY: Benton County Natural Areas and Parks Department.

Jackson-Frazier Wetland provides drainage for Jackson and Frazier Creeks, which originate in the hills of nearby McDonald Forest and eventually connect to the Willamette River by way of Bowers Slough to the northeast of the wetland and Village Green Creek to the south. Saved from development, the wetland became a Benton County park in 1992. Throughout the year, it hosts a truly astonishing number of bird species, from red-winged blackbirds to marsh wrens, as well as beavers whose handiwork is apparent in felled Oregon ash trees and dams constructed of their branches. A level, wheelchair-accessible boardwalk with informational displays makes a 0.67-mile loop around the southern portion of the wetland.

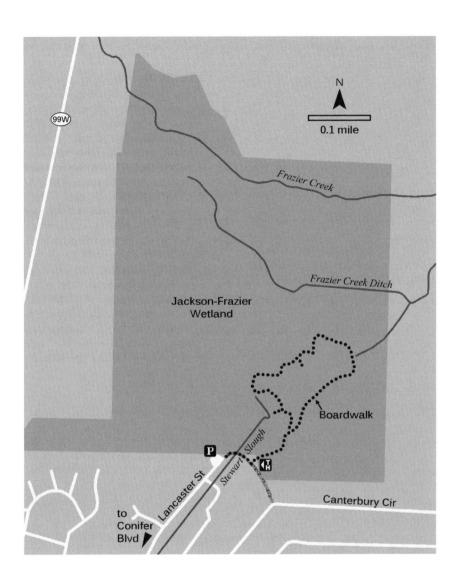

99W

N

0.1 mile

Frazier Creek

Frazier Creek Ditch

Jackson-Frazier
Wetland

Boardwalk

P

Stewart Slough

Lancaster St

to
Conifer
Blvd

Canterbury Cir

A sports park and boat ramp to the north and shaded picnic and play areas to the south anchor this popular and accessible recreational complex along the Willamette River in south Corvallis.

To get there: For the north parking area, from downtown Corvallis, take Hwy 99W south, turn left onto Crystal Lake Dr, and in 0.5 mile turn left onto Fischer Ln and go to the end. For the south parking area, travel south 1.1 miles past Crystal Lake Dr on Hwy 99W, turn left onto Goodnight Ave, and follow the road 0.9 mile to its end.

This large recreational complex includes the Crystal Lake Sports Fields (baseball and soccer), the Willamette Boat Landing, the 80-acre Kendall Natural Area, and the 287-acre Willamette Park and Natural Area (which includes a picnic area, play structure, and two soccer fields at the south end). A paved, wheelchair-accessible path runs the length of Willamette Park, with several hiking/jogging/biking trails branching off and trails leading down to the river for fishing. Kendall Natural Area encompasses informal trails through riparian and mixed woodland where restoration of native plants is ongoing.

For an easy, mostly level 2.6-mile loop, begin at the south parking area and walk north along the paved riverside path. In less than a quarter mile, where the paved path curves left, veer right onto a wide dirt trail shaded by trees. Stay on this trail and in another third mile, at a T junction, take the left fork and follow this wooded trail north for more than a half mile. At a Y after the river comes into view, take the path to the left. When you come out at the sports fields, take the paved path along the north edge of the fields, and just past the big Willamette Park sign on your right, go left onto a dirt path. Stay on this path for a little more than half a mile as it winds through the restoration area until it feeds back into the paved path. Go right to return to the south parking area.

ACTIVITIES: Walking, dog walking, biking, picnicking, soccer and baseball, disc golf, wildlife watching, fishing, boating. **FACILITIES:** Portable toilets, picnic tables, picnic shelter (to reserve, call 541-766-6918), play structure, boat ramp, disc golf course. **FEES AND REGULATIONS:** No fee. Open 6 a.m. to 10 p.m. year-round. Dogs are required to be on leash in the ball fields and on the paved path April 1 to November 10 and in the picnic shelter, playground, and parking lot areas all year; otherwise allowed off leash. **BEST MONTHS:** Year-round, though dirt trails get muddy and may flood after prolonged rain. **MANAGING AGENCY:** Corvallis Parks and Recreation Department.

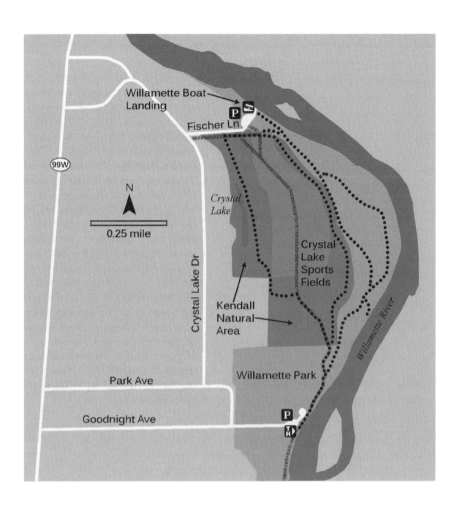

Habitats ranging from wetlands to upland oak savanna host a diverse array of birdlife, while camas fields and historic barns and buildings add interest.

To get there: From Corvallis, take Hwy 99W south 9 miles and turn right onto gravel Finley Rd, marked by a sign to the refuge. Follow Finley Rd 1.3 miles to the junction with Finley Refuge Rd; turn left here to enter the refuge. Follow this road, crossing Muddy Creek, 2.5 miles to a well-marked turnoff to the left to reach the refuge headquarters and Wild Goose Nature Store.

The William L. Finley National Wildlife Refuge, like the Ankeny and Baskett Slough refuges, was established in 1964 to provide wintering habitat for dusky Canada geese. Unlike other Canada goose subspecies, duskies

ACTIVITIES: Hiking, wildlife watching, fishing for trout in designated areas on Muddy Creek, hunting for black-tailed deer *only* during specified seasons (see fws.gov/refuge/William_L_Finley/ for info). **FACILITIES:** Refuge headquarters/nature store with ADA restrooms, observation and photography blinds. **FEES AND REGULATIONS:** No fee. Open dawn until dusk year-round, except for designated areas closed during the deer hunt and during sanctuary season from November 1 through March 31. Leashed dogs are allowed in parking areas only. No jogging, biking, horseback riding, or dogs allowed on the refuge trails. No removal of plant, animal, or mineral specimens. **BEST MONTHS:** Year-round. **MANAGING AGENCY:** US Fish and Wildlife Service.

have limited summer and winter ranges. They nest in Alaska's Copper River Delta and winter almost exclusively in the wetlands of the Willamette Valley—much of which was drained to provide open fields for agriculture and pasture during the nineteenth century. Extensive habitat restoration projects are ongoing on all 5,325 acres of the refuge. Take a driving tour and/or a walk on any of the refuge's trails to step back into the natural history of the Willamette Valley. Maps are available at kiosks in the refuge, in the refuge headquarters building, and online (fws.gov/refuge/William_L_Finley/).

From the eastern entrance of the refuge, you can work your way through one of the valley's last remaining intact wet prairies, which supports endangered plant species such as Bradshaw's desert parsley, as well as a panoply of birdlife including western meadowlark, streaked horned lark, and northern harrier. The lowlands of the refuge also include Muddy Creek's riparian habitats as well as sprawling wetlands and systems of ponds hosting western pond turtles and red-legged frogs. From there the habitat shifts to upland Oregon white oak savannas and mixed deciduous forests where you might find acorn woodpecker colonies, great

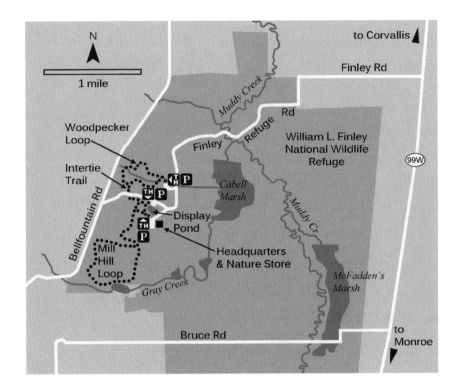

horned owls, or the resident Roosevelt elk herd.

The refuge also provides opportunities to explore the cultural history of the area. Interpretive signs mark vast camas fields once tended by the native Kalapuya people. The 1855 Fiechter House, said to be the oldest building in Benton County, provides a glimpse into the lives of European settlers and marks the track of the Applegate Trail.

MILL HILL LOOP

An up-and-down trail that can be muddy in winter takes you through oak woodland and Douglas-fir forest with marshland views along the way.

Difficulty and length: Easy, 2.5 miles round-trip with 150 feet elevation gain. **To get there:** This trail can be accessed from the headquarters parking lot or the Display Pond overlook parking area off Finley Refuge Rd (on the left just beyond the turnoff to the refuge office), which adds 0.15 mile. The trail can also be accessed on foot via the 0.5-mile Intertie Trail from Woodpecker Loop.

From the Display Pond parking area, follow the fence line down to the right and onto an alder-lined trail. A spur on the right connects to the Intertie Trail and Woodpecker Loop. For Mill Hill, continue straight and go right when the trail meets up with the headquarters entry trail. From the headquarters lot, take the paved sidewalk away from the building, cross the gravel road, and go right onto the trail at the kiosk. Stay straight at the next junction, where the trail from the Display Pond comes in, and then go left when you come to the T, where the Intertie Trail comes in from the right. In a third of a mile or so, the trail crosses a seasonally flooded streambed on a long boardwalk and then reaches a four-way intersection marked Loop Trail. Head straight across the intersection to take the Mill Hill Loop clockwise.

As the trail climbs through oaks and then Douglas-fir forest where snags show the attentions of pileated woodpeckers, you'll soon see Gray Creek to the left. Stop at a bench overlooking the marshy water to look for beavers and wood ducks. The trail continues along the crest of Mill Hill and passes several upland meadows before descending into a mixed deciduous-conifer forest and back to the start of the loop. Follow the first trail on the left to return. Take a right at the next trail connection to return to the parking areas, or stay straight to continue your hike on the Intertie Trail 0.5 mile to Woodpecker Loop.

WOODPECKER LOOP

This popular gravel trail, good for wet-season walking, winds through five different habitat types with opportunities to see up to seven different species of woodpecker.

Difficulty and length: Easy, 1.1 miles round-trip with 100 feet elevation gain. **To get there:** From the turnoff onto Finley Refuge Rd from Finley Rd, go 2.2 miles and look for the trailhead sign to a parking area on the right. The Woodpecker Loop trailhead can also be accessed on foot via the 0.5-mile Intertie Trail from Mill Hill Loop.

From the parking area, follow a short avenue lined with Himalayan blackberry to the loop. Follow the trail to the right. The trail soon opens up onto an oak savanna where an observation platform encircles an ancient Oregon white oak. From the observation platform, follow the trail as it dips down into a riparian ash swale, passes a seasonal pond, and rises again as it enters a Douglas-fir forest. Listen for drumming pileated woodpeckers or the hoots of great horned owls among the tall conifers. On the right, the Intertie Trail branches off to connect with the Mill Hill Loop.

To continue on Woodpecker, follow the trail to the left where the habitat again shifts into a mixed deciduous forest. Here songbirds abound and the chirps and calls of black-capped chickadees, dark-eyed juncos, and song sparrows can be heard from the brush lining the trail. When you reach the next junction, you have completed the loop and can follow the short avenue on the right back to the parking area.

Great horned owl © M. L. Herring

SNAG BOAT BEND UNIT, WILLIAM L. FINLEY NATIONAL WILDLIFE REFUGE

Shady backwater sloughs, riparian woodlands, and seasonal wetland habitat combined with a location on the Willamette River make this a quiet getaway rich with wildlife.

To get there: From Corvallis, take Hwy 34 east about 1 mile and turn right onto Peoria Rd. Follow Peoria Rd south for 11 miles. Turn right at the Snag Boat Bend Unit sign and proceed to the parking area.

Snag Boat Bend, a unit of the William L. Finley National Wildlife Refuge, shares the refuge's conservation goals but offers its own opportunities. The gravel bars of the Willamette River

ACTIVITIES: Hiking, wildlife watching, fishing and boating on Lake Creek. **FACILITIES:** ADA vault toilet (closed in winter), picnic table, viewing blind. **FEES AND REGULATIONS:** No fee. Open dawn until dusk year-round. Leashed dogs permitted in parking areas only. No jogging, biking, horseback riding, or dogs are permitted on the refuge trails. **BEST MONTHS:** Fall through spring. Flooding can impede access in winter and early spring. Check the refuge website (fws.gov/refuge/William_L_Finley/) for closures. **MANAGING AGENCY:** US Fish and Wildlife Service.

had been a favorite spot for hunting Canada geese long before the land was purchased to create this unit of the refuge, which was opened to the public in 2003. What sets Snag Boat Bend apart is its proximity to the Willamette River and the resulting backwater slough habitat of Lake Creek. Lake Creek's slow-moving waters make an ideal home for western pond turtles, often seen sunning themselves on logs. The tall black cottonwood trees that line the banks provide the proximity to water as well as the height and security that great blue herons prefer for their nesting rookeries.

The 2.6-mile Lake Creek Trail culminating in Turtle Loop takes you along the backwater slough of Lake Creek and through black cottonwood–dominated riparian habitat. The trail starts at the parking area with a boardwalk that meanders through a seasonally flooded wetland to an unimproved dirt path lined with blackberries and willow. The avenue soon opens up into a small picnic area with interpretive signs overlooking the backwater slough. From the picnic area continue to follow the path as it skirts both Lake Creek and the adjacent prairie. A small spur trail to the right leads to the Lake Creek viewing blind for glimpses of belted kingfisher, green heron, and river otter.

Past the viewing blind spur, the main trail skirts the edge of private agricultural fields and then reaches a gravel refuge service road. Follow the service road as it curves to the right onto a levee. At the north end of

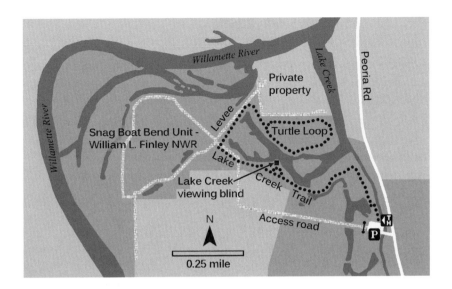

the levee road, veer sharply down to the right to pick up the loop portion of the trail. This area is often flooded in the wintertime, and in the dry months the trail tends to be overgrown with grasses and wildflowers. Follow the path as it loosely meanders around an open meadow lined with cottonwood and loops back to the meadow entrance and then the levee road. Follow the same trail to return to the parking lot.

BIKING THE MARYS WATERSHED

Corvallis has one of the best bicycling systems in the nation, and from Corvallis a number of recreational bike routes roll through farmlands and into the mountains to the west. Trails on Marys Peak and Bald Hill and in McDonald Forest all allow bikes, with some seasonal closures. For a real challenge, ride the Marys Peak Road to the top—26 miles each way from Corvallis (10 miles from the Hwy 34–Marys Peak Road junction to the peak)—or take the easy way and have someone take you to the top so you can ride down (with good brakes). For more ideas, pick up the latest *Corvallis & Benton County Bicycle Guide* at local bicycle shops, the city hall, or the Chamber of Commerce.

BIKING MCDONALD FOREST

McDonald Forest is hilly, so prepare for long climbs followed by exhilarating descents. Trails twist up hillsides, while gravel forest roads tend to have gentler slopes. The roads are a great way to roll through the forest and are accessible by hybrid bikes and mountain bikes. Most trails are open to bikes year-round, many are available from April 15 to October 31, but some are hiker-only. Refer to the free Visitor Guide and map available at most information kiosks and online from the College of Forestry (cf.forestry.oregonstate. edu/visitor-map-and-guide). Stick to officially marked trails. Wherever you ride, yield to all other users. When approaching, slow down, provide an audible warning (a bell works great), and look for acknowledgment. Take extra care when approaching horses: ask the rider for instructions and be prepared to stop and let them pass.

For an introduction to single-track mountain biking, try the Intensive Management and Calloway Creek Trails in Peavy Arboretum. The many hills are short and shallow rollers. A spur trail climbs to tranquil Cronemiller Lake.

CORVALLIS-TO-ALBANY MULTIUSE PATH

A multiuse path for bicycles and pedestrians was being developed along the railroad tracks paralleling Hwy 20 between Corvallis and Albany until controversy stalled the project. If it is ever completed, the nearly 10-mile-long pathway will run from Circle Boulevard in Corvallis to at least Spring Hill Road in North Albany and possibly onto the Lyon Street Bridge to Water Avenue. The project was first proposed in the early 2000s and was being worked on jointly by the City of Albany and Benton County. The first segment, from Circle Boulevard to Manchester Street just past Cheldelin Middle School in Corvallis, was completed in 2013.

A favorite loop in the southeast corner reaches 1,495-foot Dimple Hill. From Chip Ross Park, ride Lower Dan's Trail 0.6 mile and make a sharp right to reach Jackson Creek Rd (Rd 612). For a challenge, continue up Lower Horse Trail, beginning with a steep run through a meadow, continuing through a shady grove, and concluding with a trio of heart-pumping switchbacks. To conserve energy, instead take the road to the Dan's/Horse Connector, a longer but milder route. Either way, continue on Upper Horse's seven tight-turning switchbacks. At the top, turn left onto Rd 600 and give your legs a break. At the intersection with Rd 650, turn left and follow the road to the top of Dimple Hill to take in views of Corvallis and Marys Peak. As a further reward for the climb, enjoy the long, quick, fun descent down Upper Dan's Trail.

On the other side of Dimple awaits the Uproute Trail, which crosses Oak Creek—and the technique-testing Extendo Trail. For a hilly, all-road workout, try Soap Creek to McCulloch Peak.

PHILOMATH TO BELLFOUNTAIN COUNTY PARK

This loop through farmland along the edge of the Coast Range features several challenging climbs, a midroute picnic area at Bellfountain County Park, and a relaxing, level return trip.

Distance and climb: 37 miles round-trip, 1,084 feet total ascent. **Road surface**: Paved with some loose gravel and narrow shoulder, particularly at bends after mile 9. **Start/end point**: Sunset Shopping Center, at the intersection of Philomath Blvd / Hwy 20 and SW 53rd St between Corvallis and Philomath. **Facilities**: Restrooms on Finley Refuge Rd at William L. Finley National Wildlife Refuge, mile 11.1, and Bellfountain County Park, mile 16.

This route is a rough rectangle running south from Philomath along the Benton County Scenic Loop. You'll find light traffic and an ample shoulder as you pass through rolling farmland during the first segment of the trip. The terrain becomes hilly around mile 9 as you skirt the foothills of the Coast Range; use caution as the shoulder narrows and curves begin. Here you wind past Finley National Wildlife Refuge and climb several challenging hills with satisfying and scenic descents. The return leg of the trip follows Hwy 99W north. Traffic on the highway is significant but the large shoulder and straight, level roadway offer an easy ride home.

Turn-by-turn directions: Go south 0.9 mile on SW 53rd St and turn right onto Plymouth Rd. At mile 2, turn left onto Bellfountain Rd. At mile 15, turn right onto Dawson Rd. At mile 16, turn right into Bellfountain County Park. For the return leg, turn left onto Dawson Rd from the park. At mile 20, turn left onto Hwy 99W. At mile 34, turn left onto SW Avery Ave. Turn right at SW Avery Park Dr and ride through the park, then turn left to enter the bike path on SW Philomath Blvd. After crossing SW 35th St, bear left on the path as

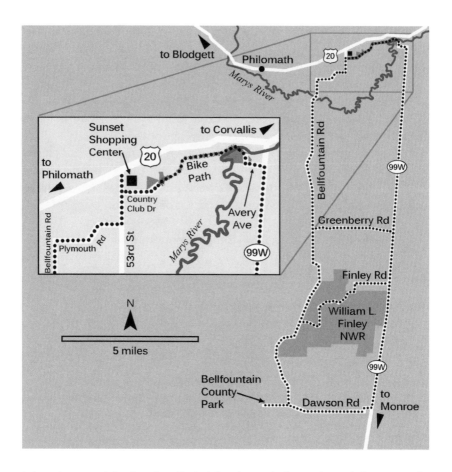

it heads toward Starker Arts Park, bike through the park, and then go right onto Country Club Dr and right onto SW 53rd St to return to your start point.

Options: If you enjoy those uphill climbs, you may want to reverse your path at Bellfountain County Park to tackle the climbs in the opposite direction. Cyclists who don't mind a little walk on gravel may opt to enter Finley Wildlife Refuge on Finley Refuge Rd and follow it to the refuge's eastern exit on Hwy 99W rather than riding on to the park. This route skips the most difficult ascents and trims the round trip to 28 miles. To trim even more miles and elevation change off the route, turn left onto Greenberry Rd at mile 8 and then left onto Hwy 99W to return, for a route totaling 21 miles and climbing 374 feet.

PADDLING THE MARYS RIVER

About 20 river miles of the Marys are runnable at certain flows from early winter to late spring, from the Coast Range town of Blodgett through Wren to Philomath and on to south Corvallis, where it enters the Willamette River. The river in its mild-mannered seasons is suitable for advanced beginner to intermediate canoers and kayakers interested in scenery, natural history, geology, and mild white water. Between Blodgett and Philomath you can see basalt headlands, old-growth conifers and oaks, grottos of wildflowers, and resident otters, beavers, herons, wood ducks, vultures, and mergansers. Occasionally a cutthroat trout (traveling to and from the Willamette River) will break the surface to feed. Railroad fans will enjoy the old railroad bridges, as the Willamette to Toledo railroad tracks follow the river. Below Wren, Fitton Green Natural Area borders the river on its left bank.

Between Blodgett and Philomath, the river has a higher gradient and flows faster, with some little rapids where the river flows over basalt shelves. A class-2 series of shelves starts about 0.5 mile below Harris Covered Bridge upstream of Wren. Between Philomath and Corvallis, the Marys flattens out into farm country. Winter storms can bring down trees here, and large logjams can form in this lower reach, turning a placid journey into a slog of portages. Watch out for poison oak on the banks and be prepared to scout if you can't see around the bend and to portage anytime there's an obstacle or the flow is too low for your boat. Even though this river may seem small and tame, it is powerful, so wear a personal flotation device at all times.

The Marys is best run in the spring when breeding birds abound and the wildflowers are blooming on mossy basalt shelves along the river.

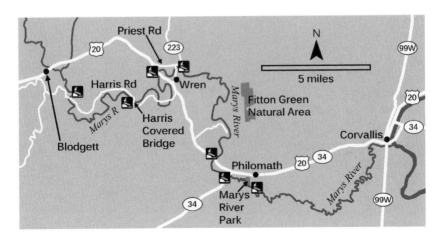

This undammed river is too low and slow (14 cfs) to paddle in summer, and too high and wild to paddle in winter, when the flow can spike to almost 14,000 cfs. The Marys is relatively easy and safe to float between 300 and 800 cfs; these runnable flows occur from early winter to late spring. Watch for the sweet spot on the USGS gauge in Philomath. Local canoeists claim that 500 cfs is the ideal flow for their trips. With inflatable kayaks, the river can be floated down to about 200 cfs.

Each section—Blodgett to Wren, Wren to Philomath, and Philomath to Corvallis—is about a two-hour float. You can put in south of Blodgett where Harris Rd crosses the river. Near Wren, the access points are Harris Covered Bridge on Harris Rd, the Hwy 20 bridge, and the Hwy 223 bridge near the Priest Rd intersection. In Philomath, you can access the river at the Hwy 20 bridge, the Hwy 34 bridge, and Marys River Park. Park carefully in these places. Use road rights-of-way and do not trespass.

CALAPOOIA RIVER
WATERSHED

Named after the Calapooia band of Kalapuya, who harvested camas bulbs from its marshes for thousands of years, the Calapooia River flows 72 miles from the flanks of Tidbits Mountain (elevation 5,185 feet) in the Cascade Range down a narrow valley to rolling pasture and hay fields around Holley and Crawfordsville. Below Pioneer Park in Brownsville, the river makes its slow, meandering way through wheat and grass seed fields to Albany. The confluence with the Willamette River is between Bryant and Monteith Parks in downtown Albany (elevation 210 feet).

The Calapooia is a free-flowing river, but it wasn't always. Three small diversion dams built in the late 1800s—the Brownsville, the Sodom, and the Shearer—once supported a thriving mill industry, including woolen and lumber mills and the state's oldest water-powered grain mill. Yet the dams also created significant barriers to migratory fish. Sediment and logjams built up behind the dams, affecting downstream fish habitat and increasing the power of winter floods. Starting in 2002, in partnership with the local community and agencies, the Calapooia Watershed Council worked to remove the dams and eight barrier culverts, and the last dam was removed in 2011. Threatened spring chinook and winter steelhead runs now have a clear path to spawning grounds, and conditions are also improving for other fish in the river, including cutthroat trout, red-sided shiners, dace, and Pacific lamprey.

Even though 94 percent of the Calapooia watershed is in private ownership, eager explorers can find rich opportunities to enjoy the natural world here. Public lands include the headwaters of the river in the Willamette National Forest (US Forest Service), McClun County Wayside and McKercher County Park (Linn County), Pioneer Park (City of Brownsville), Thompson's Mills State Heritage Site (Oregon Parks and Recreation Department), and Bryant and Monteith Parks at the mouth (City of Albany). Rock hounds love the Calapooia for the Holley blue agate found only here, as well as pale blue agate, green and purple jasper, and petrified wood found on Forest Service lands. Excellent fishing for both rainbow and cutthroat trout can be had in the headwaters of the Calapooia during summer months.

SPLASH DAMS

From the McClun Road bridge, the banks of the upper Calapooia River appear encased in concrete, but a closer look reveals this to be bedrock. The bedrock here, and throughout much of the upper Calapooia River, is an important clue to the historical use of Oregon rivers.

Beginning in the 1800s, before logging roads, rivers transported timber to mills. Loggers yarded felled trees into a river and waited for rains to increase water flows and drive the logs downstream. Then logging companies began to build temporary dams of logs or boards to hold back the water so it could be released in a large flood to transport the logs to mills on a regular schedule year-round. The upper Calapooia had two splash dams; streams of western Oregon—including tributaries of the Marys, the Luckiamute, the Yamhill, the Pudding, and the South Santiam, as well as the Calapooia—had 232 all told.

The torrents of water and logs scoured streams to bedrock, removing gravels essential for spawning salmon and destroying rearing habitats. To make log transport easier, streams were simplified by blocking side channels (critical overwinter refuges for salmon and trout) and by removing large boulders and natural logjams with dynamite. These practices were outlawed in the 1950s, but their effects linger: researchers have found that splashed streams are still less hospitable to fish than streams that were never dammed, because they have more exposed bedrock, fewer deep pools, and fewer pieces of large wood to create spots for fish to hide and rest.

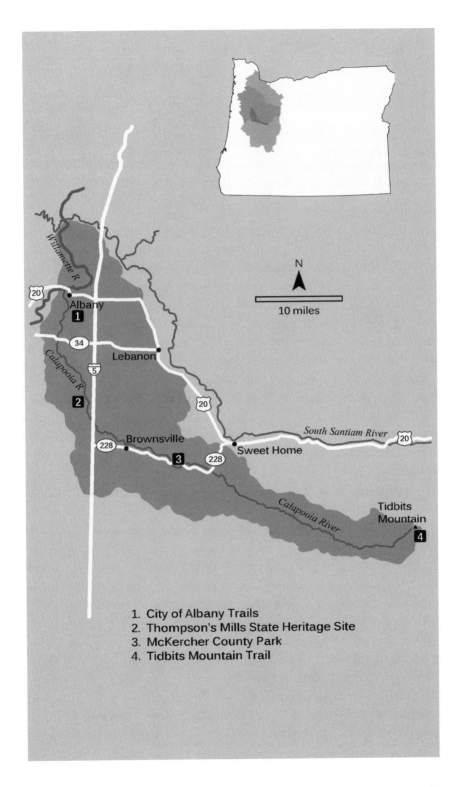

N

10 miles

20

Willamette R

20

Albany
1

34

Lebanon

5

Calapooia R

2

20

Brownsville
228

228

3

Sweet Home

South Santiam River
20

Calapooia River

Tidbits
Mountain
4

1. City of Albany Trails
2. Thompson's Mills State Heritage Site
3. McKercher County Park
4. Tidbits Mountain Trail

The Beginnings of the Kalapuya People

ESTHER STUTZMAN, traditional story-keeper

I am Kalapuya and Coos, and one of the stories that I heard from my relatives was about the beginnings of the Kalapuya people and how it all came to be. You see, the world was made of stone. There were stone mountains and stone valleys. At the very top of the stone mountain something came to life, and that life became known as Le-lu, First Woman, who walked down from that stone mountain with two babies clutched to her breast. As she walked, with every step she took the grass began to grow. And as she sat and as she touched the ground, the rivers began to flow.

And she walked until she came to the valley, the valley of the stone. And there she met Quartux, Mother Wolf, who looked at her and said, "Who are you?" And she said, "I am Le-lu, First Woman." And Quartux said, "And where did the babies come from?" And Le-lu, First Woman, said, "I dreamed of them and they came to me, but I need someone to watch them while I go out and look around in the world."

Quartux looked at her and smiled and her teeth flashed in the sun. Mother Wolf said, "I will watch them."

Le-lu was a bit afraid, but something inside of her made her trust Mother Wolf. So she wove a pack basket of wild iris, kliskwis. And she put the babies in the pack basket and strapped them to the back of Mother Wolf; and just to make sure the babies would be safe and would not fall out, Le-lu also wove a wide strap and strapped those babies around their heads in that basket. Then she went away to look around in the world.

She was gone a long time, but when she came back the babies were safe. Quartux, Mother Wolf, had taken good care of them. As Le-lu lifted those babies out of that basket, she saw that something was different. As she unstrapped them from that basket, took the straps from their heads, she noticed that their foreheads were flattened. She said, "This is good. From now on our people will flatten the foreheads of the babies in honor of

Mother Wolf, who took such very good care of the babies." Indeed, that's how life came to this earth.

The people of the Kalapuya did flatten the foreheads of babies to honor Mother Wolf, who also has a forehead that is flattened. This was a practice that was kept until about a hundred years ago when it was considered to be cruel and it was outlawed by the government. So our people did come to earth and we honor Mother Wolf. We honor Quartux and we believe that she is the protector of the babies.

The Calapooia River wends its way northward along the west edge of Albany and enters the Willamette between Bryant and Monteith Parks. A visit to Bryant Park is the best way to view the Calapooia, particularly during the winter months, when parts of the park can be flooded by the river. Or wade in the Calapooia in the summer, when Monteith Park hosts Albany's popular River Rhythms concert series. Simpson Park to the northeast also offers public access to the Willamette and shares a parking area with Talking Water Gardens, an innovative reclamation project. Periwinkle Creek, an Endangered Species Act–listed stream for coho salmon, flows into the Willamette in Bowman Park, and a path runs along it in the middle of town. You can also walk along the Willamette and through redevelopment projects on Albany's waterfront on the paved Dave Clark Riverfront Path, which runs for 1.5 miles between Monteith and Bowman parks. Takena Landing offers access to the other side of the river. For a map of City of Albany trails, go to cityofalbany.net/images/stories/parksandrec/trails/TrailMap.pdf.

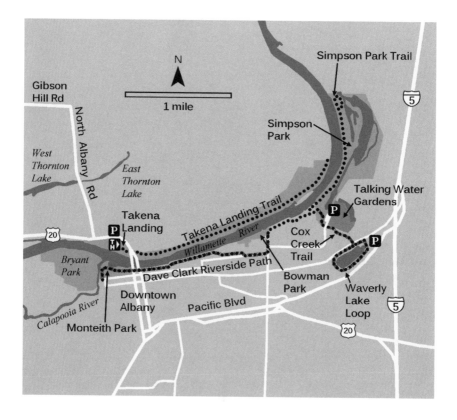

BOWERS ROCK STATE PARK

In 1973, the State of Oregon acquired 148 acres of land in a bend of the Willamette River a couple of miles west of downtown Albany as part of the Willamette River Greenway program. Since then, it has acquired 420 more acres for Bowers Rock State Park, but as of 2015 there are no improved trails or any other amenities. Though the state might develop the park in the future, access is limited by the fact that the park is bordered on all but the river side by private land. In 2014, Oregon Parks and Recreation, in partnership with the Calapooia Watershed Council, began phased restoration of native fish passage and habitat in the backwater areas of Bowers Rock.

The park is located at River Mile 123–121, just upriver from where the Calapooia joins the Willamette, across from Hyak County Park. Foot access to Bowers Rock is via the end of the private, gravel portion of Bryant Way (extending west from the intersection of paved Bryant Way and Bryant Drive), where parking is prohibited. Past the state park kiosk at the end of the gravel road, the unmarked trail (which can be blocked by water during the rainy season) skirts a grass-seed field and follows a dirt road west from a 50-acre pond. The best access is by boat along the Willamette River or the Little Willamette River backwater.

SIMPSON PARK TRAIL

A wide, shady trail along the Willamette offers vistas of the river and access via several short side trails.

Difficulty and length: Easy, 2.4 miles round-trip with no elevation gain. **Facilities:** Portable toilets (one wheelchair accessible), pet waste station, picnic table. **Fees and regulations:** No fee. Open 6 a.m. to 10 p.m. Dogs allowed on leash. **Best months:** Year-round. **To get there:** From downtown Albany, take Second Ave north for 1.1 miles, turn left at Geary St, and take the second right onto Front Ave, which becomes Waverly after the sharp curve to the left. End in the gravel parking lot at Talking Water Gardens.

Simpson Park Trail is a wide, bark-chipped path accessible to walkers, bikers, and perhaps even sturdy strollers and wheelchairs. At the start of the trail, you pass the boat launch for First Lake, which used to be a log pond back when a lumber mill operated nearby. It is fed by Talking Water Gardens and is prone to algae overgrowth in summer, so keep your pets away. At the north end of the trail in about 1.2 miles, take either fork to enter a short roundabout that feeds back into the trail for the return trip.

Options: About 200 yards along the Simpson Park Trail, a wide gravel trail to the left leads to Bowman Park and connects there to the Dave Clark Riverfront Path. This trail passes through the middle of an 11-acre wetland

and riparian restoration site being managed by the Calapooia Watershed Council. You can also pick up the paved Cox Creek Trail heading east from the parking lot, which reaches the Waverly Lake Loop and passes a dam removal site and 5 acres of new riparian planting done by the local watershed group.

TALKING WATER GARDENS

Several easy connected trails through a constructed wetland offer a chance to view diverse vegetation, overwintering birds, and wildlife.

Difficulty and length: Easy, mostly level trails of various lengths that you can combine any number of ways, totaling about 2 miles of trails. **Facilities**: Same as for Simpson Park Trail. **Fees and regulations**: No fee. Open sunrise to sunset. Dogs allowed on leash. No swimming (water may be toxic) or smoking. **Best months**: Year-round.

Talking Water Gardens is a 39-acre engineered wetland created on the site of an abandoned lumber mill. You can wander at will through a series of wide, interconnected, primarily gravel (some wood-chipped) paths and bridges that meander around constructed marshes, ponds, and waterfalls. Most trails are suitable for strollers, bikes, and wheelchairs.

Native plants, including wapato, red-flowering currant, camas lily, and creeping spikerush, abound in spring and summer. An oak savanna fronts the eastern edge of the park. Migrating birds flock to the wetlands in huge numbers during the fall and winter; more than eighty bird species were identified within the first three years of the wetland's existence. Abundant other wildlife, including minks, otters, beavers, foxes, and bullfrogs, make the wetland their year-round home.

A WATER-TREATMENT WETLAND

Talking Water Gardens is the first public-private engineering project of its kind in the United States. Construction of the project began in 2010 as a partnership between metals manufacturer ATI Wah Chang and the cities of Albany and Millersburg. The purpose of the engineered wetland, which was fully implemented by spring 2013, is to provide an extra level of natural treatment for wastewater from the cities and from the industrial plant. The system mimics natural processes and cools treated wastewater to meet regulatory standards before it is discharged into the Willamette River. A series of heavily vegetated holding ponds is fed by rock waterfalls that aerate and mix the treated water to enrich oxygen, encourage beneficial organisms, and enhance plant growth.

EAST THORNTON LAKE NATURAL AREA

East Thornton Lake is Albany's only natural lake, an old oxbow of the Willamette River that still catches river overflow during heavy winter rains. Located in North Albany off North Albany Road, the lake is home to breeding populations of rare western painted and pond turtles, as well as foxes, river otters, and migratory birds. The 27-acre property was acquired by the City of Albany in 2010. A consortium of conservation organizations has plans to restore East Thornton Lake to the landscape that existed before white settlement. The natural area will host school groups, researchers, cultural workshops, and historical displays when it is completed.

The wetland is surrounded by industrial activity, so you may want to adjust your expectations accordingly. Algae bloom during the warmer months is purposely uncontrolled as part of the cooling process. Although the water meets regulatory standards for treated wastewater, it is not potable, and you and your pets should avoid it.

TAKENA LANDING TRAIL

A shady, level path along the bank of the Willamette River across from Albany offers an easy-access respite from urban sights and sounds.

Difficulty and length: Easy, 3.5 miles round-trip with insignificant elevation gain. **Facilities**: Restrooms, picnic tables, boat ramp. **Fees and regulations**: No fee. Park open 6 a.m. to 9 p.m. Dogs allowed on leash. Bikes okay. **Best months**: Dry season; part of the trail turns to mud in the rainy season and may even be submerged. **To get there**: From Albany, drive west on Lyon St and cross the Willamette on the Hwy 20 bridge. Turn left into Takena Landing Park at the second stoplight, North Albany Rd. The trailhead is under the highway bridge.

Takena Landing is one of two Albany city parks with boat landings (Bowman Park is the other). The name of the 72-acre park was inspired by Albany's original name, Takenah, a Native American term meaning "large pool or depression," referring to the place where the Calapooia River joins the Willamette, which is actually across the river from and a little upstream of the park. (The city was renamed because the word was too often translated as "hole in the ground.")

The trail offers occasional glimpses of the river and spur paths down to the pebbly shore, but most of the route proceeds through a corridor thickly edged with Himalayan blackberry, ivy, and other vegetation. A few cottonwoods tower overhead and, along with other canopy trees, provide plenty of shade, making this a popular exercise trail for locals in the sunny months. The trail borders a golf course and passes under a railroad trestle in the first half mile and then becomes quieter, wilder, and rougher when the wood chips spread by local Eagle Scouts give way to packed dirt. The trail makes a loop inland at the end and shortly returns you to the main trail.

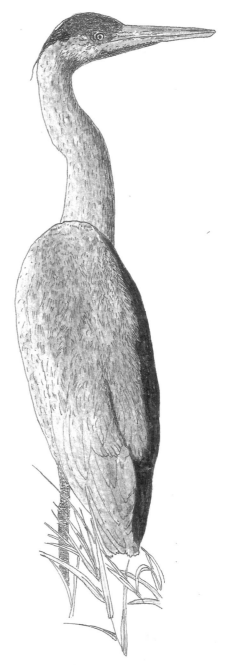

Great blue heron © David Wagner

CALAPOOIA RIVER WATERSHED

THOMPSON'S MILLS STATE HERITAGE SITE

A living history museum in a bend of the Calapooia River demonstrates mill technology from the 1850s and provides a shady respite for bikers on the Willamette Valley Scenic Bikeway.

ACTIVITIES: Picnicking, educational tours. **FACILITIES:** Vault toilets and picnic tables. **FEES AND REGULATIONS:** No fee. Open 9 a.m. to 4 p.m. daily except Thanksgiving, Christmas, and New Years. Dogs allowed on leash. **BEST MONTHS:** Year-round. **MANAGING AGENCY:** Oregon Parks and Recreation Department.

To get there: From Albany, take Hwy 99E south about 12 miles and turn left onto Boston Mill Rd. Go 2 miles and look for the park on your left.

Thompson's Mills State Heritage Site preserves Oregon's oldest water-powered gristmill, still in operating condition. A short millrace diverts water from the Calapooia River to a reservoir, and the backed-up water turns

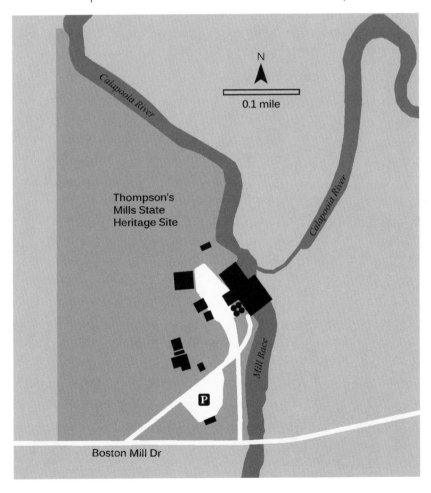

the mill wheels and powers the elevator machinery. Originally called Boston Mill, the structure was built by pioneer Richard Finley in 1858 and served Linn County farmers, selling flour under the Delicious and Valley Rose labels. The state bought the mill in 2004 and opened it to the public in 2007. Free one-hour tours are given at 10 a.m., noon, and 2 p.m. every day; you can also do a self-guided tour. Call 800-551-6949 for recorded information or 541-491-3611 to reach a park employee.

The mill was the reason the Sodom and Shearer Dams—removed in 2011—were built. The 7-mile Sodom Ditch was dug in the late 1800s to divert high water from the Calapooia River and minimize flooding. But the ditch began to divert nearly the entire flow of the river, so the Sodom Dam was built on the ditch around 1890 to divert water back into the Calapooia during low flows. (Now that the dam is gone, the renamed Sodom Channel conveys most of the Calapooia River's winter flows and half of its summer flows.) The Shearer Dam was built on the Calapooia to divert river flows to the mill via the millrace. Now water is pumped into the millrace, and new waterworks on the millrace were built in 2013.

A stretch of pools, riffles, and cascades in the Calapooia River offers places to swim and splash, while tall Douglas-firs provide shade for summer picnics.

ACTIVITIES: Picnicking, swimming, inner tubing, fishing. **FACILITIES:** Vault toilets, picnic tables. **FEES AND REGULATIONS:** No fee. Open dawn to dusk. Dogs allowed on leash. **BEST MONTHS:** May through September. **MANAGING AGENCY:** Linn County Parks and Recreation.

To get there: From I-5 south of Corvallis, take Hwy 228 toward Brownsville. At mile 9.6, a pullout to the right offers views of the small falls reached from the park, along with interpretive signs. At mile 9.8, turn right into the McKercher Park parking lot.

McKercher County Park, located along the banks of the Calapooia River 7 miles east of Brownsville, is one of the few pieces of public land along the river. It's a nice place to stop for a picnic if you're driving the Over the River and Through the Woods Scenic Byway. It's also a worthy extension if you're riding from Albany to Brownsville on the Willamette Valley Scenic Bikeway.

Several picnic tables, some overlooking the river, are pleasantly situated in a small, mostly second-growth Douglas-fir forest. The cascades just downstream swell in size in the winter and provide a cool retreat in the summer, when you'll find lots of people swimming in the deep, protected pools below the little falls. The area above the cascades is also fun to splash around in. Head toward the river and take one of the many trails down to the water. To reach the cascades, follow the trail west as it skirts the highway and take one of the spur trails down to the water.

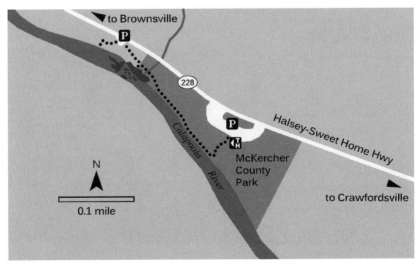

A trail from the west or an alternate from the south takes you through forests to a 5,185-foot pinnacle with a 360-degree view of the Cascades and Coast Range.

DIFFICULTY AND LENGTH: From the Tidbits West Trailhead accessed from Hwy 20, easy/moderate, 3.3 miles round-trip with 925 feet elevation gain. From the Tidbits South Trailhead accessed from Hwy 126, moderate, 4 miles round-trip with 1,100 feet elevation gain. **FACILITIES:** None. **FEES AND REGULATIONS:** No fee. Open to horses and mountain bikes. Dogs allowed on leash. **BEST MONTHS:** July through October. Road and trail closed by snow in winter and spring. **MANAGING AGENCY:** US Forest Service, Sweet Home Ranger District (Tidbits West) and McKenzie River Ranger District (Tidbits South).

To get there: To reach the Tidbits West Trailhead, take Hwy 20 east from Sweet Home for 14.2 miles, and just past Cascadia State Park turn right onto Canyon Creek Rd (Rd 2022). From here drive 17.5 miles on good gravel logging roads, accessible to passenger cars. First go 7 miles and turn right onto Rd 2026 (Owl Ridge Rd). Cross two bridges, over Canyon Creek and Owl Creek; stay left at the Y after the second bridge to continue on Rd 2026. Follow this for another 7.2 miles past six spur roads and turn left onto Rd 335. Travel 3.1 miles to the trailhead on the right, marked by a sign on the left, and park along the road.

To get to the Tidbits South Trailhead, from Blue River take Hwy 126 east for 4 miles and turn left (north) onto Blue River Reservoir Rd (Rd 15). Follow Rd 15 north for 4.7 miles past Blue River Reservoir and when the road turns to gravel continue straight ahead onto Rd 1509. Continue uphill on Rd 1509 for 8.3 miles and turn left onto Rd 877 (marked with a trailhead sign). Drive a steep 0.2 mile until the road ends and park there.

The trail from the Tidbits West Trailhead ascends gently through a young forest and then runs along a ridge and through a mature noble fir forest nearer the summit. Along the trail, bear grass, wild rhododendron, copious wildflowers, and succulents in a sunny scree rock garden bloom in July; look for red elderberries and huckleberries in August. As you approach the top, stay right at a fork where the trail from the other side of the mountain comes in.

Trillium © Wendy Thompson

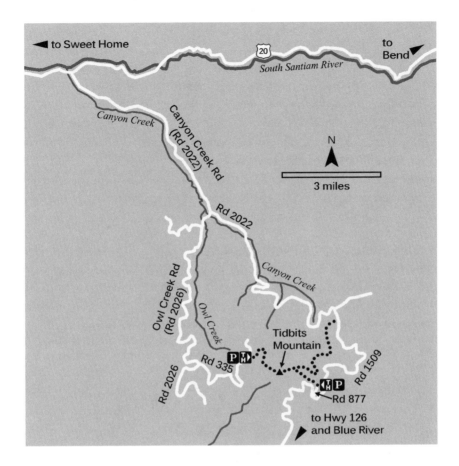

From the Tidbits South Trailhead, the trail ascends through a magnificent lower-elevation old-growth Douglas-fir and western hemlock forest for 1.2 miles before coming to a clearly marked junction with the Gold Hill Trail. Go left at the junction and soon cross a series of scree fields. At mile 1.7 you reach an unsigned junction with the western summit trail; keep left (uphill) at this junction.

From this point where the two trails meet, the climb steepens but only for a short distance. Round the top of the mountain and watch your footing as you scramble to the rocky summit, where a concrete pad marks the site of a former fire lookout. On a clear day, you can see many High Cascade peaks, including the Three Sisters, Mount Washington, Mount Jefferson, and even the top of Mount Hood. You can also sight practically all the way down the forested watershed of the Calapooia River, which originates on Tidbits Mountain. Return to the trailhead the same way you came up.

BIKING THE CALAPOOIA WATERSHED

Many quiet farm roads in the Calapooia watershed can be combined into a bike ride. For an easy 13.6-mile out-and-back ride from Brownsville to McKercher County Park, follow Kirk Avenue from downtown for 0.8 mile, turn right onto Northern Drive for 5.7 miles, and turn left onto Highway 228 for 0.3 mile to the park. Or ride the middle segment of the Willamette Valley Scenic Bikeway, Oregon's (and the nation's) first scenic bikeway, from Bryant Park in Albany to Pioneer Park in Brownsville, a total of 30.3 miles with 150 feet total ascent. Each turn on the route is clearly marked. Download maps at oregonscenicbikeways.org. Links to exportable GPS files and cue sheets are also available at rideoregonride.com.

RIVER VALLEY LOOP FROM ALBANY

This ride along rolling rural back roads traverses open farmland between the Willamette and Calapooia Rivers and passes the historic Oakville Presbyterian Church.

Distance and climb: 26.9 miles round-trip, 148 feet total ascent. **Road surface**: Paved with narrow shoulders and high-traffic crossings at miles 8 and 19.7. **Start/end point**: Bryant Park, Albany. **Facilities**: Restrooms at Bryant Park.

This route is a loop running south from Bryant Park in Albany along a portion of the Willamette Valley Scenic Bikeway. Traffic is light as you leave Bryant

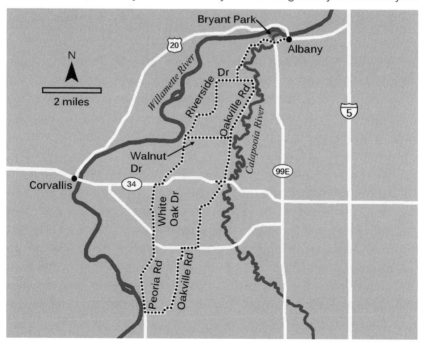

Park on rolling back roads but increases at mile 2.5 as you turn onto Riverside Drive. Then you wind through rural residential neighborhoods until you cross heavily trafficked Highway 34 at mile 8; use caution here. Traffic thins considerably during the next 11.5 miles as you roll through open farmland, but you may encounter large farm equipment on the single-lane road from mile 12.7 to 14.5. The return leg of the loop features more rural residential neighborhoods and small farms. It takes you past the Oakville Presbyterian Church, built in 1878, and ends back at Bryant Park.

Turn-by-turn directions: From Bryant Park, go right onto Bryant Wy, and at mile 1.2, turn left onto Bryant Dr. Stay on this road as it jogs left at mile 2.2. At mile 2.7, turn right onto Riverside Dr and continue south for nearly 5 miles. At mile 8, turn right onto Hwy 34 for 0.2 mile and cross to turn left onto White Oak Rd. Head south on White Oak Rd for 2 miles. At mile 10, merge onto Peoria Rd and head south for 2.75 miles. Turn left onto Oakville Rd at mile 13 to start the loop back.

Pedal east and then north on Oakville Rd for approximately 3 miles, passing the Oakville Presbyterian Church. At mile 15.9, turn right onto Harvest Dr and then make an immediate left onto Oakville Rd. Stay on Oakville Rd as it jogs right and then left before reaching Hwy 34 again at mile 19.7. Turn right onto Hwy 34 and cross traffic to turn left onto Oakville Rd. Continue north on Oakville Rd for nearly 4 miles. At mile 23.8, turn left onto Riverside Dr. At mile 24.3, turn right onto Bryant Dr. Jog right to continue on Bryant Dr, and at mile 25.7, turn right onto Bryant Wy to return to your starting point at Bryant Park.

Options: For a shorter ride, cut the loop to 12.9 miles by turning left onto Walnut Dr at mile 5.9. Follow Walnut Dr for 1.7 miles and turn left onto Oakville Rd at mile 7.6. At mile 9.8, turn left onto Riverside Dr. Then turn right onto Bryant Dr at mile 10.3 and retrace your route to return to your starting point at Bryant Park.

BROWNSVILLE TO PEORIA LOOP VIA THOMPSON'S MILLS

This pleasant, mostly flat ride takes you through farmland and several early communities along the Calapooia and Willamette rivers, with a stop at Thompson's Mills State Heritage Site.

Distance and climb: 30.9 miles round-trip, 255 feet total ascent. **Road surface:** Paved, mostly with paved shoulder. **Start/end point:** Linn County Historical Museum, 101 Park Ave, Brownsville. **Facilities:** Restrooms at the museum, Thompson's Mills State Heritage Site, Peoria County Park, and Snag Boat Bend.

Wide-open landscapes and pioneer history await you on this easy half-day (depending on the wind), mostly flat ride out of historic Brownsville through grass seed, wheat, hazelnut, and meadow-foam fields. You will see several century-old farmsteads along the route, part of which overlaps the

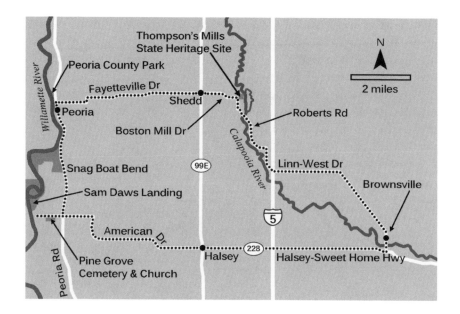

Willamette Valley Scenic Bikeway. Outbound from Brownsville, the shoulders are wide all the way to Roberts Road. At Thompson's Mills, you can take in the informational signs if you miss the guided tours. From Shedd to Peoria Road, you have a great view of Marys Peak. After you turn south onto Peoria Road, you arrive immediately at Peoria County Park with its toilets and picnic tables; shoulders are paved the rest of the way back to Brownsville. Just past Oxbow Orchard is Snag Boat Bend, a unit of the William L. Finley National Wildlife Refuge.

Turn-by-turn directions: From the museum, ride to Main St and turn right. Stay on Main as it jogs left through town. In a few blocks, turn left onto Depot Ave, ride two blocks, and bear right onto Linn Wy, which becomes Seven Mile Ln. At mile 3, bear left onto Linn-West Dr. Cross over the Sodom Channel and I-5, and at mile 5.2 turn right onto Roberts Rd. At mile 8.2, turn right onto Boston Mill Dr and detour 0.2 mile to visit Thompson's Mills State Heritage Site.

Then continue west 1.3 miles on Boston Mill Dr to Shedd, located on Hwy 99E. Cross the highway and continue 5 miles on Fayetteville Dr. At mile 15, turn left onto Peoria Rd, stopping at Peoria County Park or Snag Boat Bend if you choose. At mile 18.8, turn left onto American Dr. At this intersection, you can also take Pine Grove Dr to the right a quarter mile to detour to Pine Grove Cemetery (1853) and Community Church (1901). Headed back east on American Dr, pass through Halsey at mile 24, where the road turns into Hwy 228, and continue east 6.5 miles back to Brownsville. Turn left onto Main St to return to the Linn County Historical Museum.

PADDLING THE CALAPOOIA RIVER

Tucked between the better known McKenzie to the south and South Santiam to the north, the smaller, warmer Calapooia River is appreciated by locals who canoe and kayak the middle stretches in May and June, then turn to leisurely inner-tubing adventures as the water levels drop in July. The very uppermost section of the river offers class 3 and 4 rapids for those up to tough and technical white water, while the stretch from 4 miles above Holley to Brownsville is the most accessible, lively, and reliable section for the novice to intermediate kayaker. Below Pioneer Park in Brownsville, the river slows markedly as it reaches the floor of the Willamette Valley. Blackberries, willows, and fallen trees often block the segment from Brownsville to Albany.

Highways and farm roads parallel the river or bisect it at frequent intervals, offering the agile kayaker many places to launch a lightweight boat and get away from it all. Upper Calapooia Drive (County Road 759) closely follows the upper third of the river and in the past has offered access to advanced kayakers who enjoy the technical white water during the rainy season from 22 miles above Holley to 4 miles above Holley, but the road runs through private timberland and is gated at 8.5 miles above Holley. (While access rules change frequently, the headwaters are usually open to walk-in or bike-in anglers during summer months.) To reach the put-in points, from I-5 between Albany and Eugene take Exit 216 and head east on Highway 228 through Brownsville.

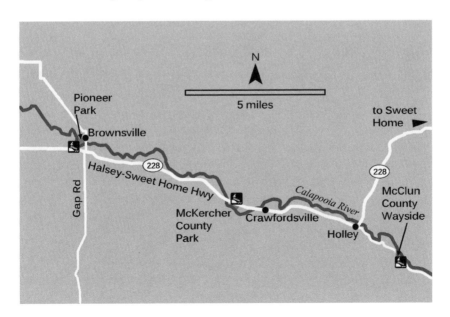

McCLUN COUNTY WAYSIDE TO McKERCHER COUNTY PARK

This quiet and pristine stretch of relatively easy rapids and riffles takes you through farmland, past occasional mossy grottos, and under a historic covered bridge.

Skill level: Beginning/intermediate (class 1 and 2). **Duration**: 2.5 to 3 hours. **River miles**: 7.2. **Put-in point**: McClun County Wayside, 1.8 miles up Upper Calapooia Dr from the Holley Store (where the road leaves Hwy 228). The wayside is just downstream from McClun Bridge. Of the two unimproved paths to the river, use the downstream one. **Take-out point**: McKercher County Park. **Facilities**: Portable toilet at McClun Wayside; vault toilets at McKercher. **Season**: Best in May and June for a beginning kayaker, April for a more experienced paddler; canoes do best in May. Rainfall can make the river's flow fluctuate greatly in a short time.

On this stretch, the Calapooia empties out of its narrow gorge to enter pasture land, but it keeps a steady pace. This run is suitable for open canoes early in the season, but by the end of June shallower-draft kayaks are a better choice. Be sure to wear closed-toed water shoes and have a length of cord with you to line your boat through stretches too shallow to run from July 1 onward.

Sweepers and debris jams come and go from one rainy season to the next so do as much scouting as roads and time permit. In particular, check out the class 2 rapids just below Crawfordsville where you pass under double bridges—one the modern bridge over Highway 228 and the other the 1934 covered bridge adjacent to it that was bypassed by the new bridge in 1963. From here the final mile to McKercher Park is well shaded and isolated from the road. Take out on the right when you see the picnic tables at the up-stream end of McKercher Park before you reach the class 4 rapids and falls just below.

BROWNSVILLE'S PIONEER PARK

Pioneer Park offers a place to swim in the Calapooia as well as base-ball diamonds, an outdoor basketball court, covered horseshoe pits, covered and outdoor picnic tables, and year-round camping (for information, call 541-466-5880). The huge maple trees provide an oasis of shade for the Linn County Pioneer Picnic, which happens on the third weekend in June. The event has convened here annu-ally since 1888, when the original wagon train families realized that the shared experiences of wagon train and early pioneer life were in danger of fading away. On the Fourth of July, local loggers compete in traditional events such as chopping, sawing, choke setting, and axe throwing. The Antiques Fair on the first Saturday in August fills the spacious park with vendors and browsers. For a full calendar of events: historicbrownsville.com/

McKERCHER COUNTY PARK TO PIONEER PARK IN BROWNSVILLE

This pleasant flat-water float through farmland is ideal for novice kayakers and canoeists.

Skill level: Beginning/intermediate (class 1 and 2). **Duration:** 3 to 4 hours. **River miles:** 7.5. **Put-in point:** McKercher County Park. Take the trail down from the parking lot and put in immediately below the falls at a small sandy beach. **Take-out point:** Pioneer Park, Brownsville. **Facilities:** Toilets at McKercher and Pioneer Parks. **Season:** Best in May and June for a beginning kayaker, April for a more experienced paddler; canoes do best in May. Rainfall can make the river's flow fluctuate greatly in a short time.

Many enjoyable hours can be spent on this slow-moving section of river exploring quiet bayou-like stretches that are the refuge of herons, mergansers, and things that go ker-plop in the dim light. Shade is provided by a verge of trees along the upper reaches; the lower reaches closer to Brownsville are bordered by open pasture. By mid-July most years you'll be bottoming out now and then even in a kayak.

Brush, brambles, and sweeper logs are the main hazards, and it seems the current always wants to drag you through them. One more serious hazard, depending on river flow, is the remains of the dismantled Brownsville Dam 4 miles below McKercher. Avoid the logs and concrete on the right and stick to the left side or portage. You can scout this spot from Northern Drive, 3.7 miles from McKercher Park.

Once you pass under Brownsville's iconic green bridge and make a big sweeping turn to the right, be prepared to take out on the right before reaching the high banks that mark the end of public property.

LUCKIAMUTE RIVER WATERSHED

The first thing you notice about the 368-square-mile Luckiamute (pronounced LUCKY-mute) River watershed is the river's circuitous route from its origins on the western peaks to the Willamette River floodplains at its eastern confluence. Following the path of a raindrop that falls on a southern Polk County ridge—maybe 3,232-foot Monmouth Peak or the slightly higher Fanno Ridge in the Coast Range—tells the story. If the raindrop leans slightly to the south, it will fall into the Siletz River and rush 40 miles to enter the Pacific Ocean just south of Lincoln City. But this raindrop falls on Monmouth Peak, also known as Bald Mountain for its naturally treeless subalpine meadow. It seeps into one of the tiny first-order streams that begin here, where the average rainfall is more than 140 inches a year. This drop's journey to the sea via the Luckiamute River will be nearly seven times as far as by the Siletz River route.

At first, its 62-mile ride to the Willamette River seems a quick one. The water rushes down steep slopes from Bald Mountain along logging roads, through commercial forests, over ancient volcanic basalt and marine sediment pushed up by the subductive dance of the Juan de Fuca Plate. But near the beginning of the public roads, where Luckiamute and Gage Roads meet, the Luckiamute River begins to slow. On its banks, homes appear and small farms, some built by families who have lived here for generations. At the community of Hoskins in Benton County, the river bends north around Fort Hoskins Historic Park, which commemorates a brief and solemn chapter in Oregon's history book. At Kings Valley, a tiny community settled since the 1840s, the river rushes past the store and the 1892 church that still serves as a community hall. At the historic Ritner Creek covered bridge, the river comes within view of bikers picnicking at the small park, Kings Valley Highway being a favorite rural biking route.

The river then turns north and slightly east, flowing past the tiny community of Pedee, through low foothills spread with Christmas trees and past homes in the rural Maple Grove area. There it turns away from narrow Kings Valley, choosing the fields that broaden to accommodate orchards, dairies, nurseries, and small farms along Maple Grove, Airlie, and then Elkins Roads. Just south of Elkins Road, a few miles west of Highway 99W, the now-meandering Luckiamute meets up with the Little Luckiamute, which has its start at the top of Fanno Ridge. As if to catch up on news from Falls City, the combined currents here slow to a crawl, and in the winter they pool and flood, raising giant jams of logs and debris from the mountains, creating impromptu dams that send the waters over the banks to mix with rich silty loam before they return to the lower Luckiamute.

In the summer, the muddy Luckiamute idles through Sarah Helmick State Recreation Site, where swimmers and waders find refreshment before the river crosses Highway 99W south of Monmouth. Now, as the river turns south and then east, it passes the outpost of Parker, with its historic homes and farms, meandering in broad U shapes through the bottomland on its way to its destination a few miles south of Buena Vista. Near where Soap Creek and the Luckiamute merge, Indian arrowheads are found on the Willamette half a mile to the east, pressed into its banks by members of the Luckiamute band of Kalapuya.

Past the state boat ramp on the west side of Buena Vista Road, the river wends through Luckiamute Landing State Natural Area, home to camas bulbs that send up their blue and white flowers along the trails, rare western pond turtles and wapato, and native birds, fish, and reptiles. Once joined with the Willamette at 150 feet above sea level, just downstream of where the Santiam River comes in on the other side, the raindrop that fell on Bald Mountain still has 108 miles to go to reach the Columbia River, and then another 100 river miles to navigate to the sea. Its roundabout journey has taken it through lands both ruggedly wild and bucolic, which the public can experience at state and county recreation sites and in the OSU-owned Paul M. Dunn Forest.

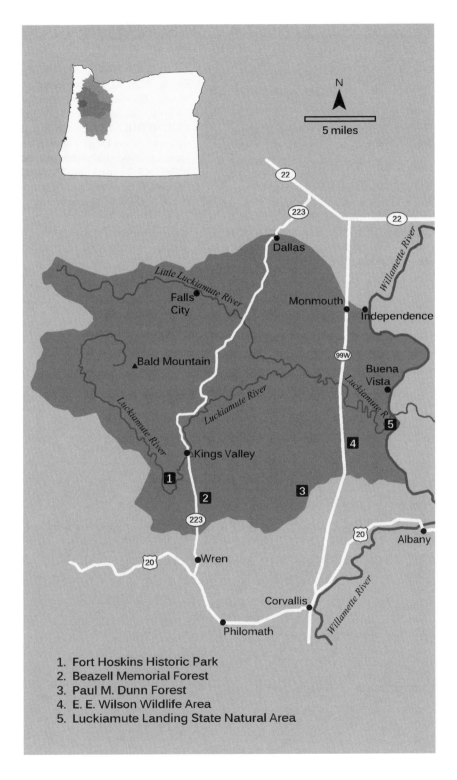

1. Fort Hoskins Historic Park
2. Beazell Memorial Forest
3. Paul M. Dunn Forest
4. E. E. Wilson Wildlife Area
5. Luckiamute Landing State Natural Area

FORT HOSKINS HISTORIC PARK

The site of a Civil War–era Army fort in the Coast Range foothills offers fine views from a knoll overlooking the Luckiamute River.

To get there: From Corvallis, take Hwy 20 west for 10 miles and turn right onto Hwy 223 at a big sign for Kings Valley. Follow the highway for 6.4 miles and turn left onto Hoskins Rd. After 1.8 miles, continue straight onto Luckiamute Rd where Hoskins Rd goes off to the left. After another 0.2 mile, turn right onto Fort Hoskins Rd and drive up this steep entrance road for 0.4 mile to the paved parking area.

ACTIVITIES: Hiking, picnicking. **FACILITIES:** ADA restrooms, historic buildings, picnic shelter (to reserve, call 541-766-6871). **FEES AND REGULATIONS:** No fee. Open dawn to dusk. Dogs allowed on leash or under voice control. **BEST MONTHS:** Year-round. **MANAGING AGENCY:** Benton County Natural Areas and Parks Department.

At 128-acre Fort Hoskins Historic Park, a picnic shelter in an old apple orchard looks out across the fort site to the distant Luckiamute River and a few scattered farmhouses, all that remains of the town of Hoskins. If you know the story here, this view across the head of Kings Valley is really a view across 150 years of Oregon's history.

As in the neighboring Willamette Valley, the Kalapuya tribe in Kings Valley used fire to manage the land, burning off grass and fir seedlings

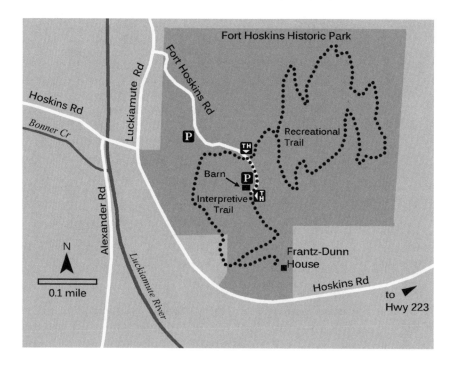

each year. The resulting oak savanna provided a wealth of food—edible camas flower bulbs, acorns, and tarweed seeds, as well as easily huntable deer. Beginning in the 1770s, however, disastrous plagues of smallpox and other "white man's" diseases killed up to 95 percent of the native people. When Nahum King led a group of twenty-five Oregon Trail pioneers to stake out farms in Kings Valley in 1846, the decimated tribe offered no resistance.

Wild turkey © David Wagner

Nonetheless, the Army rounded up Indians from all of western Oregon onto two reservations, the Siletz and the Grand Ronde. When it opened in 1856, Fort Hoskins stood at the intersection of two major Indian trails and monitored traffic entering and leaving the coastal Siletz Indian Reservation. The fort changed its focus during the Civil War, keeping an eye on settlers sympathetic to the Confederacy. When the war ended in 1865, the Army abandoned the fort. The site was sold to a family that lived and farmed there until 1992, when Benton County bought the land and developed it into a park that opened to the public in 2002.

The park has two trails: the Interpretive Trail with signage describing fort history and the Recreational Trail looping through a woodland setting. For the first, a 0.6-mile tour of the fort site, walk down the gated road by the picnic shelter and turn right at the bottom of the hill on a wide gravel path. Just beyond a sign describing the fort's parade grounds, detour briefly left down a road to the Frantz-Dunn House, built in 1869 by the family who bought the fort. Then continue on the gravel loop trail back up to the picnic area.

For a longer hike, look for a vertical trail marker opposite the restrooms. Take this path up through Douglas-fir woods 200 yards and fork to the right. The 1.2-mile loop that begins here switchbacks, steeply at times, up a hill through a restored oak savanna. Park managers have cut invasive firs to release the old oaks favored by the Kalapuyans' ancient system of management by fire.

Options: To combine with a visit to Beazell Memorial Forest, go back to Hwy 223, turn right, go 1.6 miles, and turn left into the park at the sign.

BEAZELL MEMORIAL FOREST

The largest park in Benton County offers Douglas-fir forests, oak savannas, hilltop meadows with grand vistas, and a lush riparian area along Plunkett Creek, a tributary of the Luckiamute.

To get there: From Corvallis, take Hwy 20 west for 10 miles and turn right onto Hwy 223 at a big sign for Kings Valley. Follow the highway for 4.8 miles to a sign for Beazell Memorial Forest and turn right into the gravel parking turnaround.

ACTIVITIES: Picnicking, hiking, biking, horseback riding, nature education. **FACILITIES:** Restrooms, picnic tables, forest education center, pioneer farmhouse, creekside gazebo. **FEES AND REGULATIONS:** No fee. Open dawn to dusk. Dogs allowed on leash. Plunkett Creek Trail closed to bikes and horses October 31 to April 15. **BEST MONTHS:** Year-round. **MANAGING AGENCY:** Benton County Natural Area and Parks Department.

Three miles from Fort Hoskins on the other side of the Luckiamute River, another early pioneer family settled. Ashnah Plunkett, the first white child born in Kings Valley, had met her husband at a local dance. He was a California soldier serving as a drummer at Fort Hoskins. Together they built a white clapboard farmhouse along Plunkett Creek in 1875 and raised a family. Ashnah lived there until her death in 1933. The original farmhouse still stands in the middle of the parking loop.

Fred Beazell, an employee at a high-tech company in California's Silicon Valley, bought the Plunkett farm as a vacation retreat in 1966 and finally persuaded his wife to move to Oregon in 1991. But Dolores Beazell died just two years later. Grieving, and without children, Fred decided to leave the 586-acre property to the public in memory of his beloved wife. Today Benton County manages the land to provide hiking trails and education.

For a 1.8-mile loop that gains 288 feet alongside splashing Plunkett Creek, take the gravel trail from the parking area past the Plunketts' 1930s barn, restored as a forest education center. Stay left at the first junction (going right would take you to the South Ridge Trail), cross a footbridge, and turn right onto an old roadbed (going left would take you to the 1.2-mile Bird Loop Trail, ideal for bird-watching). This wide trail follows Plunkett Creek up a canyon shaded by mossy bigleaf maples, Douglas-firs, and alders. At 0.5 mile, fork to the right on the Plunkett Creek Loop, a smaller gravel path closer to the creek. Stay on this path as you cross three wooden-railed footbridges and eventually connect up with the old roadbed again, where you turn left to return to your starting point.

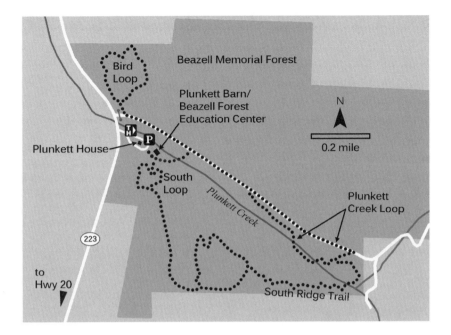

For a more vigorous hike, 2.8 miles total with 600 feet elevation gain, take the Plunkett Creek Loop as above for nearly a mile but just past the second footbridge, turn right at the easy-to-miss junction with the South Ridge Trail. This route climbs in switchbacks to a big junction with a mapboard. If you turn right here and keep right at junctions you'll climb 0.2 mile to a forested hilltop, zigzag down 0.3 mile beside a meadow, and follow an old roadbed 0.7 mile back to your car.

PAUL M. DUNN FOREST

An OSU research forest north of McDonald Forest offers miles of mostly shaded gravel roads for recreation.

To get there: From Corvallis, take Hwy 99W north 6 miles past Walnut Blvd and turn left onto Tampico Rd. There are four entry points to the forest on Tampico Rd, all on the left: the Rd 400 gate (2.5 miles from 99W), the Rd 300 gate (3.1 miles from 99W), the Rd 200 gate (4.5 miles from 99W), and the Rd 100 gate (5 miles from 99W).

ACTIVITIES: Hiking, horseback riding, mountain biking, hunting. **FACILITIES:** None. **FEES AND REGULATIONS:** No fee. Dogs allowed on leash. Timber harvesting and walk-in hunting for deer, elk, and turkey may restrict recreational use at times; for a recorded message about current restrictions, call 541-737-4434. **BEST MONTHS:** Year-round. **MANAGING AGENCY:** Oregon State University College of Forestry.

Paul M. Dunn Forest was once part of Camp Adair and was acquired by OSU in 1949 while Paul M. Dunn was dean of the College of Forestry. Most of the 4,030-acre forest is devoted to Douglas-fir plantations, with the southern portion on thirty-five- to forty-five-year rotations and the northern portion on sixty- to ninety-year

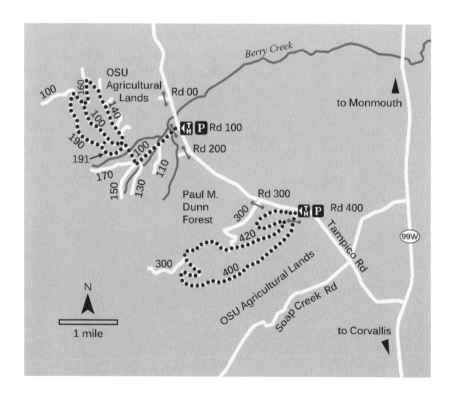

rotations. The southern portion has a few scattered stands of old growth with trees more than 160 years old. Unlike McDonald Forest, Dunn Forest doesn't have any recreational trails, but it does have miles of gravel roads that are visited by fewer people than McDonald Forest and are mostly open year-round to hikers, equestrians, and mountain bikers. The roads pass through the whole gamut of sites, from freshly harvested to recently planted to second growth and old growth, so be prepared for some cutover areas that lack shade. Access is from four trailheads at the Rd 100, 200, 300, and 400 gates. A map is available online at cf.forestry. oregonstate.edu/sites/cf/files/Dunn_Final.pdf.

For a 6.4-mile loop that gains 1,150 feet and offers views in all directions from the top, start at the Rd 400 trailhead and walk up Rd 400. Some nice views to the north open up at about mile 1.5. At mile 3, the road flattens out after a steep stretch and offers some wide Cascade views to the east as it curves broadly to the right. Rd 400 soon merges into Rd 300; go right here and stay on Rd 300 until it intersects Rd 420, where you take a right. This section of the hike is mostly downhill or flat, with views across farmland to the north and west. When Rd 420 reaches Rd 400, turn left to get back to your starting point.

The Rd 100 trailhead also offers loop possibilities. For a 5-mile trek that gains 400 feet and crosses the north fork of Berry Creek, a tributary of the Luckiamute River by way of Soap Creek, follow Rd 100 from the gate as it ascends gently through open fields managed by the OSU College of Agriculture. Stay straight where Rd 110 and later Rd 130 split off to the left. Where Rd 150 continues straight ahead, make a sharp turn to the right to stay on Rd 100. Just after Berry Creek, stay right on Rd 100 as Rd 191 splits off to the left. At the top of the next rise, take Rd 140 as it splits off to the right and offers open views to the northeast across a cutover area. Stay on Rd 140 past all spurs until it comes to

Equisetum © David Wagner

COUGARS AND BLACK BEARS

Cougars (mountain lions) and black bears live in McDonald and Dunn forests and are occasionally sighted. The odds are that you won't see one, but if you do, be sure to report your sighting. Black bears are omnivores that live mainly on leaves, berries, nuts, insects and their larvae, and fish. Deer and elk are cougars' principal prey, but they also hunt coyotes, rabbits, rodents, raccoons, beavers, and on occasion, pets and livestock. They have also been known to attack people. Cougars tend to be out at dusk and dawn but otherwise take cover. If you do happen to see one, remember that it is likely more afraid of you than you are of it. Stay calm, speak softly, and continue to face it while slowly moving out of its way, leaving it an escape route. Do not run, as that may trigger its natural pursuit instincts.

a Y; go left here onto Rd 160. When Rd 160 reaches a T, go left onto Rd 100 and follow it back to the starting point. To add on another mile or so and another 350 feet of elevation, go right onto Rd 100 when Rd 160 reaches the T, and then left onto Rd 190 at the next intersection. Rd 190 merges back into Rd 100 eventually.

E. E. WILSON WILDLIFE AREA

The street grid from a World War II Army training camp gives easy access to 3 square miles of woodlands, wetlands, and fields, plus a remnant of upland oak savanna in the Coffin Butte Tract.

To get there: From Corvallis take Hwy 99W north about 8 miles, or from Monmouth take Hwy 99W south about 10 miles, then turn east onto Camp Adair Rd and park in any of the designated parking areas. For the Interpretive Trail, park at the Public Viewing Area on the north side of Camp Adair Rd. For the Coffin Butte Tract and trailhead, use the gravel parking area 0.4 mile north of Camp Adair Rd on the west side of Hwy 99W just north of the landfill. Weekday bus service is available from downtown Corvallis to the southwest corner of the wildlife area on the 99 Express (co.benton.or.us/pw/stf/schedules.php)

ACTIVITIES: Walking, jogging, biking, horseback riding, fishing, hunting, skeet shooting, picnicking, wildlife viewing. **FACILITIES:** ADA restroom at the Public Viewing Area (closed in winter), fishing pond (with benches and picnic tables) that's stocked with trout February to June, historic buildings and displays, interpretive signs, wildlife viewing blind. **FEES AND REGULATIONS:** Parking permits required; must be purchased in advance from ODFW online (dfw.state.or.us) or anywhere hunting/fishing licenses are sold. Open daily 4 a.m. to 10 p.m. Dogs allowed year-round but must be on leash March through August. **BEST MONTHS:** Year-round. Expect to encounter hunters anytime from September through February; hunting use peaks during pheasant season in November. **MANAGING AGENCY:** Oregon Department of Fish and Wildlife.

This wildlife area offers a fascinating look at how nature is reclaiming the landscape of a World War II Army camp. Seasonal wetlands that were drained for the camp are being restored, and the area is home to many animal species of concern, including the western pond turtle, red-legged frog, and yellow-breasted chat. One of the largest known remaining populations of threatened Nelson's checkermallow is also found here.

The area offers a multitude of possible walking or bicycling routes on the street grid of what was effectively Oregon's second-largest city during the war years. Your best route is to follow wherever your curiosity takes you at each intersection. Grades on the main part of the wildlife area are gentle. However, to avoid a longer-than-expected route back to the parking areas, you should be aware of the main gaps in the street grid.

To the south of Camp Adair Rd, the wildlife area is divided into southeast and southwest quadrants by a waterway that's too deep to cross in most seasons. The first east-west crossing of this waterway is more than a mile south of Camp Adair Road, so unless you have time for a 2-mile loop, you'll want to stick to one quadrant. To the north of Camp Adair

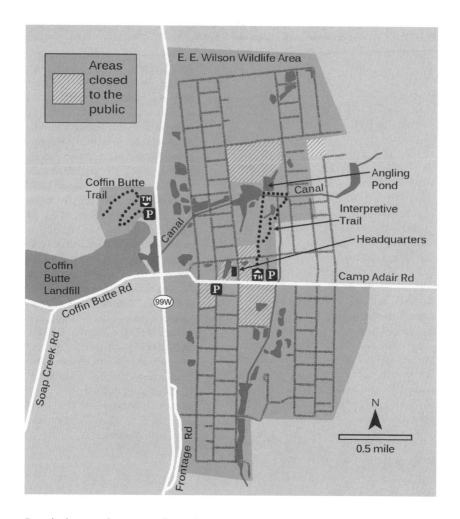

Road, the northwest and northeast quadrants are separated by an area used for ODFW operations that's closed to the public starting just north of headquarters. If you want to make a loop through both quadrants of the north end, you'll need to circumnavigate this closed zone. Finally, access from north to south on the east side of the wildlife area is limited by a canal that flows east out of the wildlife area, and another closed-to-the-public area (the site of a proposed BOMARC surface-to-air missile installation at the height of the Cold War in the 1960s).

For a well-defined walking route, try the gravel-and-boardwalk Interpretive Trail, which makes an easy, nearly level 1.5-mile loop to the Angling Pond and back through woodland and wetland. Start from the Public Viewing Area parking lot next to the Camp Adair Memorial Garden and head north past the pheasant show pens, a legacy from when the area was used to breed game birds. Follow the "Trail" signs to reach the gravel path. When you reach the Angling Pond, go right and follow the south shore, then bear right as the trail splits off and descends from the pond road. Just before meeting up again with the gravel path you came in on, the trail crosses a mowed grass expanse with a cluster of small wooden buildings formerly used for scouting jamborees.

For a more vigorous hike that offers a view of the valley and traverses a patch of legacy oaks and upland prairie, take the Coffin Butte Trail in the westernmost tract of the wildlife area. This easy/moderate 1.7-mile out-and-back route is steep in places, with 375 feet of elevation gain. You'll also have a prime view into the operations of a state-of-the-art regional landfill. Methane gas generated by decomposing garbage is piped to turbines that generate enough power for about four thousand homes. From the gravel parking lot off Hwy 99W, the trail follows a gravel service road uphill for 100 yards before a short side road branches off to a quarried area where you can see excellent exposures of some of the oldest rocks in the mid-Willamette Valley. You soon pass another quarry, where a vernal pond hosts Pacific chorus-frog tadpoles in spring. Back on the main trail, pause at the viewpoint and imagine the quiet farming and ranching community along the sleepy highway below this butte in the early 1940s, just before its sudden transformation for the war effort.

Continue up the trail through oak woodland to a grassy meadow. A metal-roof water guzzler (a structure designed to catch and hold rainwater so that wildlife such as deer can "guzzle" from it) on the north side of this meadow is set among madrones and cascara trees that draw warblers in spring, tanagers in fall, and Hutton's vireos in winter. In another 200 yards, you'll come to the end of the trail at a sign designating the highest point in E. E. Wilson Wildlife Area (604 feet).

PILLOW BASALTS

The exposed rocks you pass on the Coffin Butte Trail are pillow basalts of the Eocene age, which are interpreted as having formed from underwater lava flows similar to those that are now seen offshore of Hawaii. These basalts, together with intercalated marine sediments, were originally described by OSU geologists as the Coffin Butte Volcanic formation but now are usually counted as part of the Siletz River Volcanic formation. They most likely formed in a tropical or subtropical island setting before they accreted to the North American continent through the ongoing process of plate tectonics.

A newer park in a floodplain landscape on the Willamette River offers packed dirt and gravel trails through a patch of old farmland and native forest as well as paddle access to the Luckiamute River.

To get there: There are three access points. From Albany, take Hwy 20 west and cross the bridge over the Willamette River, then turn right onto Springhill Rd and go for about 6 miles. Turn right onto Buena Vista Rd and look for the South Luckiamute sign in about 0.25 mile on the right. Continue a mile farther and turn right at the North Luckiamute sign, cross a bridge, and follow a gravel drive 0.25 mile to the parking area. Paddler's Access is another 0.25 mile north of the North Luckiamute sign on the other side of Buena Vista Rd.

ACTIVITIES: Picnicking, hiking, fishing, bird-watching, boating, boat-in camping. **FACILITIES:** ADA portable toilet at the north parking area, vault toilets at the south parking area and at the paddle access, picnic tables. **FEES AND REGULATIONS:** No fee. Open dawn to dusk. Dogs allowed; must be leashed from April 1 to July 31 during ground bird nesting season. No bicycles, horses, or target shooting. Avoid entering restricted areas around the ponds and watch for poison oak. **BEST MONTHS:** Year-round. Trails can be puddled and muddy when it rains and can be underwater during floods. **MANAGING AGENCY:** Oregon Parks and Recreation Department.

Luckiamute Landing State Natural Area covers 926 acres in two tracts separated by private property. Habitat restoration work is ongoing in the natural area, which was acquired in pieces over time and opened to the public in 2011. Western meadowlarks winter in sizable flocks in open areas of the park.

The south tract encompasses 311 acres and features two ponds that were originally quarried for gravel in the construction of Camp Adair during World War II. The west pond, accessible by a short trail that continues in a mile-long loop around a restored prairie, offers good fishing on the south bank; the east pond is closed to fishing. Both ponds provide excellent habitat for the native western pond turtle.

The 615-acre north tract contains one of the Willamette Valley's largest remaining and best-preserved bottomland gallery forests (defined as a forest that forms a corridor along a waterway in a landscape that is otherwise sparsely inhabited by trees). This forest is dominated by a mix of bigleaf maple, black cottonwood, and Oregon ash. The north tract provides paddle access to the Luckiamute River; a removable floating dock is available from late spring until late fall. The north tract offers a choice of easy walks on fairly level terrain.

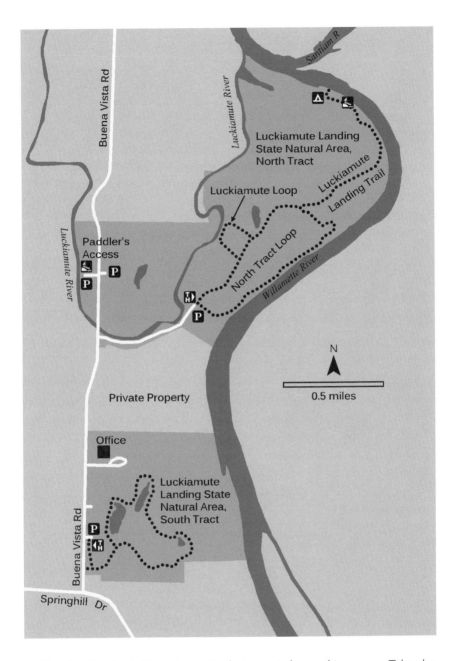

The 2-mile North Tract Loop Trail starts at the parking area. Take the trail on the right through the gap in the post-rail fence to traverse the loop counterclockwise and reach the Willamette River sooner rather than later. Near the trailhead, volunteers have planted native wildflowers in a demonstration prairie. You soon reach the banks of the Willamette

WESTERN POND TURTLES

The western pond turtle is listed in the "critical" category on the Oregon Department of Fish and Wildlife Sensitive Species List primarily because the young are a favorite meal of invasive bullfrogs. The pond turtle has a dark brown to olive shell with a cream-colored underside, grows up to 10 inches long, and can live to be forty years old in the wild. Besides flooded gravel pits, habitats include ponds, rivers, reservoirs, and seasonal wetlands. Pond turtles can also live on land part of the year and can burrow into mud to survive when a pond or river dries up.

Pond turtles breed from mid-May to late July and lay from one to thirteen eggs. They nest in areas of short grass or weeds on south- or southwest-facing slopes. They eat mainly insects but can also eat some plants and scavenge dead meat. Turtles bask in the sun on large rocks or logs in order to regulate their body temperature and digestion. To report sightings or for more information: oregonturtles.com.

and catch occasional views of the river through the trees before the trail swings left into an open patch of old farmland. At mile 1.2 you reach a junction. Turn left to return to the parking area or right to follow the 2-mile (out and back) Luckiamute Landing Trail. This trail follows a service road through the gallery forest to a rocky beach and a boat-in camp near the Luckiamute-Santiam-Willamette confluence.

The 0.5-mile Luckiamute Loop Trail takes off from the North Tract Loop Trail about 0.5 mile past the metal gate at the parking lot and is indicated by a post with a hiker symbol and directional arrow on it. This trail heads west toward the Luckiamute River and then northeast to bring you back to the North Tract Loop about 0.3 mile past where you hopped off.

BIKING THE LUCKIAMUTE WATERSHED

Lots of mountain biking adventures are to be had in Dunn Forest and the Black Rock Mountain Bike Area west of Falls City. The latter has been under development since 2002 in the George T. Gerlinger State Experimental Forest on Mount Brown. In cooperation with the Oregon Department of Forestry, volunteers have developed a system of four trails there for beginning to advanced riders. There are many looping opportunities and a variety of routes to choose from. To get there from Falls City, take Main Street west through town and bear right on Mitchell. Turn left onto Black Rock Road and continue for 3 miles, watching for logging trucks. Turn right at Camp Tapawingo and park at the trailhead. Do not drive past or block the gate. For route maps and more info: brmba.org.

For road bikes, a very popular route through the watershed is Kings Valley Road (Highway 223) between Dallas and Wren, with a detour to Monmouth via Airlie Road to Elkins Road to Helmick Road. Another favorite is the route from Kings Valley to Independence or Albany via Maxfield Creek Road to Airlie Road to Suver Road. Airlie and Emerson wineries are on that route.

CORVALLIS TO THE BUENA VISTA FERRY

A ride northeast from Corvallis crosses the Luckiamute River and rolls through hilly farmland to the Buena Vista Ferry or optionally Ankeny National Wildlife Refuge or the Rogue Hopyard.

Distance and climb: 35 miles round-trip, 614 feet total ascent. **Road surface:** Paved, some loose gravel from driveways. **Start/end point:** Osborn Aquatic Center, 10th St and Circle Blvd, Corvallis. **Facilities:** Restrooms at Osborn Aquatic Center; vault toilet at South Luckiamute parking lot on Buena Vista Rd, mile 14, and at Buena Vista County Park, mile 17.5.

This ride takes you through the E. E. Wilson Wildlife Area and past mounds of compost at Pacific Region Compost fueled by the debris bins of Corvallis. In tiny Buena Vista, the park / boat launch is a nice place to have lunch or a snack while the ferry shuttles between the Willamette River's shores. From there you have the option of crossing on the ferry and riding on to Ankeny National Wildlife Refuge or continuing north to the Rogue Farms Hopyard, where food and drink are available.

Turn-by-turn directions: Ride north on NW Highland Dr, cross Circle Blvd and then Walnut Blvd, and ride up a challenging hill that crests at mile 1.4. At mile 3, turn right onto Lewisburg Rd. At mile 4, turn left onto Hwy 99W. At mile 7.8, in Adair Village, you can stay on Hwy 99W and climb another hill or take the frontage road just east of the highway to climb a less steep hill and

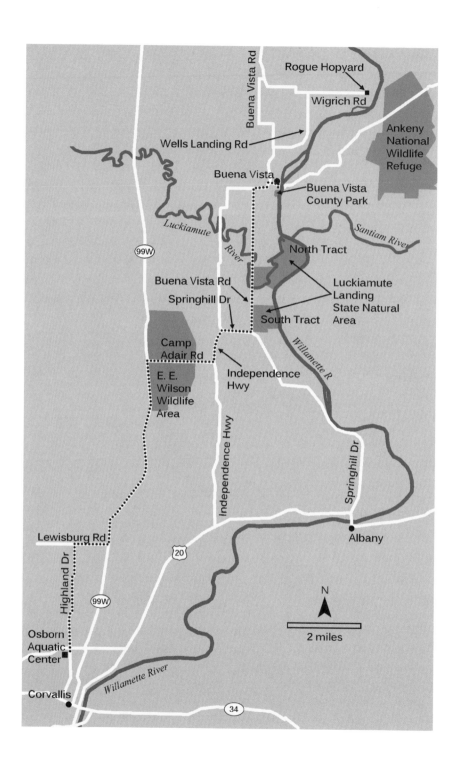

get away from traffic. The frontage road rejoins Hwy 99W at mile 8.6. At mile 9.1, turn right onto Camp Adair Rd.

At mile 11.1, turn left at the T onto Independence Hwy. At mile 12, turn right onto Springhill Dr. At mile 12.8, turn left onto Buena Vista Rd, and cross the Luckiamute River at mile 14.2. At mile 16.8, at the top of a mile-long hill, take the right fork to stay on Buena Vista Rd. At mile 17, turn right onto Main St at the sign to the ferry and right again onto Park St, which leads into the park/boat launch. If this is your final destination, you can ride back to Corvallis the way you came.

Options: If you want to ride to Ankeny National Wildlife Refuge, it's about 5 miles from the east side of the ferry landing along a lightly traveled road with pleasant rural scenery. If you happen to have a thirst for fine brews and a hunger for pub food, do not cross on the ferry but ride on to the Rogue Hopyard (round-trip 47 miles from start point in Corvallis). Follow Buena Vista Rd north for another couple of miles and at mile 19.1 turn right onto Wells Landing Rd. At mile 21.3, turn right at the T onto Wigrich Rd and ride a couple more miles to enter the Rogue Hopyard. The road dead-ends at mile 23.3 just before it reaches the Willamette River.

PADDLING THE LUCKIAMUTE RIVER

The Little Luckiamute and the Luckiamute converge 4 miles upstream from Sarah Helmick State Recreation Site and meander another 17.5 miles to the Willamette River. Once scoured by splash dam logging operations, most of the upper reaches of both rivers now run wild, though steep drops and technical portages limit this water to expert paddlers. Some extreme kayakers are willing to bushwhack down to the water and embrace stretches of class 4 and 5 rapids in spring when the river flows at 500 cubic feet per second (cfs). A few people have kayaked the major falls at Falls City when the river was running at 700 cfs. The lower stretches below the cataract at Falls City are navigable by canoe and kayak yet still

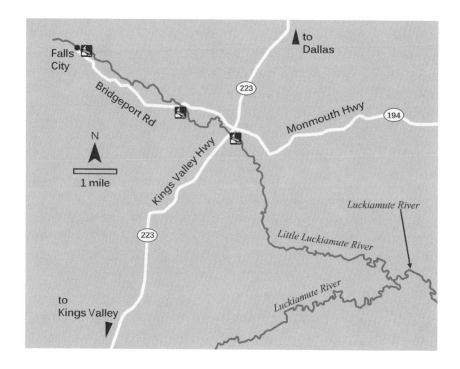

snarled with timber and brush, until the clear passage around Luckiamute Landing State Natural Area.

Intermediate and beginning paddlers can launch into the Little Luckiamute behind City Hall on Mill Street in Falls City and bounce and glide 3.5 miles down a mossy boulder garden to the bridge at Bridgeport Road or another mile past the mouth of Teal Creek to the span at Kings Valley Highway (Hwy 223). A gauge on this bridge can help boaters keep track of water levels (2.5 indicates a medium flow). Medium flows in fall or spring provide relatively clear passage through some class 2 rapids and downed trees that come and go. Summer flows require a few drags over gravel bars; winter can bring intense flows through dangerous strainers.

After Kings Valley Highway, the increasingly turbid Little Lucky sieves through downed trees and logjams and pushes under heavy brush, especially near its confluence with the Luckiamute. The next section to Helmick State Recreation Site can also be treacherous and exhausting, with numerous sweepers, logjams, and steep banks snarled in nettle and blackberry. Fit, properly suited, experienced paddlers may thrill to the challenge of extensive portages and brushy surprises, but for most, recreational paddling begins at Helmick.

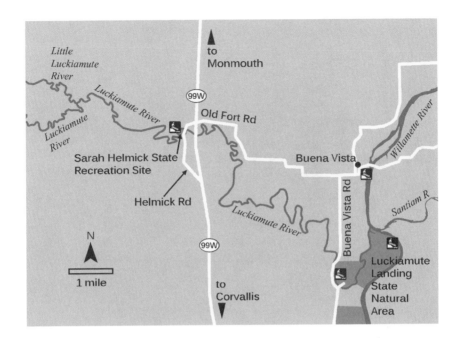

Several paths at Helmick lead down to the river, some steeper and slicker than others. A popular paddle from here loops and twists 13.5 miles through Luckiamute Landing into the Willamette and another 1.5 miles to Buena Vista County Park. This trip may take eight hours or more in summer, or as little as five hours during moderate spring flows (1000–1500 cfs). Here on the valley floor the muddy Luckiamute meanders under five bridges, including a railroad trestle, where again frequent logjams and tall banks make passage precarious.

The simplest, snag-free paddle begins at Luckiamute Landing State Natural Area. The paddle launch on Buena Vista Road is well marked. There is no fee for parking overnight, but the park ranger encourages a heads-up (541-924-8492). Here the current is often mild and paddlers can explore upriver or head downstream 2 miles to the Willamette.

SOUTH SANTIAM RIVER WATERSHED

The 66-mile-long South Santiam River runs clear and cold out of the Cascades from its origin at the confluence of Latiwi and Sevenmile creeks just west of Jumpoff Joe Mountain. At higher elevations, the river's mountainous terrain is thickly forested with mostly second-growth Douglas-fir, western hemlock, red cedar, bigleaf maple, and red alder. East of Sweet Home, its waters are impounded in Foster Reservoir, completed in 1968 to control flooding, generate hydroelectricity, and provide recreation and irrigation. This is also where it gathers in the waters of the Middle Santiam River and Quartzville Creek, both of which are impounded above Foster Reservoir behind Green Peter Dam, completed in 1967 and providing the same services. Below Foster, the South Santiam receives the waters of numerous other tributaries, including Wiley Creek, McDowell Creek, Hamilton Creek, Crabtree Creek, and Thomas Creek. It flows through an agricultural and residential landscape past Sweet Home, Waterloo, Lebanon, and Crabtree before finally meeting the North Santiam south of Jefferson.

Santiam was a Kalapuyan leader who lived near the confluence of his namesake river and the Willamette. The Santiam Molalla and Santiam Kalapuya peoples lived in the valleys of the middle and south forks of the Santiam until forced to the Grand Ronde Reservation in 1856. Hudson's Bay Company trapper Thomas McKay followed the South Santiam River in 1846 looking for a suitable wagon route from Albany to the Malheur River but found none. Not until 1861 was a route laid out that closely followed Indian trails; the Santiam Wagon Road was completed in 1868 and provided a vital commercial link connecting the Willamette Valley with central Oregon into the late 1930s. In 1905, the road was on the route of the first transcontinental auto race, pitting two 1904 Oldsmobile Runabouts against each other in a journey from New York City to the Lewis and Clark Exposition in Portland. The advent of railroads beginning in the early 1900s considerably reduced freight traffic on the wagon road, as did completion of the McKenzie Pass Highway in the 1920s. The Santiam Highway (Highway 20), completed in 1939, supplanted and closely follows the route of the Santiam Wagon Road, which was listed on the National Register of Historic Places in 2010.

The South Santiam watershed, 30 to 40 percent of which is publicly owned, offers plenty of opportunities for hiking, camping, swimming, fishing, boating, cross-country skiing, and even climbing on the rock spires of Menagerie Wilderness. The Willamette National Forest and two wilderness areas at higher elevation offer camping and hiking, as do Cascadia State Park, BLM recreation sites, and Linn County parks along the lower reaches. The Sweet Home Ranger District of the US Forest Service offers a series of guided hikes and events throughout the year; for information, call 541-367-5168.

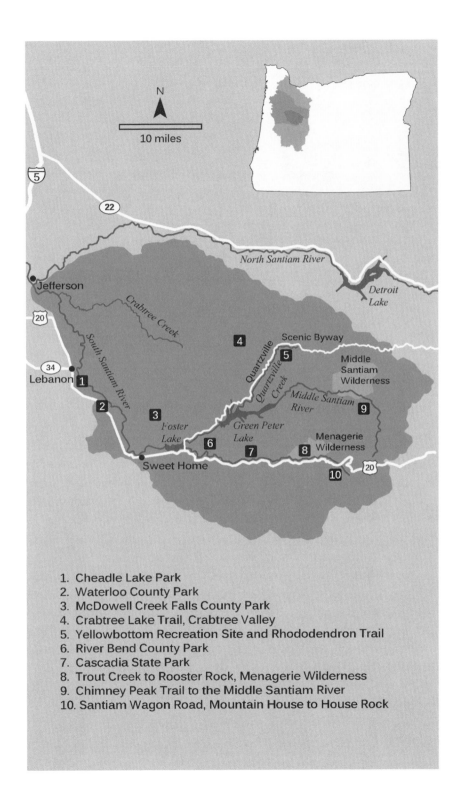

1. Cheadle Lake Park
2. Waterloo County Park
3. McDowell Creek Falls County Park
4. Crabtree Lake Trail, Crabtree Valley
5. Yellowbottom Recreation Site and Rhododendron Trail
6. River Bend County Park
7. Cascadia State Park
8. Trout Creek to Rooster Rock, Menagerie Wilderness
9. Chimney Peak Trail to the Middle Santiam River
10. Santiam Wagon Road, Mountain House to House Rock

Salmon on the Santiam

HENRY HUGHES

It's May, and a few days without rain have lifted my spirits and settled the river. At first light, I walk between the towering firs of Sweet Home's Waterloo Park, down through the ferns and holly to the mossy alder banks of the South Santiam and start casting for salmon, what Izaak Walton called "the King of fresh-water fish." I mull over some problems at home—my son's grades, my wife's teaching load, and the cost of a needed new roof. By late morning, two other anglers speaking Russian walk away defeated, and I'm tempted to whistle a little Tchaikovsky. Hours go by and other people come and go, asking "Any action?" and "Where's the fish?" The afternoon sun lights the wooded east bank, a deer nibbles young willow spears. The water glows an opalescent blue-green, and I watch it braid white over the cobbled basalt and down through the throat of the falls.

Time and motion swirl. Kalapuya Indians once came down to these falls to trap and spear fish, and early white settlers netted, snagged, and pitchforked salmon out by the thousands, filling wagons and smokehouses. The salmon has always been an important food source and cultural icon for peoples of the Pacific Northwest. Where are the fish today?

A salmon leaps, a silvery arc of muscled amazement; then another, and my heart leaps with them. *They're here*, I whisper to myself, snapping on a bright new spinner and casting into the frothy boil below the falls, reeling the lure deep through the bubbling tailout. Another fish rolls just a few feet away. As I retrieve a little more slowly on the next cast, the line suddenly stops. Arcing back on the rod, I feel the living weight and see a huge bright crescent erupting into the broad splash of a spotted tail.

The fish dives and runs deep, as chinook salmon almost always do, tearing downstream nearly to the steel bridge, where a couple of truant boys yell and point. I stay tight to its runs, steer it away from a log, delight in the fight, and just hang on as it makes one more plunge into the pool, coming up slowly and showing a chrome flank that melts away—at least for a moment—any of life's little worries. A young man fishing on the bank a few feet away reels in his line and offers to help. "Thanks," I say, relieved. We step carefully over the sharp stones, and I guide the fish into the green mesh of his net. "Nice springer," he says. "Gotta be twenty pounds. A real bright buck!"

The spring chinook salmon is one of the great treasures of the Willamette River and its Cascade-side tributaries—the South and North Santiam, Clackamas, Molalla, Calapooia, Middle Fork Willamette, and McKenzie Rivers. Before settlement, these waters teemed with chinook salmon and with steelhead, cutthroat, bull, and rainbow trout. Land development, industry, agriculture, logging, overfishing, hatcheries, and thirteen major dams have forever changed the life of the Willamette's king of fish, but the odyssey of the salmon I hold seems no less amazing.

This fish was one of the 28,000 spring chinook to leave the river, survive life at sea, and be counted on its homebound journey at Willamette Falls in 2013. The average annual number of spring chinook coming up the Willamette in the last ten years has been 46,000, in addition to

FISH PASSAGE AND HABITAT

The South Santiam River watershed sustains populations of native spring chinook salmon (the official state fish of Oregon) and winter steelhead trout, listed as threatened under the Endangered Species Act. The watershed is also home to coastal cutthroat trout and Pacific lamprey, listed as sensitive. The Foster and Green Peter Dams make it hard for salmonids to migrate to and from prime spawning and rearing habitat in the upper reaches of the basin. Green Peter Dam completely prevents fish passage to the Quartzville Creek and Middle Santiam River watersheds. Upstream passage systems at Foster Dam allow adult migration to spawning habitat in the upper South Santiam basin but create problems for smolts migrating downstream. To compensate, spring chinook and summer steelhead are reared at the South Santiam Hatchery on Foster Reservoir for release into the South Santiam River.

Because of past timber management and stream cleaning practices, the river lacks the large pieces of wood needed to prevent erosion, protect spawning gravels and nutrients, and create complex fish habitat, especially in its lower reaches. The South Santiam Watershed Council is actively partnering with landowners on several tributaries of the South Santiam to plant native trees and shrubs along stream banks, improve stream conditions for native fish, and eliminate passage barriers for steelhead and resident trout.

a decade-long yearly average of 20,000 summer steelhead, 8,500 coho salmon, 2,000 winter steelhead, and 1,200 fall chinook.

The fish in my net has no adipose fin, just a healed bump on the dorsal ridge a few inches from its tail, so I know it was raised in a hatchery. The smooth scar of a clipped adipose fin is the way anglers distinguish hatchery-raised salmon, steelhead, and trout from their wild and often protected kin. Sometime between May and August four or five years ago, the parents of this springer swam into the trap at the South Santiam Hatchery in Sweet Home, convinced it was, in fact, home sweet home. Like many anglers, I have seen returning chinook salmon in their truer homes, up in the narrowing rivers and wooded, pebbly shallows, their silver sheen tarnished to a golden brown that blushes red, then deepens into black, their noses and fins worn and sore from the long struggle up-river. The male's upper jaw curves slightly, the female is heavy in the belly as she tail-digs her redd, the gravelly nest where she'll lay more than four thousand eggs. The male wards off rivals and sprays the eggs with his sperm-rich milt. But it's a one-way trip home for the Pacific salmon. Soon after spawning, starved, beaten, and plagued with pale fungus, the fish hang like shrouded ghosts in the clear water until they lean over and die.

In September, the nervous parents of the springer I caught were herded into an anesthetic tank, sorted for ripeness, killed with a swift blow to the head, and placed on a conveyor belt where hatchery workers dumped their eggs and milt into buckets for fertilization. The living eggs were incubated in shallow tanks circulating clean water chilled to 50 degrees. Some died, but most developed into black-eyed embryos that were driven to the Willamette Hatchery on Salmon Creek near Oakridge for early rearing. The surviving fry were trucked back to the South Santiam for fin clipping and release.

As a 7-inch smolt, this salmon was piped back into the river in October, February, or March to begin its journey downstream, eating plankton, insect larvae, and small fish, joining thousands of other salmon raised at the South Santiam, Marion Forks, Willamette, and McKenzie hatcheries as well as the wild spring salmon still naturally born in these rivers. Fewer than 25 percent of the watershed's spring chinook are wild (all of the Willamette's fall chinook and coho salmon are remnants or wanderers from introduced stocks), but great efforts are made to truck those returning wild fish over the dams into the upper reaches of the North and South Santiam, Middle Fork Willamette, and South Fork McKenzie Rivers where salmon fishing is prohibited and it's hoped that they will pair up, dig redds, and spawn.

Chinook salmon © M. L. Herring

The ride downstream over dams, however, is very rough on young salmon. According to one of Oregon's leading salmon experts, biologist Tom Friesen, "The survival rate for juvenile salmon over the high-head dams at Detroit, Lookout Point, and Cougar is generally very low because the dams weren't designed with fish passage in mind." Survival at the smaller Foster Dam is better. But even small dams can create obstacles for migrating fish, and groups are following the example of the Calapooia Watershed Council, which presided over the removal of the Brownsville, Sodom, and Shearer Dams to help salmon and steelhead move and spawn.

In addition to the extensive damming of rivers, factors such as pollution, riverbank development, and silting due to agriculture, logging, and construction have seriously impaired salmon, steelhead, and trout reproduction all through the Northwest. According to University of Washington professor David Montgomery, "Salmon returns to Pacific Northwest rivers are just 6 to 7 percent of historic levels." Michael Cairns, who spent thirty years as a fisheries biologist with the US Environmental Protection Agency, believes that "unless environmental policies and practices change, salmon will become extinct in the Willamette and its tributaries by the end of the century."

Hatcheries supplement declining fish populations but remain controversial because many experts believe they disguise greater, human-caused environmental degradations and weaken the overall biological fitness of the species. "Some studies have shown declining production in populations influenced by hatcheries," explains Friesen. "The fish don't replace themselves, so the population continually declines." In the case of Oregon's beloved steelhead, a race of rainbow trout that cycles from river to sea and back again (and thus is labeled anadromous) like the salmon, genetic pollution is a serious issue. All winter steelhead are native and wild to the Willamette and its tributaries, but their numbers are steadily dropping. Summer steelhead have been introduced and are heavily stocked in this system. Many anglers, like me, are delighted to find lots of returning summer steelhead to catch and eat, but many biologists believe that stocking summer steelhead may harm threatened winter steelhead through hybridization and competition. David Montgomery writes that "hatchery fish can genetically swamp a small wild population, thereby reducing its genetic diversity and increasing its vulnerability to environmental change." Hatchery fish, in a sense, are domesticating and endangering those that are wild in the Willamette.

Different species and races of anadromous fish have different strategies for survival. Some bolt down the river, some linger. Heavy winter rains and raging high water can mean crushing death for young fish, and that's where small creeks and streams with ample cover are so crucial. After weeks of endless rain, when the Willamette is brown and roiling, I have seen salmon smolts seeking calmer water up in the brushy Luckiamute River and Ash Creek as far as Highway 99 in Monmouth. But even in the best of times, many small salmon are eaten by birds, northern pike minnows, and larger piscine and pinniped predators as the waters of the Santiam pour into the Willamette, the Columbia, and the Pacific Ocean. The fat spring chinook I caught at Waterloo probably spent a year in fresh water and four years at sea, gorging on herring, squid, and krill, evading sharks and orcas and the much more deadly lines and nets of vast international fishing fleets.

Somewhere out at sea in the depth of winter, a powerful urge turned this fish back home. Recruiting with thousands of other chinook to the mouth of the Columbia River, it cut through a hundred miles of cold spring water and found, probably by smell, the mouth of the Willamette River. It passed below the lights and bridges of Portland through hungry gangs of sea lions and seals and the hook-tangled waters of Multnomah Channel and Oregon City. Pacific salmon stop feeding once they hit fresh water—the stomach of the big male I caught was completely empty—but their instinct to chase and bite "food" or glitzy curiosities and annoyances continues, and many fish will be taken by lures and bait as they run the epic gauntlet back to their natal streams.

At the grand Willamette Falls, salmon and steelhead experience the strange drama of a fish ladder. At the end of the last ice age when the Missoula floods backed up water all through the valley to Eugene, fish easily entered the upper rivers. Geologic gouging and dams have dropped water levels, and though some salmon and steelhead still pulse over this cataract during high flows, the fish ladder, built in 1882 and rebuilt in 1971, offers a crucial step up. I enjoy watching fish enter the ladder, seemingly determined to fight the current and fulfill their destiny. It's estimated that 95 percent of the migrating adults successfully climb the falls, though some drop back and never make it home.

The springer I'm unhooking got over Willamette Falls sometime in April and swam a hundred miles to the mouth of the Santiam, near my home, where I first tried to catch him. He eluded me and charged another 12 miles into the South Santiam and another 20 up to Lebanon's Waterloo Park, where he met his end. I take my knife and cut the gills, letting him bleed out into the water. Later I fillet the bright orange muscle, season simply with salt and pepper, and set the glistening wedges on the hot grill. The meat sizzles through omega-rich veins of fat. My wife and children sit down to eat. The pink flesh is delicious, and even the skin is a crispy delight. I raise my glass of local pinot noir and make a playful toast: "God save the king." My wife sips, smiles, and eats another bright piece of fish. "God save the salmon," she says, much more like a prayer.

This city park under development features a large oxbow lake, walking trails, and views of the Cascade foothills.

To get there: For the north lot (boat ramp, fishing platform, north trailhead), from I-5 take Hwy 20 east for 13.5 miles through the heart of Lebanon. Turn left onto Russell Dr. In 0.5 mile, the road becomes River Dr, and the entrance to the park is another 0.3 mile on the right. For the south lot (events space, south trailhead), continue on Hwy 20 all the way through Lebanon and turn left onto Weirich Dr. The park is on the left in about 0.5 mile.

ACTIVITIES: Walking, biking, fishing, boating, wildlife viewing. **FACILITIES:** Portable toilets, boat ramp, ADA accessible fishing platform, pet waste stations, picnic tables, sports fields. **FEES AND REGULATIONS:** No fee. Day use only, 7:30 a.m. to 8 p.m. No swimming or horses. Dogs allowed on leash. **BEST MONTHS:** Year-round. **MANAGING AGENCIES:** City of Lebanon (Cheadle Lake), Lebanon Community Foundation (adjacent property).

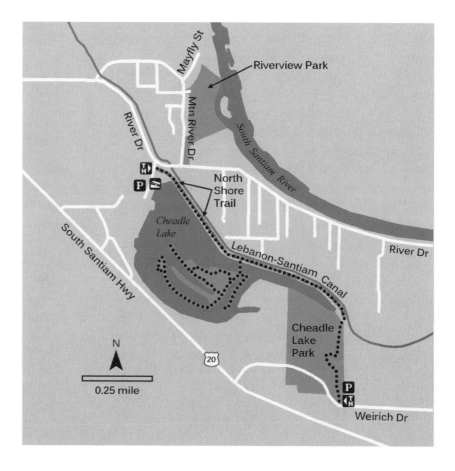

THE LEBANON-SANTIAM CANAL

The historic Lebanon-Santiam Canal is part of a larger 18-mile canal system called the Albany-Santiam Canal. The early towns of Albany and Lebanon, separated by the great expanse of the Albany Prairie, each had a plan for a canal, but at different times and originally for different reasons. The canals were later combined into one long water-way that flows from the Lebanon Diversion Dam on the South Santiam River northwesterly through Lebanon and across level farmland until it spills into the Calapooia River at Albany.

The idea for a canal to power mills and other industry in Albany originated in the 1850s and was added to by pioneer Thomas Monteith, who envisioned a navigational canal similar to the Erie Canal that passed by his hometown of Albany, New York. This 12-mile canal from the Santiam River to Albany was built in 1872–73. The 6-mile Lebanon-Santiam Canal, built in 1891–92, was conceived as a new source of municipal water and waterpower to run mills and manufacturing plants in Lebanon. The canal meandered north through Lebanon to connect with the Albany Canal.

Both cities eventually used the canal for hydroelectric power generation and municipal water supply. Water for a series of Albany powerhouses on the Calapooia River was fed from a flume extending from the canal; the flume-fed brick powerhouse reconstructed in 1924 is still in use as part of Albany's water treatment plant. Today the canal is a municipal water source for both Albany and Lebanon.

Lebanon's largest and newest park is undergoing restoration and development to become a regional multipurpose event center. The 135-acre park was part of what was once the world's largest forest products complex, covering more than 200 acres and processing logs felled in nearby forests. The 35-acre property south of Cheadle Lake was purchased in 1998 by the Lebanon Community Foundation and now hosts the Strawberry Festival (the first full weekend in June), Lebanon's annual Fourth of July celebration, and many other activities. The North Shore Trail and the Cheadle Lake Water Trail invite walking and paddling throughout the year.

Cheadle Lake, centerpiece of the park, was an oxbow of the South Santiam River before 1853. The oxbow lake was drained in 1936 and used for pasture and grazing before being resurrected in the early 1940s as the log pond for a mill producing high-grade plywood and marine plywood, both of which were in great demand during World War II. The mill ceased operation in the late 1980s, and in 2005 Freres Lumber donated

100 of Cheadle Lake's 106 acres (except for the northernmost portion close to the remnants of the industrial plant) to the Lebanon Community Foundation, which donated the lake to the City of Lebanon in 2008. Since 2009, the lake area has been open to the public.

You can launch a kayak, canoe, or small boat from the paved boat ramp at the north parking lot and paddle around Cheadle Lake's large central island, exploring channels and backwaters. Although boats with electric motors are allowed, the thick algae and lily pads in the lake could pose a problem, and sunken logs are a definite risk in summer when water levels are lower. Look for Oregon's two native turtle species, the western pond turtle and the western painted turtle, resting on logs.

The wide, level, gravel-and-asphalt North Shore Trail runs straight along the eastern edge of Cheadle Lake, between the lake and the Lebanon-Santiam Canal, for 1.25 miles between the north parking lot and the south trailhead on Weirich Drive. A graveled land bridge near the trail's halfway point provides access to the large island in the middle of the lake, most likely formed from dredging during the lake's years as a mill pond. You can walk down to the end of any or all of the fingers that jut out into the water or follow the main gravel trail to loop through the central section.

BUILD LEBANON TRAILS

Since 2005, a partnership between Lebanon's city government, the community hospital, and volunteers has focused on developing a net-work of 50 miles of interconnected trails that will link parks, schools, and businesses within Lebanon's urban growth boundary. The Lebanon Trails Committee is in the process of making its Build Lebanon Trails vision a reality through easements and property purchases. Its intention is for these trails to be open to all; most will be paved and wheelchair accessible.

The Mark's Slough Trail, the first official trail in the system, was completed in 2007. This flat, paved 1-mile trail starts at a parking lot across from the City of Lebanon Wastewater Treatment Plant on Tennessee Road, makes a loop around a slough that drains to the South Santiam River, and crosses Tennessee Road to access a short segment along the river. The North Shore Trail at Cheadle Lake was completed in 2009. Other planned trails will meander along both sides of the South Santiam River, take visitors to the top of Ridgeway Butte, and lead through historic downtown Lebanon. For updates and current information: buildlebanontrails.com.

Western pond turtle © Wendy C. Thompson

Options: You can add a walk from the north parking lot at Cheadle Lake to Riverview Park and back (approximately 1.5 miles round-trip) or through Riverview Park to Gill's Landing Park and back (approximately 4 miles round-trip). From the parking lot, go right on River Dr, cross the road, and head north on Mountain River Dr. Just before Mayfly St, turn right onto an unmarked road to a paved parking lot to enter Riverview Park, an undeveloped green space and future city park on the banks of the South Santiam River. To reach Gill's Landing, continue downstream (north) beside the concrete retaining wall behind a row of houses and enter the woods on a packed dirt path. The path proceeds along the top of a protective flood dike as it traverses a forested area with the river to the right and abandoned industrial land to the left. This will one day be developed into the West River Trail.

WATERLOO COUNTY PARK

This well-maintained, older park along the South Santiam River offers a shady loop trail, more than a mile of river frontage, and grassy open space for outdoor activities.

To get there: From Lebanon, take Hwy 20 east for about 6 miles and turn left at Waterloo Rd, which becomes Gross St as it enters Waterloo. Just before the road turns sharply to the left, becoming 1st St, turn right at the sign for Waterloo County Park. To access the loop trail and off-leash dog park, stay straight on the main road into the park and pull into the first parking lot on the right. To get to the Claude Cox Addition, drive past the main park entrance and go a couple of blocks on 1st St to the park on the right.

Waterloo Park and the town of Waterloo probably exist because of Waterloo Falls, where the town's founder, Elmore Kees, built a grist mill. The falls, located at the entrance to the park and clearly visible upstream from the Waterloo Bridge, are nothing more than a 5-foot drop where the South Santiam narrows

ACTIVITIES: Camping, hiking, swimming, picnicking, fishing, boating, inner tubing, disc golf, horseshoes.
FACILITIES: Restrooms and showers, picnic tables with BBQ grills, three picnic shelters, off-leash dog park, children's playgrounds, baseball diamond, boat ramps (one in the main park above the falls and another in the Claude Cox Addition below the falls), 18-hole disc golf course (map at oregondiscgolf.com/course_maps/Waterloo.html), horseshoe pits, dump station, 120 RV and tent campsites (the A loop is open year-round and can be reserved; the B-loop campsites are first-come, first-served but are closed during the wet months, typically October through March).
FEES AND REGULATIONS: No fee for individual day use; fees for camping and group day use of picnic shelters (for reservations, call 541-967-3917). Day-use areas open dawn to dusk. Dogs allowed on leash except in off-leash area.
BEST MONTHS: Year-round.
MANAGING AGENCY: Linn County Parks and Recreation.

between small boulders, but they were enough to power a mill and today represent the last rapids on a float trip down the river.

At 128 acres, Waterloo Park is big enough that kids can enjoy riding bikes or scooters from one end to the other. The acres of grass and shade are a huge draw in the summer, as is the water. Anglers come for the summer steelhead as well as the fall and spring salmon runs. The river has a mud bottom here, but good swimming holes can be found near each boat ramp, as well as at several spots along the loop trail. The trail, which can be muddy in the winter, is an easy hike of about 1.5 miles with insignificant elevation change. It takes you through a thick forest of old oaks, pines, and maples (keep an eye out for poison oak here), then cuts between the two camping loops and wanders along the South Santiam River.

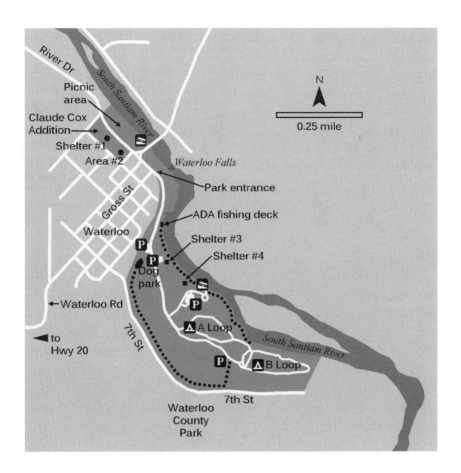

N

0.25 mile

River Dr

South Santiam River

Picnic area

Claude Cox Addition

Shelter #1

Area #2

Waterloo Falls

Park entrance

Gross St

ADA fishing deck

Waterloo

Shelter #3

Shelter #4

P

P

Dog park

P

Waterloo Rd

7th St

A Loop

to Hwy 20

South Santiam River

P

B Loop

7th St

Waterloo County Park

McDOWELL CREEK FALLS COUNTY PARK

This lush, low-elevation park on crystal-clear McDowell Creek offers peaceful paths to views of tiered and curtain waterfalls.

To get there: From Lebanon, take Hwy 20 east about 4 miles. At the sign for McDowell Creek Falls, turn left onto Fairview Rd, then go right at the stop sign for 0.9 mile. Turn left onto McDowell Creek Dr and drive 7.5 miles to reach the lower parking lot.

ACTIVITIES: Hiking, picnicking, fishing, wading. **FACILITIES:** Vault toilets, picnic tables, grills. **FEES AND REGULATIONS:** No fees. Dogs allowed on leash. Day use only, dawn to dusk. **BEST MONTHS:** Year-round. The waterfalls are fuller in the winter, but the wooden stairs, bridges, and platforms can be slick when wet. **MANAGING AGENCY:** Linn County Parks and Recreation.

An easy drive and a peaceful, temperate rain forest make this park a pleasing alternative to more well-known and crowded waterfall destinations. For a family-friendly 1.8-mile loop with 200 feet of elevation gain, start at the lower parking lot. Cross the bridge over McDowell Creek, from which you can view Lower McDowell Creek Falls. At about 0.2 mile, you reach the base of Royal Terrace Falls, a triple cascade on Falls Creek that drops 119 feet. The trail splits just before the bridge below the falls; go right to ascend a long flight of concrete and slate steps to a platform from which you can view the falls before continuing on the trail.

From here the trail crosses the creek, then dips and climbs through the woods above the canyon for a third of a mile (ignore the fork to the left) before intersecting the paved road. Cross the road and continue on the winding trail through the woods another third of a mile to the upper parking lot. Cross the gravel road here and continue on the trail, taking the stone steps down to the creek and following the trail downstream to a viewpoint deck above 39-foot Majestic Falls on McDowell Creek. Then climb down a couple of flights of wooden stairs to another viewpoint deck. From here, climb down another flight of wooden stairs and cross the creek on a long wooden footbridge. The trail follows the creek downstream past Crystal Pool's 20-foot cascade and crosses the road again. Continue down the trail, cross two wooden footbridges (the last below Royal Terrace Falls), and bear right at the Y to return 0.2 mile to the lower parking lot.

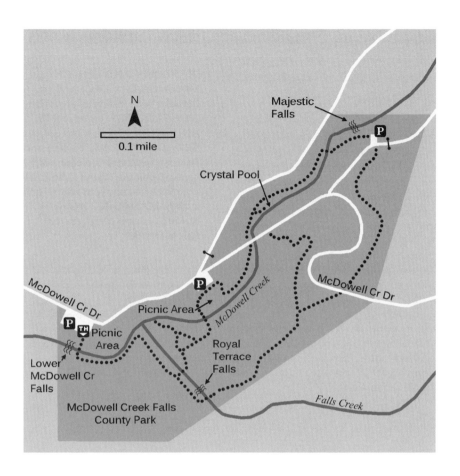

N

0.1 mile

Majestic
Falls

Crystal Pool

McDowell Cr Dr

McDowell Creek

McDowell Cr Dr

Picnic Area

Picnic
Area

Royal
Terrace
Falls

Lower
McDowell Cr
Falls

Falls Creek

McDowell Creek Falls
County Park

A remote trail in the Cascade foothills follows an abandoned logging road as it descends into a remarkable valley containing some of Oregon's oldest and largest trees.

DIFFICULTY AND LENGTH: Moderate, 4.2 miles round-trip to the lake with 900 feet elevation gain. **FACILITIES:** None. **FEES AND REGULATIONS:** No fee. **BEST MONTHS:** July to November. Access roads and the trail (with its highest point at about 3,850 feet) are closed by snow in winter and spring. **MANAGING AGENCY:** Bureau of Land Management, Salem District.

To get there: From Sweet Home, take Hwy 20 east for about 2 miles, and just past Foster Reservoir turn left onto Quartzville Rd. Drive 20 miles and at milepost 20 split off to the left onto paved Rd 11-3E-35.3, indicated by a small BLM marker. From here you will travel 7.2 miles to the trailhead, 6.3 of which are on paved but minimally maintained roads. Watch for rocks on the road, and during wet weather be prepared for mud on the last unpaved leg. From Quartzville Rd, travel 2.1 miles on the paved road to a Y and stay left on paved Rd 11-3E-35.3. Travel 0.8 mile to another Y and go right onto paved Rd 11-3E-35.1. Stay on this paved road for 3.4 miles, ignoring spurs, until you reach another Y. Turn left here onto a dirt-and-gravel road and follow this road for 0.9 mile, staying left for the last rough 0.1 mile, until you reach the rocky berm blocking the road.

Crabtree Valley is an island of ancient trees in a sea of previously clear-cut BLM forestlands, providing an outstanding example of what much of the Old Cascades looked like before industrial logging. The valley's north-facing slope, surrounding rock buttes and outcrops, and wet meadows have protected it from fire for hundreds of years, allowing massive six-hundred- to nine-hundred-year-old Douglas-fir, western hemlock, and western red cedar to thrive. Crabtree Valley was private timberland destined for harvest in the 1970s, but conservationist and public pressure led to one square mile being transferred from Willamette Industries to the BLM in a 1985 land swap. Crabtree Valley gathers multiple sources into Crabtree Creek, which flows eventually into the South Santiam River. The core of Crabtree Valley is designated an Area of Critical Environmental Concern. The valley's trees, lake, and meadows shelter spotted owls, Pacific giant salamanders, and other woodland wildlife.

From the trailhead on a clear day, look east for outstanding views of Mount Jefferson and the tops of Three Fingered Jack and the Three Sisters. The trail begins just past the rocky berm and follows the roadbed as it ascends for 0.3 mile before wrapping around a massive basalt outcrop to the right and descending 1.1 miles of rough road into silent

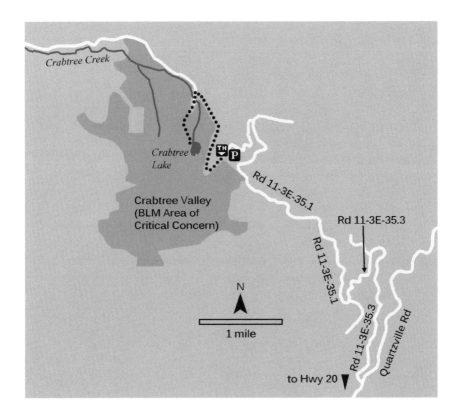

Crabtree Valley. You have to jump across several deeply incised rivulets on the way down. At a columnar basalt outcrop on the right about 0.2 mile after you begin the descent, look to your left over the valley to catch glimpses of Crabtree Lake and the Willamette Valley and Coast Range far to the west.

At mile 1.4, the road ends at a berm of logs, rocks, and dirt backed up by a set of concrete barricades. Scramble around either end of the berm to reach the logging road below and follow it sharply left toward Crabtree Lake. At mile 1.8 you reach another set of concrete barricades on the road. Go around the barricades and continue on the trail straight ahead another 0.3 mile through an alder thicket to the outlet of Crabtree Lake. Two small campsites near the shore of the lake, which is stocked with rainbow trout, make this a worthy destination for a short overnight trip.

Options: A small trail goes part of the way around the lake. Take the trail to the left at the lake, cross Crabtree Creek, and shortly take a spur to the left to reach a huge flat-topped rock outcrop with a campsite and views of Waterdog Meadow below. Continue on the user path around

QUARTZVILLE SCENIC BYWAY

Quartzville Creek is the centerpiece of a recreational corridor managed by several public land management agencies. The upper creek, a favorite of skilled kayakers during the rainy season, is known for its crystal-clear water, verdant old-growth forests, and short, thrilling drops caused by its boulder-strewn course. Lower down, the creek is impounded in Green Peter Reservoir. The 9.6-mile portion of Quartzville Creek just above where it enters the reservoir was added to the National Wild and Scenic Rivers system in 1988 in recognition of its outstanding scenic driving, white-water boating, and recreational mining opportunities.

Quartzville Road, which wends its way upward for 50 miles from Highway 20 to Highway 22 along Green Peter Reservoir and Quartzville Creek, is designated a BLM Back Country Byway. Above Yellowbottom Recreation Site, the road enters Willamette National Forest. A number of forest roads take off toward trailheads for hikes into the Middle Santiam Wilderness and national forest lands beyond. During the summer, traffic is moderate to high and you'll see tents, campers, and RVs in every pullout. Drive the byway after mid-September for vivid fall colors and lower traffic volume. Snow closes the road at higher elevations in the winter.

the east side of the lake to encounter gigantic trees. If you're a serious tree hunter and don't mind bushwhacking, you might want to seek out a native guide for help finding King Tut, a Douglas-fir estimated to be eight hundred years old, west of Crabtree Lake.

Wild ginger © Wendy C. Thompson

YELLOWBOTTOM RECREATION SITE AND RHODODENDRON TRAIL

A small campground in old-growth forest along Quartzville Creek offers a great swimming hole and a short but steep loop trail into a silent old-growth cathedral and wild rhododendron garden.

To get there: From Sweet Home, take Hwy 20 east for about 2 miles, and just past Foster Reservoir, turn left onto Quartzville Rd. Drive 24 miles on this paved road until you see the Yellowbottom Recreation Site sign on the right. For day use, park in the lot on the right just before the sign.

A couple of short trails descend from the parking lot at Yellowbottom to a

ACTIVITIES: Camping, hiking, swimming, picnicking, recreational mining. **FACILITIES:** Vault toilets, RV and tent campsites, dump station, picnic tables. **FEES AND REGULATIONS:** No fee for day use; fee for camping. Day-use area open dawn to dusk. Dogs allowed on leash. **BEST MONTHS:** Year-round, though loop trail can be muddy in the winter. Visit in late spring for rhododendron blooms; between Memorial Day and Labor Day for swimming. **MANAGING AGENCY:** Bureau of Land Management, Salem District.

large, deep swimming hole in Quartzville Creek. A wide gravel bar provides easy access to the water, and a rope swing on the other side of

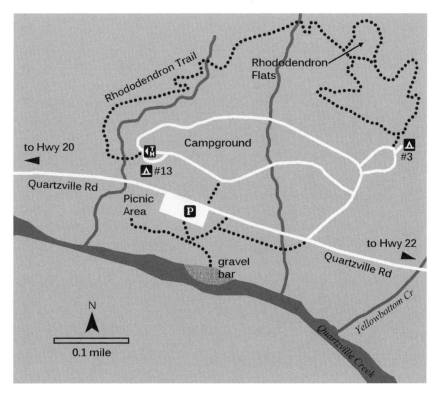

MINING ON QUARTZVILLE CREEK

Quartz rock formations around Quartzville Creek contained gold that inspired a minor gold rush to this area in the 1860s. The first mining claim was established in 1863, and within four years, five hundred mining claims had been staked and Quartzville was a town of wooden buildings and tents populated by more than a thousand people. The mills were inefficient, though, making large-scale mining there unprofitable, and by 1870 the town was abandoned.

Another flurry of mining activity between 1888 and 1892 led to the building of two new towns, Anadiem and Bryant, but they too went the way of Quartzville. Today the old townsite is on private land but recreational mining and rock hounding are allowed on Quartzville Road between Rocky Top Bridge and the Willamette National Forest boundary at Galena Creek. Anyone can pan for gold in dry gravel beds within a quarter mile on either side of Quartzville Creek; permits are required for suction dredging. The swimming hole at Yellowbottom is closed to recreational mining between Memorial Day and Labor Day.

the creek offers the possibility of a splash into the center of the creek.

Directly opposite on the other side of Quartzville Road, take a short trail into the 13-acre campground and go left on the paved road to find the trailhead for the 1.2-mile Rhododendron Trail. The gravel path takes off to the left just beyond Campsite #13. It switchbacks upward steeply over forest duff and up log stairs, crossing a couple of streams before reaching Rhododendron Flats, an area of wild rhododendrons and old-growth firs and hemlocks. Take the fork to the left to loop around the flats and then bear left again to complete the larger loop by descending back into the campground alongside Campsite #3. If you want to retrace your steps back to where you began the hike, thus adding 0.5 mile to the loop, bear right when you've looped around Rhododendron Flats.

RIVER BEND COUNTY PARK

A newer park nestled in a large bend of the South Santiam offers a shady loop trail and a half-mile of frontage on a shallow, pebbly stretch of the river.

To get there: From Sweet Home, take Hwy 20 east for about 6 miles and turn left at the sign for River Bend County Park. To access the loop trail, stay straight on the main road into the park and follow the signs to Cabin #5. Park in the lot to the left of the cabins and look for the trail sign on the gravel road that passes in front of Cabin #5. You can take the loop trail in either direction, but go clockwise to reach the river immediately. There is also paved river access off of the D camping loop.

ACTIVITIES: Camping, hiking, picnicking, fishing, boating, inner tubing, river walking. **FACILITIES:** RV and tent campsites, dump station, restrooms and showers, cabins, picnic shelters, playgrounds, playing fields, boat ramp, group meeting and camping areas (for reservations, call 541-967-3917). **FEES AND REGULATIONS:** No fee for individual day use; fees for camping, cabins, and group day use of picnic shelters. Day-use areas open dawn to dusk. Dogs allowed on leash. **BEST MONTHS:** August for water play; camping and cabins year-round. **MANAGING AGENCY:** Linn County Parks and Recreation.

River Bend, opened in May 2006, has a young forest and attractive facilities built with local logs and river cobble. Land for the park (76 acres) was

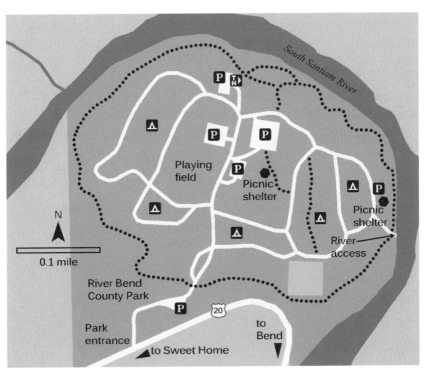

YELLOW-LEGGED FROGS

The foothill yellow-legged frog, found from northern Oregon down the California coast to Baja California, lives in and around the South Santiam in River Bend County Park. The frog's numbers have been dwindling, and the River Bend dwellers are among the last populations in northwest Oregon. The frogs are usually from 1.5 to 3 inches long with rough skin, legs with yellowish undersides, fully webbed hind feet, and mottled gray, brown, or reddish backs. They have a habit of jumping into moving water, and they lay

Yellow-legged frog © Wendy C. Thompson

their eggs in masses attached to underwater rocks. The tadpoles subsist on algae, detritus, and diatoms, while the adult frogs eat bugs such as flies, ants, moths, hornets, grasshoppers, and water striders. You can help the species survive by not collecting tadpoles or adult frogs.

donated by the Northwest Area Foundation after it was logged in the early and mid-1990s. The previous managers of the site (Cascade Timber Consulting) allowed recreational use, and local residents know the area as a longtime swimming and fishing spot. The big draw is the clear, cold, shallow water of the upper South Santiam, an appealing place to wade and inner tube on a hot summer day. The water rushes over a bed of multicolored pebbles, around gravel bars, and between large, low rock islands. Be sure to wear appropriate footgear for river walking.

The easy, level loop trail, surfaced with gravel and forest duff, is about a mile long. It traverses the outer perimeter of the campground through mixed woods and follows the edge of the river for about a quarter mile, mostly on a bank above it. Several wooden benches offer unobstructed river views.

CASCADIA STATE PARK

Tall Douglas-fir, cedar, and hemlock trees tower over this tranquil park on the site of a former mineral springs resort along the South Santiam River.

To get there: From Sweet Home, take Hwy 20 east for about 13 miles. After passing milepost 41, turn left at the Cascadia State Park sign. Cross the river on a bridge and bear right into the park.

This land in the Cascade foothills has long served as a stopping place for travelers over Santiam Pass. Kalapuya and Molalla Indians passed through to hunt, fish, and pick huckleberries. Later, white settlers drove their wagons along the north side of the river on the Santiam Wagon Road. What started as

ACTIVITIES: Hiking, camping, fishing, boating, picnicking, swimming. **FACILITIES:** Vault toilets and restrooms, tent campsites and showers, picnic tables, group shelters and campsites (call 1-800-452-5687 to reserve). **FEES AND REGULATIONS:** No fee for individual day use; fee for camping. Campsites available on a first-come, first-served basis May 1 through September 30. Dogs allowed on leash except for off-leash area near group camping. East picnic area open May through September, west picnic area open year-round. **BEST MONTHS:** Spring through fall; August for water play. **MANAGING AGENCY:** Oregon Parks and Recreation Department.

a stage stop grew into popular Cascadia Mineral Springs resort, which flourished in the early decades of the 1900s. In 1941 the State of Oregon bought the resort land and established Cascadia Springs State Park, as it was known in its early years; more land was acquired to bring the total acreage to 253 in 1980.

Signs of the park's past still linger. Art and artifacts from the Kalapuya can be found just outside the park at Cascadia Cave. Wagon ruts still remain near the confluence of Soda Creek and the South Santiam River. The stone patio of the long-gone hotel built by George Geisendorfer in 1898—which had thirty rooms, tennis courts, a lawn for croquet, a garden, and even a bowling alley—has a replica of the pump that once drew water loaded with calcium, potassium, and iron from Soda Creek, although the old spring has been cemented over.

Today, eight-hundred-year-old Douglas-fir trees tower over Oregon grape, huckleberry bushes, ferns, and salal. About 2 miles of trails give hikers access to an 80-foot waterfall on Soda Creek and the South Santiam's enticing swimming holes. The trail to the waterfall, Lower Soda Falls, begins along the road to the day-use area, just beyond the first parking lot. This gentle trail follows Soda Creek for about three quarters of a mile, crossing it twice on wooden footbridges, until it dead-ends at the base of the falls.

For river access, follow the paved Soda Springs Trail from the parking lot near the entrance. The trail leads past the old stone patio and pump replica, then down steps to the broad rock slabs, pebbly beaches, and inviting pools of water that make this a popular place on a hot summer day. If you're willing to walk a little farther, quiet pools await you upriver. Park in the day-use parking area and follow the gravel road through the group camps to where it becomes a wide path through the woods along the river. Short side paths drop down to secret pools and short, tumbling cascades. In about 0.3 mile, the trail bears uphill to the left, looping back to the parking lot. Another branch of the trail continues along the river toward Cascadia Cave, which is on private property and can only be visited on a guided tour.

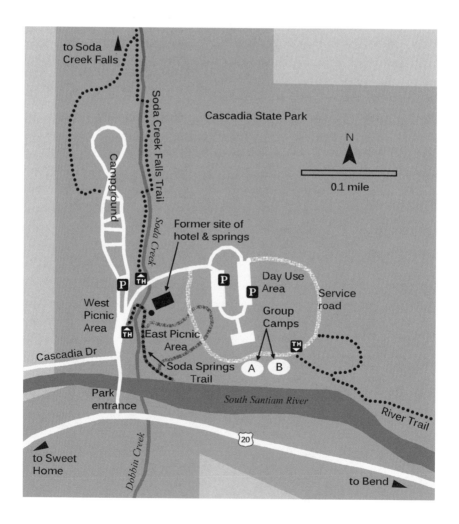

SOUTH SANTIAM RIVER WATERSHED

CASCADIA CAVE

Cascadia Cave, formed by an overhanging rock, has some of the oldest rock art, or petroglyphs, in the Pacific Northwest, dating back eight thousand years. From a distance, visitors can easily spot zigzag lines, bear prints, and large holes ground into the cave wall. Upon closer inspection, more subtle markings appear: faces, salmon, and abstract figures.

The first expedition documenting the petroglyphs was led in the 1960s by Thomas Newman, who published a record of the expedition in 1966. Since then, archaeologists from around the world, shamans, native people, and ordinary visitors have contributed additional observations and insights about the cave. Vandalism and looting in the last couple hundred years have destroyed some of the cave's original features. State, county, and local agencies are currently collaborating on a plan to protect this fragile and important historical site.

Archaeologist-led tours of the cave are offered twice yearly through Sweet Home Heritage Hikes. The tour is an all-day event, including displays of Native American artifacts and replicas plus a walk to Cascadia Cave. Call the Sweet Home Ranger District (541-367-5168) for more information

Options: Oregon has more covered bridges than any other state west of the Mississippi. To see the only covered bridge across the South Santiam in Linn County, drive 1 mile west on Cascadia Dr from the park entrance and turn left onto High Deck Rd. Cross the Short Bridge over the river to get back to Hwy 20.

TROUT CREEK TO ROOSTER ROCK, MENAGERIE WILDERNESS

A long, steady climb through a fire-regenerated forest ends at a former fire lookout site with a view of Menagerie Wilderness and the canyon of the South Santiam.

To get there: From Sweet Home, take Hwy 20 east for about 20 miles. Past milepost 48, pass the entrance to Trout Creek Campground on the right, cross the bridge over Trout Creek, and make an immediate left turn into the pullout with trailhead kiosk.

Rooster Rock (elevation 3,567 feet) is the best known of the volcanic rock pinnacles in Menagerie Wilderness that mountaineers from around the Pacific Northwest use to hone their technical climbing skills. Two dozen other pinnacles with names like Chicken Rock, North Rabbit Ear, and the Porpoise complete the menagerie and are remnants of the volcanoes that built this part of the Old Cascades. The area was protected primarily because of these pinnacles, but the rare forest that blankets the area is reason enough to visit. This forest of Douglas-fir and hemlock is native and mature, but it's not old growth, having sprung up after a

DIFFICULTY AND LENGTH: Moderate/difficult, 6.6 miles round-trip with 2,300 feet elevation gain. **FACILITIES:** Vault toilets and water at Trout Creek Campground May through September. **FEES AND REGULATIONS:** Self-issue wilderness permit required to enter wilderness from Memorial Day weekend through October 31. Dogs allowed on leash. Horses allowed. **BEST MONTHS:** April through November. The trail can be muddy in spring and is closed by snow in winter. **MANAGING AGENCY:** US Forest Service, Sweet Home Ranger District.

THE OLD CASCADES

The Cascade Range actually encompasses two mountain ranges, the High Cascades and the Old Cascades. Ten million years before the lofty volcanic peaks of the High Cascades were formed, a chain of volcanoes gave rise to the Old Cascades. This range caught the precipitation moving east from the ocean and caused eastern Oregon's semi-arid climate, and it forms the foundation of the higher peaks such as Mount Jefferson and Mount Hood. Notable peaks of the Old Cascades—all 4,000 to 5,000 feet in elevation—include Crescent Mountain, Three Pyramids, Trappers Butte, and Scar Mountain, all to the northeast of Menagerie Wilderness. In the Menagerie, erosion over time has reduced the volcanic cones of the Old Cascades to the remnant plugs seen today.

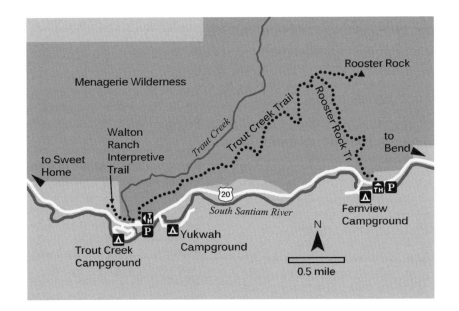

Rooster Rock

Menagerie Wilderness

Trout Creek

Trout Creek Trail

Rooster Rock Tr

Walton
Ranch
Interpretive
Trail

to Sweet
Home

to
Bend

20

South Santiam River

Fernview
Campground

N

Yukwah
Campground

Trout Creek
Campground

0.5 mile

high-intensity fire burned through most of the area about a hundred years ago.

Just west of the trailhead, Trout Creek tumbles by on its way to the South Santiam. The trail makes a relatively gentle but steady ascent through the forest along a south-facing slope above the highway. At mile 2.8 the Rooster Rock Trail comes in from the right. Continue uphill here as the climb steepens through a dry upland forest of madrone, chinkapin oak, and manzanita and crosses a couple of scree fields below basalt outcroppings. After two switchbacks the trail reaches the base of Rooster Rock. Take the switchback to the left and continue upward for a short distance, and when the trail forks, go right to a viewpoint on a bare rock knoll where the base cabin for the fire lookout once stood. (The lookout itself, an 8-by-8-foot cabin built in 1927 and abandoned in 1963, was wedged atop Rooster Rock and reached by a 100-foot ladder.) On a clear day, you can see pinnacles to the north and Iron Mountain, North Sister, and Middle Sister to the east.

Options: If you park a shuttle car or bicycle at the trailhead for the Rooster Rock Trail 2.6 miles farther up Hwy 20, you can descend via the steeper and shorter Rooster Rock Trail, which measures 1.6 miles back to the trailhead from the junction with the Trout Creek Trail. From the Trout Creek trailhead, you can also take the gravel Walton Ranch Interpretive Trail across Trout Creek 0.25 mile to two viewing platforms overlooking a ranch site with a wintering elk herd.

CHIMNEY PEAK TRAIL TO THE MIDDLE SANTIAM RIVER

A short descent through ancient Douglas-firs and red cedars takes you to an old trail shelter and an enticing swimming hole below 20-foot Shelter Falls.

To get there: From Sweet Home, take Hwy 20 east for about 23 miles. After passing milepost 52, turn left onto Soda Fork Rd (Rd 2041). From here you travel nearly 13 miles on a one-lane logging road that is usually passable for passenger vehicles; use caution and watch out for fallen rocks, holes, and other traffic. After the turnoff from Hwy 20, keep left at a fork at mile 0.9, staying on Rd 2041, and drive 7 more miles uphill to a six-way junction. Continue downhill on the main road for a little more than 4 miles to a three-way junction. Take the middle road, marked 646 and Chimney Peak Trail. Drive 0.7 mile farther to the trailhead and parking area at the end of the road.

DIFFICULTY AND LENGTH: Easy/ moderate, 1.6 miles round-trip with 315 feet elevation gain. **FACILITIES:** None. **FEES AND REGULATIONS:** No fee. Camping at the trailhead allowed up to 14 days. Dogs allowed under voice command or on leash. Between Memorial Day and October 31, day-use and overnight visitors to the Middle Santiam Wilderness (which you won't reach unless you take the option of crossing Pyramid Creek) must fill out a self-issue wilderness permit at the kiosk. **BEST MONTHS:** May or June through November. The road is closed by snow in winter and prone to wash-outs (for current road conditions, call 541-367-5168). **MANAGING AGENCY:** US Forest Service, Sweet Home Ranger District.

The 38.5-mile-long Middle Santiam River originates in the Old Cascade Crest just west of Iron Mountain. Because much of the river flows through the Middle Santiam Wilderness or along a private road, not many people see it, although a few adventurous kayakers have floated the river to Green Peter Reservoir. The Middle Santiam Wilderness Area (designated in 1984) is notable for containing one of the first contiguous old-growth forests protected as wilderness. Shelter Falls is not in the wilderness; the Chimney Peak Trail enters the wilderness past Pyramid Creek.

From the Chimney Peak trailhead, the trail descends through second-growth woods at first but soon switchbacks through a silent ancient forest carpeted with moss-covered logs, ferns, and occasional wild rhododendrons. Ford three streams before reaching three-sided, peak-roofed Shedd Camp Shelter, which provides a sleeping platform out of the rain as well as a bench in front of a campfire. The original shelter on this site was built in 1915 as an overnight stop for trail workers and firefighters on their way to the high country from the Cascadia Ranger Station; the shelter was rebuilt in 1938 by the Civilian Conservation Corps.

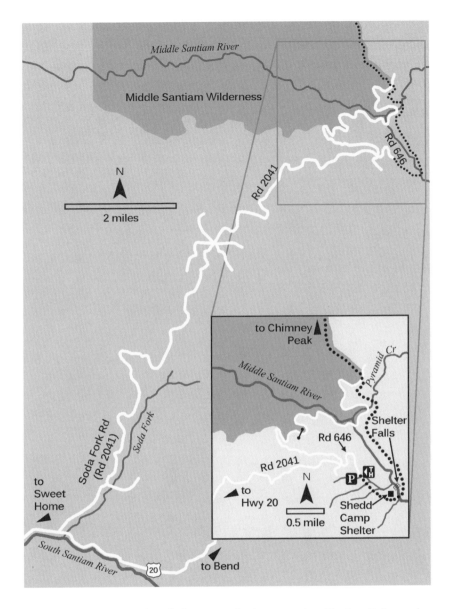

The trail continues briefly but steeply downward to Shelter Falls on the Middle Santiam River. Large boulders frame the swimming hole below the falls; to enter, scramble down on paths through the forest. Always look for hazards before jumping into the river, as winter flows may have deposited logs and debris.

Options: You can continue on the Chimney Peak Trail for 5.7 miles of generally easy ups and downs to small, green Donaca Lake, which has native cutthroat trout and a few nice campsites. The trail crosses the

Middle Santiam River above the falls (use logs when the water is low, wade when it's higher), goes left at a fork in 0.3 mile, and travels north before requiring another ford of Pyramid Creek. After that it crosses an abandoned portion of Rd 2041 (blocked by landslides and washouts) and continues on to the lake.

From Donaca Lake, follow the gradually ascending trail another 6.5 miles to reach the base of Chimney Peak, once adorned by a fire lookout tower. A summit bid requires a scramble up the last rocky few hundred feet.

SANTIAM WAGON ROAD, MOUNTAIN HOUSE TO HOUSE ROCK

This hike along a historical roadbed takes you through old-growth forest, loops past a cave beneath a house-size boulder, and drops down to 30-foot House Rock Falls.

To get there: From Sweet Home, take Hwy 20 east for about 23 miles. After passing milepost 52, cross the Soda Fork bridge and pass the former Mountain House restaurant (now a private residence) on the left before turning right into a small gravel parking area in front of a green gate.

The Santiam Wagon Road stretching from Albany to Camp Polk, just north-east of present-day Sisters, was built

DIFFICULTY AND LENGTH: Easy/moderate, 5 miles round-trip with 300 feet elevation gain. **FACILITIES:** Vault toilets and water at House Rock Campground May through September. **FEES AND REGULA-TIONS:** No fee. Dogs allowed on leash. Horses and mountain bikes allowed on wagon road but not on House Rock loop. **BEST MONTHS:** May or June through October. The trail can be muddy in the rain and is under snow in the winter and early spring. **MANAGING AGENCY:** US Forest Service, Sweet Home Ranger District.

between 1861 and 1868 to allow settlers in the mid-Willamette Valley to drive their cattle and sheep to summer grazing lands in central Oregon and to supply miners in the John Day area. The road closely followed trails the native peoples had established. During the 1870s and 1880s, the road was used heavily to move freight, passengers, and mail as well as livestock. Four- and six-horse teams pulling wagon trains up to half a mile long transported raw wool from eastern Oregon to mills in Brownsville,

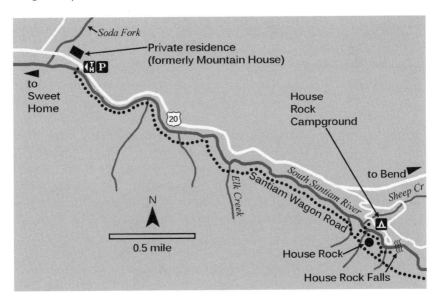

Waterloo, and Jefferson and returned laden with fruit, vegetables, and other supplies.

Start this hike along the roadbed by crossing the wooden bridge across the South Santiam and bearing left to enter an extensive stand of red alder that has grown up to fill in the site of an old mill pond. The trail soon climbs high above the river, and in the first mile you cross two small step-across fords and begin seeing old-growth Douglas-fir. When you come to Elk Creek at mile 1.2, you can pick your way across on stones at lower flows, but you may have to get your feet wet at higher flows. After another easy ford right after milepost 2, you reach a junction marked by a large brown sign giving historical information about the wagon road. Descend on the trail to the left to do the loop to House Rock and House Rock Falls.

Near mile 2.2 you come to a T-junction. The trail to the left leads to an impressive bridge across the South Santiam River to House Rock Campground. Go right at the junction to reach enormous House Rock, where both Native Americans and American settlers took shelter. When it rains, streams trickle through the cave, but it provides a place to have lunch out of the weather. Continue on the trail to the right as it drops down near enough to the river to scramble down to good swimming holes. You will soon reach another junction with a sign directing you to turn left and go 0.2 mile on a spur trail to reach House Rock Falls. After enjoying the falls, return to this junction and go uphill to the left for 0.1 mile to return to the Santiam Wagon Road. Turn right to return to the Mountain House trailhead.

SANTIAM WAGON ROAD TRAIL SYSTEM

The developed trail system following the Santiam Wagon Road runs for 19.5 miles and ranges from 1,500 to 3,200 feet from its start at the Mountain House trailhead to its terminus at Fish Lake. From there, you can cross Highway 126 to connect with the McKenzie River Trail System, which extends all the way to Big Lake. You can access the wagon road at various spots along Hwy 20 and string together different segments for a hike of the length and difficulty you choose. Starting at the west end, the different sections are Mountain House to Latiwi Creek Road (3.3 miles one way), Latiwi Creek to Sevenmile Trailhead / Horse Camp (3.3 miles one way), Sevenmile Trailhead to Tombstone Pass (4.2 miles one way), and Tombstone Pass to Fish Lake (8.7 miles one way). The *Sweet Home Ranger District Trail Guide*, available at the Sweet Home Ranger District office at 4431 Highway 20 in Sweet Home, gives detailed descriptions and directions.

BIKING THE SOUTH SANTIAM WATERSHED

East of Cascadia State Park, the Willamette National Forest offers miles and miles of mountain biking opportunities. Gravel forest roads follow or cross Canyon Creek, Moose Creek, Falls Creek, Soda Fork, and Latiwi Creek. For a short jaunt to a nice swimming hole, take the gravel road that ascends gently beside Moose Creek, a stream with intact riparian areas and opportunities to view winter steelhead. From Sweet Home, drive east about 15 miles on Highway 20 and turn left onto Moose Creek Road. Just after you cross the bridge over the river, turn left into a parking area where you can leave your car. Ride up Moose Creek Road, staying left at the first fork. Cross a bridge over Moose Creek and turn right on Road 2025. The mostly shaded gravel road follows the creek for 3.5 miles. A short trail from the large open area just before the road ends takes you down to the creek and a nice swimming hole under a fern-planted wall.

For road bikes, many routes through farm fields and rolling oak savanna are possible from starting points in Lebanon and Sweet Home.

LEBANON TO ROARING RIVER COUNTY PARK

This out-and-back ride through farmland northeast of Lebanon takes you up and down small hills to pretty Roaring River County Park, where you can picnic and dip.

Distance and climb: 29.6 miles round-trip, 470 feet total ascent. **Road surface**: Paved with some shoulders. **Start/end point**: River Park on Grant Street in Lebanon. **Facilities**: Restrooms and picnic tables at River Park and Roaring River County Park; vault toilets and picnic tables at Larwood Wayside.

This route takes you from the banks of the South Santiam River in Lebanon over rural roads to a quiet county park on the Roaring River (actually a creek rushing over a stony bottom). On the way, you pass Larwood Wayside, a quaint little park with covered bridge where the Roaring River empties into Crabtree Creek, the only spot in the entire United States where a river empties into a creek (and featured in *Ripley's Believe It or Not* for that reason). Roaring River Park is a perfect midpoint, with shady picnic areas in groves of evergreens and a walking path along the creek. You'll find light traffic on the sections of this route without shoulders (everything but Brewster and Richardson Gap Roads).

Turn-by-turn directions: Go left onto Grant St to cross the bridge over the South Santiam and start onto Brewster Rd. At mile 1.1, turn right onto Mount Hope Dr. At mile 4, go straight onto Bond Rd where Mount Hope Dr turns off to the right. Cross Lacomb and at mile 6.2, turn right onto Baptist Church Dr. At mile 7.2, turn left onto Richardson Gap Rd. At mile 10.5, turn right

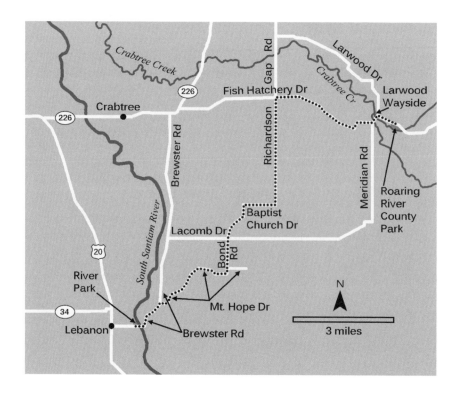

onto Fish Hatchery Dr. Cross Meridian at mile 13.9, cross the Larwood Bridge over Crabtree Creek at mile 14.1, and turn right to stay on Fish Hatchery Dr another 0.7 mile to Roaring River County Park on the right. Return the way you came.

PADDLING THE SOUTH SANTIAM RIVER

The South Santiam drainage offers plenty of paddling, though much of it is best left to experienced thrill seekers. The upper South Santiam from a mile above Fernview Campground all the way down to Foster Reservoir offers a class 3–5 run of nearly 20 miles after a substantial rain or snowmelt. Tributaries to this upper section that offer white-water adventure include Soda Fork (class 3–5), Canyon Creek (class 5), and Moose Creek. North of Green Peter Reservoir, Quartzville Creek is a classic advanced kayaking run that includes some class-5 waterfalls above Galena Creek. Also above Green Peter, the Middle Santiam River offers the only Cascade wilderness run, with class 3 and 4 rapids. Below Green Peter Dam, a 2-mile run to Foster Reservoir offers some of the best summer white water in the area for experienced kayakers. Wiley Creek enters the South Santiam

River just below Foster Dam and offers class 3 and 4 rapids on a beautiful run that flows through a moss-covered canyon.

For those just starting out or wanting a more relaxing adventure, the lower South Santiam offers a good variety of runs to build your skills or drift peacefully along. Below Foster Reservoir, the river mostly has a low gradient, easy riffles and small rapids, lazy stretches of flat water, and pleasant scenery through farm fields and pastures. Foster Dam releases adequate flows for year-round paddling. Crabtree Creek also offers paddling possibilities just above (class 3–4) and just below (class 1–2) Larwood Wayside, as described in *Soggy Sneakers*.

SWEET HOME TO WATERLOO PARK

One rapid and a few small shelves offer play places on this South Santiam run before it flattens out and floats you peacefully between tree-lined banks.

Skill level: Beginning/intermediate (class 1 and 2). **Duration:** 5 or 6 hours. **River miles:** 11 miles. **Put-in point:** Pleasant Valley Boat Ramp, three miles downstream of Foster Dam; from Hwy 20 on the west side of Sweet Home, go north on Pleasant Valley Road, cross the railroad tracks, and turn right just before the bridge at the sign for the Sweet Home Public Service Area. **Take-out point:** Waterloo Park, upper boat ramp. **Facilities:** Vault toilet at the Pleasant Valley Boat Ramp, vault toilets and picnic tables in Waterloo Park. **Season:** Year-round.

The only major rapid here is the US 20 rapid, 2 miles below Sweet Home, where the river bounds off the highway embankment on the left, making large standing waves and strong eddies. You can scout this from Highway 20 before you run it. You'll encounter a few shelves just downstream but then the river flattens out for the rest of the trip to Waterloo. Take out at the boat ramp on the left in Waterloo Park above Waterloo Falls.

Options: Just below the boat ramp at Waterloo Park is Waterloo Falls, which is class 4 at high water and is normally portaged. Then 2.8 miles below Waterloo Park is the 10-foot Lebanon Dam, which must be portaged. If you're looking for an easier float, skip this stretch and consider a couple of other day trips possible downstream. In winter, spring, and late fall, this broad river moves right along and has many choppy stretches, but expect shallow spots and a slower current in summer and early fall.

Gill's Landing (1400 E Grant St, Lebanon) to the Highway 226 bridge 1 mile west of Crabtree (a poor take-out with no boat ramp) is an 11-mile float between tree-lined dirt banks offering views of farm fields and pastures. You can also take out at a better spot about 0.1 mile downstream where Crabtree Road / Old Bridge Road ends at Sanderson Bridge (the bridge is long gone but a gated parking lot remains), but you need a permit and a key to the gate from Linn County; call 541-967-3919.

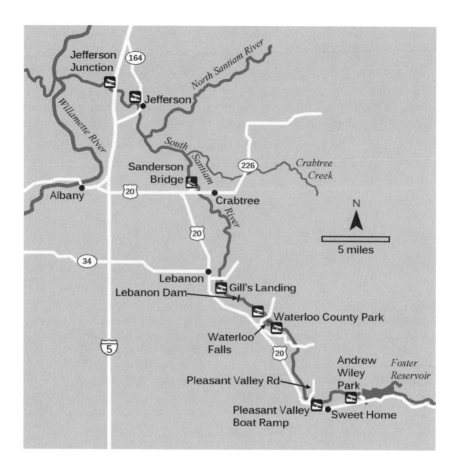

You can also float from Sanderson Bridge 11 miles to the boat ramp on the right bank under the Jefferson Highway bridge in Jefferson, or another 2 miles to the Jefferson Junction boat ramp, a concrete boat ramp on the right bank at the Santiam Rest Area on I-5 (exit 241). This stretch is slower and smoother than the one above it; at mile 8 the North Santiam comes in from the right and the volume of water increases. Even on smooth water like this, always watch for hazards such as logjams.

NORTH SANTIAM RIVER WATERSHED

The 92-mile-long North Santiam River originates on the west side of Three Fingered Jack and gathers waters from the glaciated slopes of Mount Jefferson. Flowing west through a rocky canyon, the wild river is impounded behind the massive Detroit Dam and the smaller but still impressive Big Cliff Dam, built between 1949 and 1953 for flood control and power generation. About 4 miles below Big Cliff Dam, at Niagara County Park, the river valley begins to widen and give way to foothills, farms, and fields. At lower elevation, Opal Creek and Battle Ax Creek come together in the Opal Creek Scenic Recreation Area to form the Little North Santiam, a major tributary that spills into the North Santiam near Mehama. The river emerges from the foothills into the Willamette Valley near Stayton and angles southwest, providing irrigation and drinking water for Stayton and Salem. The North Santiam reaches its confluence with the South Santiam River south of Jefferson. From there, the Santiam River flows another 12 miles west to reach the Willamette.

The Santiam Molalla lived on the western slopes of Mount Jefferson and the Three Sisters, and on the headwaters of the North Santiam, while the Santiam Kalapuya lived along the lower Santiam River, until the forcible resettlement of these native peoples to the Grand Ronde Reservation in 1856. The river canyon was a formidable obstacle to settlers until a railroad was built in 1887, opening up the canyon to settlement and logging of the surrounding mountains. Today Highway 22, the West Cascades National Scenic Byway, parallels the river along much of its course above Stayton. Chinook salmon, coho salmon, and steelhead trout return to the

North Santiam to spawn, but their journey upriver stops at Big Cliff Dam. In the reaches upstream of the dam, the river is stocked with trout, and near the river's source at Santiam Lake, wild cutthroat trout, rainbow trout, and brook trout can be found.

About 80 percent of the watershed is owned and managed by the US Forest Service, the Bureau of Land Management, and the Oregon Department of Forestry. Starting around Mehama and extending all the way east to Mount Jefferson Wilderness, the North Santiam and its tributaries offer a multitude of wild places to explore and enjoy. County parks, BLM recreation sites, state parks, state and national forests, and federal wilderness and scenic recreation areas provide swimming holes, picnic areas, hiking trails, campsites, fishing areas, bikeable logging roads, and boating put-in points.

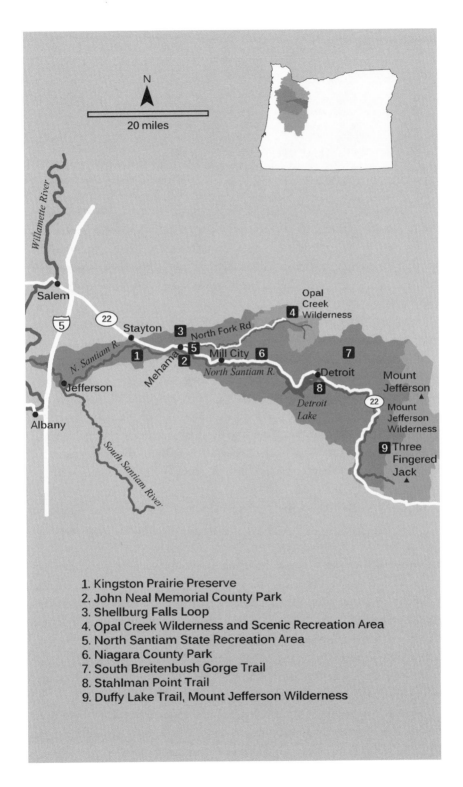

N

20 miles

Willamette River

Salem

22

Stayton

3 North Fork Rd

5 Mill City

Opal Creek Wilderness

4

1

N. Santiam R.

Mehama

2

6

North Santiam R.

7

Detroit

8

Mount Jefferson

Jefferson

Detroit Lake

22

Mount Jefferson Wilderness

Albany

South Santiam River

9 Three Fingered Jack

1. Kingston Prairie Preserve
2. John Neal Memorial County Park
3. Shellburg Falls Loop
4. Opal Creek Wilderness and Scenic Recreation Area
5. North Santiam State Recreation Area
6. Niagara County Park
7. South Breitenbush Gorge Trail
8. Stahlman Point Trail
9. Duffy Lake Trail, Mount Jefferson Wilderness

The North Santiam Microcosm

JAMIE WYANT

I wake up early. Standing in the shower, I wash myself with water that comes from the North Santiam. Later, it's in the coffee I drink, the blueberries that enliven my oatmeal. The river is in me. It flows through my life and the lives of everyone around me. I live in Salem. We take our drinking water from the North Santiam.

The North Santiam is not an epic river. No ancient civilization arose on its banks, nor does it embody the history of a nation. It's a local river.

The scale of the North Santiam is easy to hold in my mind. Spatially, the watershed is a little more than 100 miles long and maybe 20 miles wide. Motorists cover the distance in a morning, bicyclists in a day. From any of a dozen hills, hikers encounter panoramas that encompass the watershed from Mount Jefferson to the river's mouth. Even the hydrologic cycle is local. After all, the ocean is just over the horizon beyond the low coastal range.

And local people have an active, direct, and personal role in this river's future.

Today I'm driving up the canyon. My first stop is Geren Island in Stayton, the 250-acre island in the North Santiam River that's home to the City of Salem's water treatment facility. I link up with Tim, the facility manager. We take a look at how free-flowing river water becomes tap water. The North Santiam is so clean, Tim's system is as simple as it gets. It depends on slow sand filtration to remove suspended particles, and biological processes in the *Schmutzdecke* to dissolve organic contaminants. I ask, of course. Tim answers, "*Schmutzdecke*, or 'dirt cover,' is the biomass that develops naturally on top of the sand filter."

We pause to watch a bald eagle spill air and turn to look in on us. "Happens a lot," Tim says. I think, nice job.

Salem owns water rights for 155 million gallons per day, about two hours' river flow on a typical autumn day. Nine other communities draw drinking water from streams in the North Santiam watershed.

I thank Tim and move on. On my way, a center-pivot irrigation rig creates a sunny-day rainbow. The irrigation water, pumped from the North Santiam, will enter the national food distribution system frozen in corn or green beans.

I meet with Brent from the Santiam Water Control District. The water control district pulls more water from the river than any other user—with 16,832 acres under irrigation, much more water.

We touch on the first real controversy. The water control district and City of Salem co-own the upper and lower Bennett diversion dams, where North Santiam River water is diverted into a complex series of canals and natural creeks. Drift boaters hate the dams, a nuisance to navigate. Not only for boaters.

Last February I watched winter steelhead, their imperative to migrate compelling belly flop after belly flop on the upper dam's concrete apron. I imagine bruised and exhausted fish hating the dams too. Brent explains that farmers and wild fish have been at odds in the past, but ever so gradually, a personal conservation ethic is taking hold. First one landowner adopts conservation, then a neighbor; pretty soon it's a few.

I think to myself, like nature, whose secret is patience. Then I continue wending my way up the canyon.

I turn onto the road along the Little North Santiam. Don't know anyone who calls it anything but the North Fork, just the map. At the end of the road, I grab a water bottle and hike into Jawbone Flats, an old mining camp now home to the Opal Creek Ancient Forest Center. It took nearly twenty years to work through angry contentions, tinged by resentments engendered by controversy over the northern spotted owl, before the old-growth forest around Opal Creek was designated a wilderness in 1996. Today, Opal Creek and the surrounding forests enjoy international repute and see around twenty thousand visitors each year. How close we came to allowing this marvel to slip away—though by 1996 the timber bubble had already burst.

I drive up Highway 22 to Mill City, where a different beacon stands sentinel—a broken-out gray and red Texaco sign perched above an abandoned station. It's a marker, I think, of an excruciating economic cavity left behind when the land-based sensibilities that defined Oregon throughout the decades from statehood to the 1990s finally expired. Will timber ever again fuel rural Oregon's economic engine?

In Mill City I recall an earlier journey up the canyon. I met the local watershed council coordinator, a double handful of Willamette National

Forest staff, and four loggers for a tour and rambling discussion of a new twist in forest management.

We visit three areas where spindly thirty-year-old trees with sparse foliage and broken limbs tell of overcrowding, stress. Forest Service staff estimate there are about 12,000 acres of timber stands just like these within the North Santiam watershed. Overcrowded forests stop growing until some kind of disturbance comes along to thin them. In the old days, like gardeners with chainsaws, loggers would have cut out the weakest trees to release the growth of the remnant stand.

But twenty years ago the politically charged reaction to arguably unsustainable and certainly monumental timber harvests roiled the old school. In the blink of an eye, or so it seemed, we turned off the resource-extraction economy in favor of a much broader array of human and natural interest. We decided to embrace benign neglect as a forest management practice. Today, there aren't enough millable logs in the stagnant stands to cover the cost of thinning these forests.

So in that overcrowded forest we spend time hands in pockets, puzzling over thinning prescriptions, distance to markets, and operating costs. Most surprisingly, we spend a lot of time discussing "special forest products." The idea is that if an operator can't break even on selling the post- and pole-sized logs, maybe there's enough money in special products like chips and firewood, or in selling moss, boughs, cones, and bear grass to florists.

I see the old-timers, who remember the days of big timber and hungry timber markets, struggle to understand how wood chips and bear grass, boughs and cones can make up for merchantable timber. Truth be told, grass and cones can't replace the market value of big timber. For any special forest products plan to work, timber operators will have to change. They'll have to understand how to successfully maneuver in many different markets. It will take flexibility, quick access to market data, and a nimble, information-driven approach. Maybe it will take a generation versed in the technology of the twenty-first century. But will they want to work in the woods?

About three-quarters of the North Santiam watershed is forested. How the forestlands are managed matters to all of us who live here. Forests filter the water that flows in the river and fills our taps.

I'm preaching to myself and had better pay attention to the road. Detroit Dam is just ahead.

I grasp the rail in response to the temporary vertigo I feel. I'm standing on the dam rising more than 450 feet above the river. Like every high-wall dam I've ever visited, it impresses me with its audacity. What motivated those men to first imagine and then create this concrete massif? Did they understand the consequences? Because it's almost certain the Detroit Dam has had the single greatest impact of any human endeavor on the North Santiam River and all its wild fish communities, and its cities and towns from Idanha down to Salem.

As to why, it's easy to forget how the Willamette used to rage. But in the 1930s, Willamette Valley residents demanded federal flood protection. I cannot imagine anyone anticipated the dire impact flood protection would have on wild fish populations. Damming the North Santiam cut off more than 70 percent of the historic spawning habitat for migratory salmon and steelhead, and it utterly changed the river's hydrologic regime, wreaking havoc on fish migration and stressing already-decimated populations.

But there was a time when to relate to nature was to bend it to human needs, to pour a couple million cubic yards of concrete into taming a river, or cut a few million board feet of timber to feed the voracious appetites of commerce. More recently, we've come to appreciate that intervening in a complex system gives rise to unanticipated, often undesirable, consequences.

When the listing of salmon, steelhead, and chubs as endangered came hard on the heels of the shuttering of the timber industry, no one had the heart to face more economic disruption. I wonder, if it weren't for the spotted owl controversy, would we ever have agreed to depend on a voluntary system where governments, communities, and local volunteers act together with their neighbors to reconnect with nature and restore habitat important to fish?

I stand on the dam and I know there's nowhere like the North Santiam. It's an entirely local river. I've found a microcosm in its farms, fish, and forests, in the historic conflicts, and in the hopeful nurturing of a conservation ethic—a conservation ethic where we choose to see humankind as *a part of* the natural system, not *apart from* it.

The Fight for Opal Creek

CAROL SAVONEN

Owls versus jobs. Loggers versus tree huggers. Opal Creek and its old-growth watershed, so serene and pristine today, was once at the center of a bitter war over ancient forests that pitted the timber and environmental camps against each other and attracted national attention. From the late 1960s into the 1990s, many of us who loved ancient forests fought with fierce passion for the protection of this land. At the same time, timber companies struggled to keep their mills running.

Tree sit-ins, road blockades, and lawsuits were frequently in the news in those days. I lived up the McKenzie River in the late 1980s and watched, day after day, a stream of log trucks pass my house carrying one-log loads. The trees being cut down were so huge that a section of a long trunk might fill a whole trailer. New raw gashes in the mountains grew larger and more numerous, leaving bony slopes of slash and stumps. Rivers ran chocolate, silting in salmon spawning beds. Mudslides closed roads during winter storms.

Rather than sit helplessly and watch the devastation roll by, I finally felt I had to do something to help save the remaining forests. In 1989, I volunteered with the Sierra Club to lead hikes into the threatened Opal Creek area, the largest uncut old-growth low-elevation watershed remaining on the west side of the Cascades. I had never been there, for in those days there were no trails; there were only timber sale markers.

Forests such as those at Opal Creek once covered millions of acres along the west slope of the Cascades. But now the land protected in Opal Creek Wilderness and Opal Creek Scenic Recreation Area is the largest remaining area of temperate rain forest habitat in Oregon, covering more than 34,000 acres (more than 53 square miles). The towering trees there, some more than fifteen hundred years old, are a remnant of what the forests of the west slope were like before EuroAmericans arrived. Otter, beaver, elk, flying squirrels, red-backed voles, and spotted owls still abound. The turquoise waters of Battle Ax and Opal Creeks run crystal clear and still have rich spawning gravels and cool, shaded pools and riffles.

The contrast between the Opal Creek drainage and other local watersheds of comparable scale is stark—the Molalla, Santiam, and Calapooia watersheds in western Oregon's low-elevation Cascades have all been ravaged by a century of timber harvest. From the air (or in Google Earth), a dense maze of logging roads scars cutover forests. Dams hold back once free-flowing water in large reservoirs; long reaches of rivers have been silted in or suffer sluiced-out spawning gravels. Former ancient forests are now patchworks of industrial forestland, farm fields, and timber towns, crisscrossed by highways and logging roads.

Opal Creek is not untrammeled by humans. Spear points and rock artifacts dating back at least two thousand years have been found across the watershed. Archeologists believe the site that is now Jawbone Flats was once a summer camp for the Santiam Molalla people. More recent human artifacts include old mine shafts, pieces of rusting machinery, the road along Battle Ax Creek, and the Jawbone Flats settlement with its small hydroelectric station, left by miners who worked this land for gold and other metals from the 1930s until 1992.

But these signs do not mar the experience of being here. The ecosystem still thrives.

From the 1960s to the 1990s, Opal Creek was slated for timber harvest. Lumber mills stood ready to saw up the millions of board feet surveyed in the watershed. Conservation efforts began in the 1960s as well. Sierra Club Northwest representative Brock Evans first drew lines around the Opal Creek drainage on a map of areas to be considered for inclusion in the Wilderness Act of 1964. But the timber industry knew where the big trees were and pressured politicians to remove those areas from the final bill. Opal Creek, Breitenbush, the Kalmiopsis, the Middle Santiam, and the South Umpqua were wiped from the original proposal.

In the early 1970s, George Atiyeh returned from Special Forces combat in Vietnam and retreated to his childhood refuge, the old mining settlement at Opal Creek. While growing up, George and his cousins had spent their summers at Jawbone Flats in the forest with "Grandpa" Jim Hewitt, father-in-law of George's uncle, Vic Atiyeh, governor of Oregon from 1979 to 1987. Grandpa Hewitt had built the Jawbone Flats mining camp in the 1930s, mining lead, zinc, copper, and silver.

Coming back home, Atiyeh was shocked by what he witnessed from the pilot seat of his four-seater Cessna 170 when he flew over the west slope of the Cascades. For as far as he could see, most of the land was ravaged to stubble and silted-in streams. The only uncut watershed in the vicinity was Opal Creek.

With his deep personal connection to the place, Atiyeh was inspired to try to save it. He began a tireless campaign to hold off US Forest Service plans to log and road the area. For the next two decades, he flew over the landscape with politicians, conservationists, and whoever else would go to showcase the stark contrast between cut and uncut lands.

Local tensions built. The attitude of the local timber community, including the local Forest Service district ranger, was "conservationists be damned!" In 1980, the Detroit District ranger vowed publicly to "cut Opal Creek." In 1981, Forest Service workers nailed clear-cut boundary markers to the trees around the periphery of 1,800 acres of forest and mapped 11 miles of roads for logging trucks.

Media photographers, filmmakers, and reporters began to accompany Atiyeh on his flights over the western Cascades. Atiyeh and others tirelessly traveled around the Pacific Northwest and farther afield to give slideshows about the merits of the threatened watershed. More than ten thousand people around the country attended slideshow presentations about Opal Creek and the plight of west Cascades forests.

Oregon's economy was at a tipping point. Timber companies, once the economic backbone of the region, had cut almost all the easy-to-access low forests, rich with giant, high-quality, tight-grained old-growth timber. The trees in the Opal Creek watershed would keep hundreds employed at the mills and local economies fueled for a few more years, claimed the timber industry. But mills were modernizing, employing fewer workers per board foot cut.

Television specials and coffee table books showcased the consequences of modern industrial forestry to millions. Brock Evans, now vice president of the Audubon Society, helped produce the 1989 Audubon special *Ancient Forests: Rage Over Trees*, narrated by Paul Newman, bringing national exposure to Atiyeh's work to save Opal Creek. The timber industry succeeded in gaining a national advertiser boycott, but Ted Turner showed the documentary six times without commercials on his network.

As I started leading hikes into the area in 1989, forest activists were building foot trails into the watershed in an attempt to make it easier for the public to experience Opal Creek. The Forest Service threatened the trail builders with arrest for "felony destruction of government property" but backed off, afraid of a public relations nightmare, when the trail builders refused to desist. Weekend after weekend, we led groups of people into Opal Creek on the newly built trails. We wrote letters, called legislators in Washington, DC, and courted state senators and representatives. We attended demonstrations and rallies about timber and wilderness issues at the capitol building in Salem and in Pioneer Square in Portland.

The protection of the northern spotted owl under the Endangered Species Act in 1990 delayed or stopped timber sales. More than a thousand citizens signed pledges to commit civil disobedience if cutting in remaining old-growth forests of western Oregon were to begin. Much of the urban public was recognizing that an uncut primeval forest provided long-term values—clean air, water, and wildlife, not to mention a refuge from modern life.

Conservationists filed lawsuits and proposed multiple bills, state and federal, to protect the area through the 1980s into the 1990s, including an effort to establish Opal Creek watershed as a state park in 1989. All these efforts were defeated politically. In a scene environmentalist Andy Kerr likened to "the last buffalo hunt," in 1989 five hundred loggers and mill owners and a hundred log trucks circled the capitol building in Salem, honking their horns and blocking traffic to protest proposed protection of Opal Creek.

Remaining ancient forests were in the crosshairs. New technology allowed forest scientists to analyze satellite photos and realize that the Pacific Northwest had been cutting down its rain forests in the 1970s and 1980s at a faster rate than Brazil had been cutting its own. During the late 1980s, an unbelievable 2 square miles of Oregon's ancient forests were being clear-cut per week.

The conflict grew severe enough to warrant the attention of President Clinton, who convened a timber summit in Portland in April 1993 with foresters, biologists, and conservationists at the table. The resulting Northwest Forest Plan adopted in 1994 was the most comprehensive landscape management plan ever devised by a federal agency. The plan instituted a system of reserves for maintaining and regrowing old-growth habitat that fish and wildlife depend on. Yet, amazingly enough, another bill to protect Opal Creek failed that year in the Senate.

At long last, on September 30, 1996, Congress passed retiring Senator Mark O. Hatfield's last legislation, protecting 20,287 acres as the Opal

Creek Wilderness. Another 13,538 acres became the Opal Creek Scenic Recreation Area along the nearby Little North Fork Santiam and tributaries, plus an adjacent 3,066 acres around Elkhorn Creek was designated as a Wild and Scenic River.

As I write this, almost twenty years later, more than twenty thousand people visit Opal Creek a year. More trails continue to be built. Oregonians voted Opal Creek their favorite wilderness in 2013 in an online poll by Oregon Wild. Opal Creek Ancient Forest Center provides environmental education for school groups, summer camp, cabin rentals, and workshops to help people spend time in, study, and fall in love with this uncut gem.

The fact that Opal Creek is now protected in perpetuity is, to me, profound evidence of the power of grassroots efforts.

I recently returned to the forests of Opal Creek for the first time in almost fifteen years. What struck me most was the fact that such an amazing place was so close to being lost. I marvel also at the tenacity of the human spirit that helped defend it—despite defeat after defeat. I hope that this story inspires others to defend wild areas that still remain unprotected.

Opal Creek

JOHN DANIEL

A narrow, twisting trail enters this woods
of hemlock, red cedar, and Douglas-fir,
follows the stream flashing white through trees,
switchbacks across steep ridges, and grows fainter
as the tilted, mossy-barked trees grow huger
and fallen trunks lie everywhere, roots upthrust,
their solid centuries drawn back to ground,
ranks of seedlings rooted in the rotting wood.

Grow and go down, the dark earth spiring to light
and returning, the forest travels its changing way
without the need of any trail to guide it,
and neither do the varied thrush and winter wren
need direction through the shadows where they sing,
or the red-backed vole that burrows in the ground,
or the stream spuming and swirling between pools.
Only we humans who walk here need this line

that leads through stillness and muted light,
through ferns and thimbleberry sopping our pants,
through the blended dark smells of mossy ground,
through scatters of mushrooms yellow and crimson
and flaring orange, others half-black half-white—
and even we can stray, even women and men
can gradually learn to let go of the trail
as it fades among trees and underbrush

and leaves us where nothing human shows the way.
There are other ways. We can lower ourselves
on vine maple holds down a moss-slick bank,
thrash through a tangle of devil's club and briars,
climb from the thicket on a down Douglas-fir
and walk that trunk to another, and another,
and at last to one great fallen tree, thicker
than we are tall. We can climb its furrowed bark

and sit for a while, our hard breath easing,
as we listen to a bird hidden high above.
Like the spiring trees and the lives they hold,
we rest ourselves on death's generous body,
and all around us where the stillness sings
we see the green abundance of death's rising.
We came for this, to join for an afternoon
the long dance of the trees, and when we turn

to find the trail and walk out of the forest,
we take with us what surrounds us in this place
by leaving it here, where it belongs—
where mushrooms, moss, and red-backed vole,
where thimbleberry and dripping ferns,
where thrush and wren and the unseen birds,
where swirling stream and muted light,
where stillness and the ancient trees go on.

This remnant patch of native Willamette Valley prairie southeast of Stayton encompasses wet meadows, dry uplands, and breeding pairs of western meadowlarks.

ACTIVITIES: Walking, wildflower viewing, bird-watching. **FACILITIES:** None. **FEES AND REGULATIONS:** No fee. Open dawn to dusk. Stay on trails; no dogs, horses, bicycles, or motorized vehicles. **BEST MONTHS:** Late April through early June. **MANAGING AGENCY:** The Nature Conservancy.

To get there: From Salem, take Hwy 22 east for 12 miles. Take the exit to Stayton and turn right onto Cascade Highway/Stayton-Scio Rd. Drive through Stayton, cross the bridge over the North Santiam River, and turn left onto Kingston-Jordan Dr. After 1 mile, stop at the railroad tracks and then turn left onto Kingston-Lyons Dr. After 1.6 miles, where the road makes a 90-degree turn to the right, go straight onto the gravel road and park on the unpaved turnout at this junction. The preserve is divided into two parcels on either side of Kingston-Lyons Dr. Enter Roberts Meadow, the parcel that is publicly accessible, by way of a small gate to the right of the wooden Nature Conservancy sign that stands just outside the barbed-wire fence close to the parking lot.

Walking among the native wildflowers and grasses of Kingston Prairie Preserve on a sunny day in May, you will find yourself immersed in one of Oregon's rarest ecosystems, which once covered more than a million acres of the Willamette Valley. A shallow seasonal stream flows through the preserve, receiving water that trickles through wet meadows. On higher ground grow grasses and flowers characteristic of upland prairie habitat. A few solitary Oregon white oaks spread their sturdy boughs over the grass. The song of the western meadowlark draws attention to another highlight of the preserve—Kingston Prairie is one of the few places in this region where meadowlarks still nest.

Kingston Prairie is a 152-acre island of native habitat in a sea of agricultural land. It escaped development because it isn't suitable for farming—it has thin soils underlain by extensive basalt bedrock. The land is now owned by the Nature Conservancy, which works to maintain the natural state of the prairie. An undeveloped network of use paths takes the visitor around the central area of the east parcel of the preserve. Watch your step, for footing is uneven and a healthy population of moles is pushing up dirt mounds.

For thousands of years, prairies such as this were vitally important sources of food plants and game animals for Native Americans. Local tribes actively preserved the prairies and oak savannas by periodically

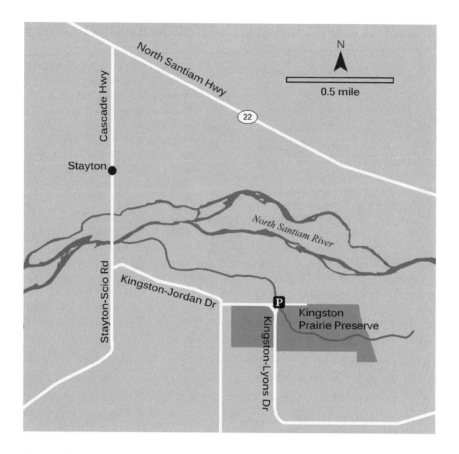

setting fire to the dry grasses. Burning promoted the growth of food plants such as camas and maintained open spaces for hunting. European-American settlers put an end to the burning and rapidly converted much of the land to farming purposes in the mid-1800s. Today less than 1 percent of the valley's native prairie remains, and the remnant patches are small and widely scattered.

Despite its isolation and small size, Kingston Prairie harbors a wealth of native plant diversity. The dominant perennial grasses are tufted hairgrass in the wet meadows and Idaho fescue in the upland prairie. Dozens of wildflower species bloom here in spring, including camas, shooting stars, and yellow monkeyflower. Rare plant species found include Oregon larkspur, Bradshaw's lomatium, white-topped aster, and Willamette daisy, which were widespread in the valley before their habitats were all but obliterated. Most of the flowers go to seed as spring transitions to summer, and color fades from the prairie. By late June all is brown or gray, and the stream will soon be dry if it isn't already.

WESTERN MEADOWLARKS

Meadowlarks have large territories and require extensive natural prairie habitats. Breeding populations in the Willamette Valley have declined dramatically in the last few decades. The western meadowlark—state bird of Oregon—is now a focal species for the conservation and restoration of the valley's prairie ecosystem. Kingston Prairie serves as a small but outstanding example of that ecosystem. Wildlife biologists have used the Kingston Prairie Preserve to study habitat needs of western meadowlark and other songbirds known to be declining in the Willamette Valley.

Western meadowlark © Wendy C. Thompson

This small gem along the North Santiam River offers a boat ramp, shady camping, and a walking trail that winds through wetlands and beaver ponds.

To get there: From Salem, take Hwy 22 east for 23 miles to Mehama and turn right on Hwy 226. Drive across the North Santiam River into Lyons and continue onto Main St. In a few blocks, turn north on 13th St (Neal Park Rd) and drive all the way to the end to enter the park.

Fishing and floating opportunities on the North Santiam are the main attraction of this park, along with a chance to view wildlife from a walking trail around the perimeter of an extensive beaver pond area. You can pick up the walking trail by passing through the opening between a couple of logs to the left just before you reach the gate into the park.

ACTIVITIES: Camping, walking, bird-watching, swimming, picnicking, fishing, boating. **FACILITIES:** RV and tent campsites (open mid-April through mid-October), ADA campsite, restrooms and showers, picnic tables, group picnic shelter, children's playground, baseball diamond, horseshoe pits, boat ramp. **FEES AND REGULATIONS:** No fee for individual day use; fees for camping and group day use of picnic shelters (for reservations, call 541-967-3917 or visit linnparks.com). Day-use areas open dawn to dusk year-round, on a walk-in basis when the campground is gated closed. Dogs allowed on leash. **BEST MONTHS:** Mid-April through mid-October. Packed-dirt loop trail may be muddy in the winter. **MANAGING AGENCY:** Linn County Parks and Recreation.

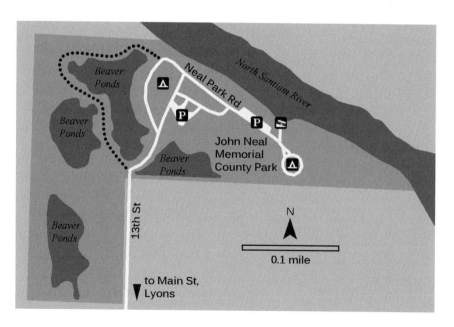

BUSY BEAVERS

North American beavers (*Castor canadensis*) were nearly trapped to extinction in the Willamette Valley by the Hudson's Bay Company in the 1800s, but their numbers have been on the rise since silk hats replaced beaver hats as the fashion of the day. Beavers fell trees to reach the inner bark—their principal food along with fresh leaves, twigs, and stems—and then use the leftover logs and branches to build dams. When water begins to pool, it's easier for the beavers to swim to trees they want to cut down for food and to pull the logs through the water to build up their lodges and dams. Each lodge has a hollowed-out chamber where the beavers sleep, eat, groom each other, and bear their young.

Because they girdle trees and cause flooding, beavers are sometimes viewed as nuisances, but their work has ecological benefits. Their dams improve the water quality downstream, provide watering holes for other wildlife, supply breeding areas for amphibians and fish, and furnish places for waterfowl to feed, rear their young, and rest.

North American beaver © David Wagner

Two waterfalls, a small seasonal campground, and 6 miles of trails through a forest of Douglas-fir and hemlock are the main draws of this state forest recreation area.

To get there: From Salem, take Hwy 22 east for 22.4 miles. For the lower (year-round) trailhead: Just before the first flashing yellow light in Mehama turn left onto Fern Ridge Rd. Follow this paved road for 1.2 miles and turn right into the small gravel lot. Park to the left of the kiosk or along the driveway without blocking the yellow gate. For the upper trailhead and campground (road open May 20 to November 1): From Hwy 22 just past the first flashing yellow light in Mehama, turn left onto Wagner Rd. Stay right and drive 2.5 miles to where the pavement becomes gravel. When you arrive at a four-way intersection, drive straight (north). Wagner Rd becomes Ayers Creek Rd. Drive 1 mile and turn left (west) onto AC 100 Rd. Drive 2.8 miles and turn left (west) at the orange gate onto Shellburg Rd. Drive 2.6 miles to the campground.

ACTIVITIES: Hiking, camping, biking, horseback riding, picnicking. **FACILITIES:** Vault toilets, water from a hand pump, picnic shelter, and seven campsites at Shellburg Falls Campground above the falls. **FEES AND REGULATIONS:** No fee for hiking; fee for camping. Shellburg Falls and Vine Maple trails for hiking only; mountain bikes and horses allowed on other trails. Dogs allowed under voice control or on leash, although cattle guards may be a challenge for dogs. **BEST MONTHS:** Year-round, but trail closures may be in effect for mountain biking and horseback riding during the rainy season (call 503-859-2151 for information). Campground accessible by vehicle May 20 to November 1 only. **MANAGING AGENCY:** Oregon Department of Forestry, Santiam State Forest.

Less than half a mile south of Silver Falls State Park as the crow flies, Shellburg Falls Recreation Area shares the same geological formation that gave rise to the waterfalls of the state park, but it's not in the same watershed—Shellburg Creek empties into Stout Creek and from there into the North Santiam River. Shellburg Falls, which is as spectacular as any waterfall in the state park, is popular with locals who appreciate being able to bring their dogs along and not having to pay a fee for day use.

An easy/moderate 4.2-mile round-trip (640 feet elevation gain) loop from the lower trailhead starts up the gated gravel road and ascends gently through rolling cattle pastures on private property. You enter a mixed forest of red alder, bigleaf maple, and Douglas-fir before passing the 1-mile mark and entering the Santiam State Forest. At 1.2 miles, the road crosses Shellburg Creek on a short concrete bridge. Immediately below the bridge is 40-foot, two-tiered Lower Shellburg Falls. The waterfall is

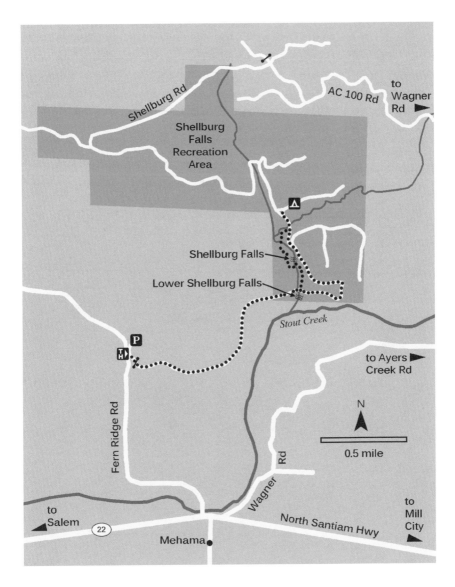

hard to see from above, but just across the bridge and past the gate is a log bench with a decent view.

Just across the bridge, take a left at the sign and head up the single-track stairs to the narrow Shellburg Falls Trail. The trail parallels the tumbling creek for about 0.2 mile before you reach 100-foot Shellburg Falls. A short side trail to the left leads to a viewpoint with a rock bench near the base of the falls. The main trail, a feat of trail building worthy of note, circles behind the waterfall in a roomy volcanic-rock grotto and climbs up a set of stairs to the top of the falls.

Once you reach the top, follow the relatively level trail 0.5 mile across Shellburg Creek on a footbridge and through a quiet old Douglas-fir forest to where it intersects the gravel road again. Turn right to follow the gravel road all the way back to the trailhead, or left to take a brief walk to the vault toilets and water pump at Shellburg Falls Campground.

OPAL CREEK WILDERNESS AND SCENIC RECREATION AREA

The largest uncut watershed in western Oregon, in the Cascade foothills east of Salem, harbors old-growth forest, crystal-clear waters, and remnants of mineral exploration and mining activity.

To get there: From Salem, take Hwy 22 east for 23 miles. Just past Mehama, turn left onto North Fork Rd. This paved road turns to gravel at mile 15.4 and becomes Rd 2209 as it enters Willamette National Forest and Opal Creek Scenic Recreation Area. Three trailheads—Henline Falls / Ogle Mountain, Henline Mountain, and Nasty Rock—are along the road, and the Opal Creek trailhead is at the gated end of the road. Access Three Pools Day Use Area and Shady Cove Campground by taking the well-marked turnoff to the right onto Rd 2207 1.4 miles beyond the start of gravel Rd 2209.

This federally protected landscape of heavily timbered slopes and crystal-line free-flowing waters encompasses nearly 21,000 acres in Opal Creek Wilderness and a little more than 13,500 acres in Opal Creek Scenic Recreation Area. The wilderness area offers solitude and relative isolation to hikers and backpackers, while the recreation area is popular for its swimming holes such as Opal Pool along Opal Creek and the Three Pools Day Use Area on the Little North Santiam River. Here you will find hiking trails along streams with sculpted emerald pools and cascading waterfalls in lush old-growth forests, as well as routes to ridgelines and peaks with spectacular views of the west Cascades.

Opal Creek, named for the wife of a ranger, is 5 miles long from its headwaters at Opal Lake to its intersection with Battle Ax Creek at Jawbone Flats. At that point the watercourse becomes the Little North Fork of the Santiam River, labeled on maps as the Little North Santiam

ACTIVITIES: Hiking, swimming, fishing, kayaking, horseback riding, biking, camping, educational work-shops and expeditions. **FACILITIES:** Vault toilets at Opal Creek gate; lodging April through November (opalcreek.org) and tiny store open summer weekends at Jawbone Flats; vault toilets and picnic tables at Three Pools Day Use Area; vault toilet and twelve first-come first-served tent sites at year-round Shady Cove Campground. **FEES AND REGULATIONS:** Northwest Forest Pass or day-use fee required for parking at trailheads and day-use area; fee for camping at Shady Cove; self-issue wilderness permit required to enter wilderness from Memorial Day weekend through October 31. Dogs allowed on leash. Horses and mountain bikes allowed to Jawbone Flats. **BEST MONTHS:** Spring through fall; trails and swimming holes are very crowded on warm summer weekends. In winter, expect snow at higher elevations and occasionally at lower elevations. **MANAGING AGENCY:** US Forest Service, Detroit Ranger District.

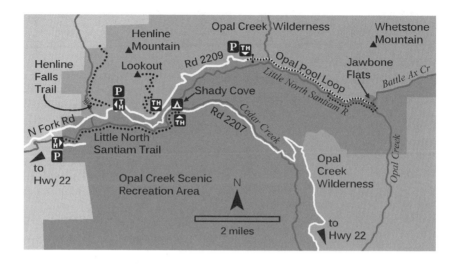

and known by locals as the North Fork. As the river flows mostly west and a little south, its waters are added to by Gold Creek, Cedar Creek, and Elkhorn Creek (which is designated as a Wild and Scenic River), along with other tributaries. The river takes on a bright shade of green; this is not the water per se but actually the green rock below magnified by the incredible clarity of the water. From its origin to the Willamette National Forest boundary, a total of 7 miles, the Little North Santiam is part of the Oregon Scenic Waterways system.

The northern part of the wilderness area is dominated by two prominent peaks, Whetstone and Henline, which offer scenic vantage points that were once used as fire lookouts. Two major forest fires burned in this watershed sometime in the 1500s and in the 1800s. A third of the wilderness and recreation area is timbered with ancient Douglas-fir, western hemlock, and western red cedar, some up to a thousand years old, that survived the fires in the cool, wet places along the streams. Elk, black bears, and northern spotted owls live in this biologically diverse temperate rain forest.

Northern spotted owl © M. L. Herring

NORTH SANTIAM RIVER WATERSHED

OPAL POOL LOOP

This popular hike follows a gravel road above the Little North Santiam River through an old-growth grove and past Sawmill Falls, then loops past Opal Pool and back through Jawbone Flats, a rustic mining camp.

Difficulty and length: Moderate, 7.1 miles round-trip with 300 feet elevation gain. **To get there:** From Hwy 22, go 20.5 miles on North Fork Rd/Rd 2209 to the gated end of the road.

As you hike down the gravel road from the locked gate, you soon cross Gold Creek on a 60-foot-high wooden bridge and begin passing some scattered eight-hundred-year-old trees. At mile 1.5 the road enters an old-growth grove emblematic of the ancient forest protected here. At mile 2.0 you come to the scattered remains of the Merten Mill. Follow a small footpath past a wooden shack toward the river to reach a 30-foot cascade known as Sawmill Falls or Cascada de los Niños (Waterfall of the Children), the latter in honor of Opal Creek's sister forest in Costa Rica.

The road forks 0.2 mile ahead. Take the fork to the right and cross the river on a log bridge, then turn left onto the Opal Creek Trail. This trail follows the Little North Santiam upstream through the woods past the point where Opal Creek joins Battle Ax Creek. After 1.4 miles, a sign points left to a short spur that gives a view of the creek as it spills into 25-foot-deep, emerald green Opal Pool.

Return to the main trail and go left to cross a footbridge over Opal Creek above Opal Pool. The trail intersects an old mining road that descends into

NORTHERN SPOTTED OWLS

The owl that sparked an epic struggle between environmentalists and the timber industry prefers to live in older forest stands with canopies that are open enough for it to fly between and underneath the trees. With a wingspan of around 4 feet, this chocolate brown owl has dark eyes, weighs 1 to 2 pounds, and stands about 18 inches tall. It hunts nocturnally for small forest mammals like squirrels, wood rats, and mice. Spotted owls primarily mate for life and nest in the tops of trees or in cavities of naturally deformed or diseased trees. They may live up to ten years in the wild, fifteen to twenty years in captivity.

In 1990, the US Forest Service listed the spotted owl as a threatened species under the Endangered Species Act. The owl lives in British Columbia, Washington, Oregon, and California, but the largest number of mating pairs (1,200 in 2013) is found in Oregon. Now the owl is threatened by competition from the barred owl, a native of the Northeast that has expanded its range westward, and the Forest Service is studying how to manage this latest threat.

Jawbone Flats, a well-preserved collection of buildings and machinery dating from the 1930s. The historic mining town is rumored to have been named after the miners' wives, who had a reputation for "shooting the breeze" while their husbands were at work. It's now managed as the Opal Creek Ancient Forest Center, "promoting conservation through educational experiences in wilderness." Stay on the road to return to the trailhead at the gate.

Options: Above Opal Pool, the Opal Creek Trail follows Opal Creek for another 0.6 mile, passing cascades, waterfalls, and swimming holes. A single-log footbridge crosses the creek at this point, and the trail goes nearly another mile before reaching Cedar Flats, a trio of ancient western red cedars.

HENLINE FALLS TRAIL

A short, wooded trail ends at a 126-foot waterfall that plunges down the side of an andesite alcove into an emerald splash pool, with a view of the main opening to the long-defunct Silver King Mine.

Difficulty and length: Easy/moderate, 1.8 miles round-trip with 400 feet elevation gain. **To get there**: From Hwy 22, go 16.9 miles on North Fork Rd/Rd 2209 to the trail kiosk and small parking area on the left.

The first 0.5 mile of this trail ascends gently as it enters Opal Creek Wilderness following the rocky, overgrown bed of a wagon road that once provided access to the Silver King Mine. When the trail forks, take the left fork and pass a sign confirming you are on the Henline Falls Trail. Even though the falls is only 0.4 mile away at this point, you won't hear or see any sign of it as you gently traverse a wooded incline until you start to hear Henline Creek far below to your left.

Nearing the falls, the trail descends gently to bring you within view of two big hunks of concrete that once supported the silver mine's hydropower plant, which used a water wheel to power machine drills. Immediately to the right of the base of the falls, known at one time as Silver King Falls, is the cavelike opening to the main working tunnel of the Silver King Mine. You can find footholds to scramble up the rocky wall below the mine opening if you want to walk 30 feet into the horizontal mine shaft. A metal gate closes off the remaining tunnel, said to extend 1,700 feet into the rock.

Options: On the way in, when the trail forks at 0.5 mile, you can take the right fork to get to the Ogle Mountain Trail, an unmaintained, steep trail that once provided access to the productive Ogle Mountain Mine. The trail follows Henline Creek for 2 miles before coming to a dead end. There is a series of seven cascades on Henline Creek above Henline Falls—dubbed Family Falls by Maynard Drawson, author of the *Treasures of the Oregon Country* series—but reaching them requires difficult off-trail scrambling and should be left to experienced bushwhackers.

MINING IN THE LITTLE NORTH SANTIAM WATERSHED

Starting with miners discovering gold in 1859, the Little North Santiam watershed was the object of extensive mining and mineral exploration. Henline Creek and Falls were named after a settler who came to the area prospecting for silver. The Silver King Mine at Henline Falls was developed and mined in the early part of the 1900s, and the Jawbone Flats mining camp was built beginning in 1930 to service mines extracting lead, zinc, copper, silver, and gold. It was not until 1992 that mining ceased around Jawbone Flats; the Shiny Rock Mining Company donated its land to the fledgling Friends of Opal Creek, established by George Atiyeh to lead the effort to secure permanent protection for the Opal Creek watershed.

The only timber ever logged in the area was cut for use in the mines. The Merten Mill on the old road to Jawbone Flats was a steam-powered sawmill built in 1943 to provide timbers for the area's mines. Five of the surrounding acres were selectively logged for the mill, but the operation proved risky and unprofitable. Artifacts still scattered around the site include an old steam boiler salvaged from the coal-burning battleship USS Oregon (which served with distinction in the Spanish-American War, was moored in Portland for many years as a floating museum and monument, and was dismantled for scrap in early 1943).

Old mine shafts and rusty mining equipment remain in the Opal Creek area to tell the tale of mines with names like Blue Jay, Silver Star, and Crown. Use caution when hiking off trails and leave artifacts undisturbed.

You can also make the difficult hike nearly to the top of Henline Mountain (elevation 4,116 feet) by driving another 0.8 mile past the Henline Falls trailhead up Road 2209 to a parking spot on the right, opposite the trailhead kiosk. Huff and puff 2.8 miles up the trail, gaining 2,200 feet in elevation, to reach a lookout site with views across Opal Creek Wilderness to Mount Jefferson.

LITTLE NORTH SANTIAM TRAIL

A trail accessible from trailheads at both ends parallels the Little North Santiam through old-growth forest, crosses streams on a series of rustic log footbridges, and climbs steeply to bypass a gorge with towering rock walls.

Difficulty and length: Moderate, 9 miles round-trip with 900 feet elevation gain. **To get there:** For the downstream (Elkhorn) trailhead, from Hwy 22 go 15 miles on North Fork Rd. Turn right onto gravel Elkhorn Dr (Rd 201), cross a one-lane bridge, and continue 0.4 mile farther to a gravel parking area on the left. For the upstream (Shady Cove) trailhead, from Hwy 22 go 16.8 miles on North Fork Rd / Rd 2209 and turn right onto Rd 2207 toward Shady Cove Campground at a well-marked turnoff. Travel 1.8 miles to the campground and continue across a one-lane timber-truss bridge to a gravel parking area on the left. The marked trailhead is on the right.

From the Elkhorn trailhead, the trail descends through young alder and Douglas-fir and then enters an old-growth forest and crosses a tributary on the first of a series of eight wooden footbridges before reaching the Little North Santiam. The crystal-clear river rolls along below, parallel to the path, meandering in and out of your field of vision. At mile 0.7 you come to a cascade where the river squeezes through chutes in a big hunk of volcanic rock. Just after you pass the cascade, the trail seems to fork, with the left fork blocked by a log. Take the left fork for a better view of the falls, but then return and take the other fork as it begins a steep ascent to bypass a rocky gorge.

From the trail's high point at 1,800 feet, you can look across the gorge for views of Henline Mountain, Triple Falls on Henline Creek, and the confluence of Henline Creek and the Little North Santiam. The trail switchbacks down to the river again and levels off at mile 2.3. The trail down can be slick, so watch your footing and use a hiking pole if you have one. The rest of the trail stays beside the river, and a handful of short side paths allow scrambling down to the water's edge. You can choose how far to go on the trail before turning around or meet a shuttle car at the upstream end for a hike of 4.5 miles.

LITTLE NORTH SANTIAM RECREATION AREA

Downstream from Opal Creek Scenic Recreation Area, the Little North Santiam Recreation Area encompasses the BLM's Canyon Creek and Elkhorn Valley Recreation Sites. These two sites and three Marion County Parks dotted along North Fork Road offer easy access to the Little North Santiam within an hour's drive of Salem. Here you can swim, fish for late summer and winter steelhead, hike, picnic, and camp, or pause while en route to Opal Creek Scenic Recreation Area. During the summer months, traffic along this road is heavy.

North Fork Park (2 miles from Highway 22) and Bear Creek (7.4 miles from Highway 22) offer good options for swimming, and Salmon Falls (13.8 miles from Highway 22) features a viewpoint of the river flowing over a 30-foot rock outcrop. These three Marion County day-use parks are open 8 a.m. to sunset, charge no fee, and provide vault toilets and picnic tables. Canyon Creek Recreation Site (7.2 miles from Highway 22) and Elkhorn Valley Recreation Site (8.5 miles from Highway 22) charge a day-use fee and offer vault toilets and picnic tables; Elkhorn Valley also offers twenty-three first-come, first-served campsites. These BLM sites typically open on Memorial Day and close on Labor Day.

A low-key state park nestled in a forest along a broad, curved stretch of the North Santiam River offers great steelhead fishing along with walking trails, picnic sites, and tent camping.

To get there: From Salem, take Hwy 22 east for 26 miles, pass North Fork Rd, and turn right at the sign for North Santiam State Recreation Area. The paved road gently descends 0.8 mile to the parking lot.

Frequented by fishermen, boaters, and tent campers, this park has a relaxed vibe and a prized angling spot. A network of short trail segments, mostly unpaved, loops through the

ACTIVITIES: Picnicking, fishing, walking, boating, tent camping. **FACILITIES:** ADA restroom, picnic tables and group picnic shelter (call 1-800-452-5687 to reserve), horseshoe pits, boat ramp; nine walk-in, boat-in tent sites (one ADA), each with picnic table and fire ring. **FEES AND REGULATIONS:** No fee for individual day use, fee for camping. Campsites available on a first-come, first-served basis May 1 to September 30. Dogs allowed on leash. **BEST MONTHS:** Year-round. **MANAGING AGENCY:** Oregon Parks and Recreation Department.

woods and along the river. A 1.4-mile trail around the perimeter of the park passes through river and forest scenery. The portion of the paved 0.35-mile River Loop that skirts the river can be combined with a paved extension and a gravel segment to make a 0.8-mile walk along the river. The 0.4-mile Anderson Loop winds through towering trees with moss-draped limbs.

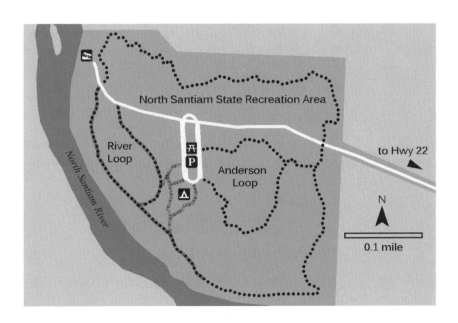

NIAGARA COUNTY PARK

A small park on the North Santiam offers historic stonework, dramatic river views, and an educational path through Douglas-fir and red alder.

To get there: From Salem, take Hwy 22 east for 37 miles. After passing milepost 37 and the little town of Niagara (which consists of about three buildings), turn right at the easy-to-miss sign for Niagara County Park. Bear right into a gravel parking lot.

ACTIVITIES: Picnicking, fishing, walking, wading. FACILITIES: ADA vault toilet and two old-fashioned outhouses (his and hers), picnic tables. FEES AND REGULATIONS: No fee. Day use only, 8 a.m. to dusk. Dogs allowed on leash. **BEST MONTHS:** Year-round. **MANAGING AGENCY:** Marion County Parks.

During times of lower flow, the North Santiam River narrows to a little more than 4 feet wide as it surges through a rocky slot at Niagara County Park. That's why brothers Frank and Edward O'Neil and their partner C. W. Callaghan thought it would be a good site to generate hydroelectric power for a paper mill. They set about building a rubble dam in the late 1890s, but year after year their work was washed away by high winter flows. They finally gave up on building the dam in 1912, but by that time stonemasons had built substantial walls and arches that remain to this day.

Take the steep but sturdy metal stairway (53 steps) down from the parking lot to the top of the volcanic extrusion upon which the stonework is built. This enormous hunk of twisted and contorted rock makes a challenging obstacle for the river and an exciting perch for dramatic views upstream, downstream, and straight across to where Sevenmile Creek tumbles in by way of a 25-foot waterfall just below the slot in the gorge. You can take a short set of stone steps to the left at the bottom of the stairway to circle under the stairs by way of the tallest archway and reach a fenced observation point.

The shady 0.7-mile round-trip Powder House Trail starts at the parking lot and makes its way upstream as it drops down close to the river. Informational displays share facts about ecology and the powder house at the end of the trail where dynamite for the dam project was kept.

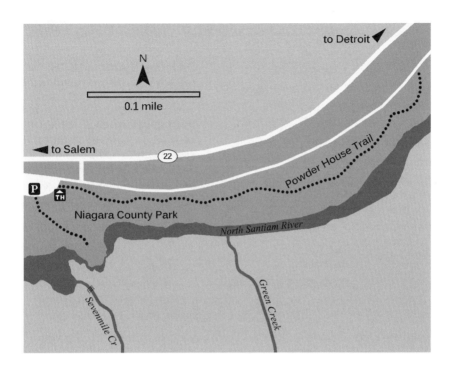

SOUTH BREITENBUSH GORGE TRAIL

This pleasant forest trail offers an exciting but safe crossing of the North Fork Breitenbush River, soft passage beneath old-growth trees within earshot of the South Fork, and a look at the gorge as well as aptly named Roaring Creek.

DIFFICULTY AND LENGTH: Easy/moderate, 5.2 miles round-trip to Roaring Creek with 700 feet elevation gain. **FACILITIES:** None. **FEES AND REGULATIONS:** No fee. Dogs allowed on leash. **BEST MONTHS:** Mid-March to mid-December. Snow blankets the trail in winter and early spring. **MANAGING AGENCY:** US Forest Service, Detroit Ranger District.

To get there: From Salem, take Hwy 22 east for 50 miles to Detroit and turn left on Rd 46 to Breitenbush River. Drive 11.2 miles on this paved road, ignoring the turnoff to Breitenbush Hot Springs at mile 9.5. Turn right onto Rd 4600-050, marked only by a stop sign, which immediately turns to gravel. Drive 0.3 mile to a wide spot next to the foundation of the former Breitenbush Guard Station and park off the road. Walk another 300 feet on the road toward the green gate into Breitenbush Hot Springs and turn left just before the gate onto the marked trail.

Near the start of this hike, the trail crosses the braided North Fork on a series of fallen logs with handrails; then the trail follows the course of the South Fork, with the river always within earshot but only infrequently in

OLD-GROWTH FORESTS

Old-growth forests once covered much of Oregon, but today fewer than 10 percent of these stands remain. These are conifer forests dominated by several species of large old trees that have not undergone any major changes (such as logging, large fires, or big windstorms) for more than 100 to 150 years. Some old-growth forests in Oregon are ancient, such as the 600- to 1,000-year-old groves of cedar in Opal Creek Wilderness and the 800-year-old Douglas-fir stands in Crabtree Valley. The most common type of old-growth forest in Oregon is dominated by Douglas-firs and western hemlocks that are 350 to 750 years old.

Many second-growth forests in western Oregon contain the occasional giant old tree, but old-growth forests are distinct in that they have four layers: big trees, large snags (standing dead trees), large fallen trees on the forest floor, and a multilayered or continuous canopy formed by the big trees, smaller trees, and shrubs. These forests still host all or most of the species of wildlife, fish, and plants that are native to them. This intact ecosystem allows them to recover relatively quickly from natural events like fires or windstorms.

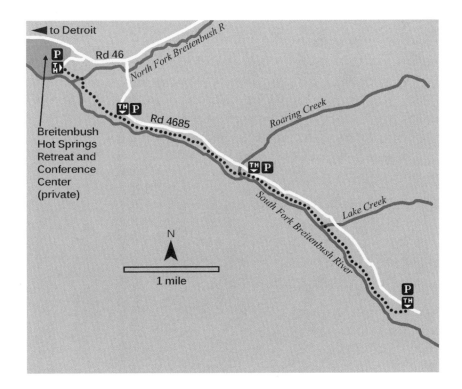

to Detroit

Rd 46

North Fork Breitenbush R

Roaring Creek

Rd 4685

Breitenbush
Hot Springs
Retreat and
Conference
Center
(private)

South Fork Breitenbush River

Lake Creek

N

1 mile

view. At mile 1.4 you have the option of taking a fork to the right onto the Emerald Forest Trail, which reaches Breitenbush Hot Springs in 2.6 miles. If you stay on the main trail, around mile 2 you encounter an area of the forest that was hard-hit by a winter windstorm in 1990, felling enough trees to close the trail for more than a year. Before you reach the area of greatest damage, you see the upended roots of three or four fallen giants right next to the trail, allowing an instructive look at their relatively shallow root systems.

At 0.3 mile past the damaged area, an easy-to-miss spur trail marked by a couple of small parallel cut logs sticking out into the trail descends briefly to the right to a viewpoint from which you can see the gorge, a 300-foot-long basalt narrows through which the water thunders. Walk another 0.3 mile on the main trail to reach photogenic Roaring Creek, which the trail crosses on a sturdy footbridge. A log bench here offers a spot to have lunch before returning to the trailhead by the same route.

Options: You can make the hike a one-way trip by parking another car at a trailhead just beyond Roaring Creek, reached by driving 0.5 mile beyond the first trailhead turnoff on Road 46 and turning right on paved Road 4685, which turns to gravel after crossing the North Fork. Ignore the first marked trailhead, cross Roaring Creek, and park at the second trailhead, on the right.

If you continue another couple of miles on Road 4685, you will come to the third trailhead, a large gravel parking area with trails into Mount Jefferson Wilderness to Bear Point (3.8 miles) and Jefferson Park (6.2 miles). If you park a shuttle car here, you can continue on the trail past Roaring Creek along the river for another 3.5 miles.

Shaggy parasol © Wendy C. Thompson

STAHLMAN POINT TRAIL

High above the powerboats and campgrounds of Detroit Lake, the former perch of a fire lookout offers breathtaking views at the end of a steady ascent.

To get there: From Salem, take Hwy 22 east for 53 miles. At the upper end of Detroit Lake, just past milepost 53, turn right onto Blowout Rd (Rd 10). Cross the river and drive 3.7 miles on the paved road to the small wooden Stahlman Point Tr. sign on the left. Turn left into the small gravel parking lot.

DIFFICULTY AND LENGTH: Moderate, 5 miles round-trip with 1,300 feet elevation gain. **FACILITIES:** None. **FEES AND REGULATIONS:** No fee. Dogs allowed on leash. No overnight camping. Be careful with children and dogs, as the rocky top drops into the surrounding forest by way of tall cliffs. **BEST MONTHS:** Mid-March to December. Snow blankets the trail in winter and early spring. **MANAGING AGENCY:** US Forest Service, Detroit Ranger District.

Stahlman Point (elevation 3,058 feet) had a fire lookout from 1948 to 1966, marked by nine concrete footings today. The trail begins next to a stream and ascends to traverse a series of steep, wooded ravines with occasional glimpses of Detroit Lake through the trees. Most of the trees are second growth, but the trail passes through a couple of pockets with old giants still standing.

Labor up the last few switchbacks and clamber up a few yards of rock, and suddenly Mount Jefferson looms straight ahead (if you're lucky enough to be here on a clear day). Down below you can see the last section of the free-flowing North Santiam River before it joins Detroit Lake.

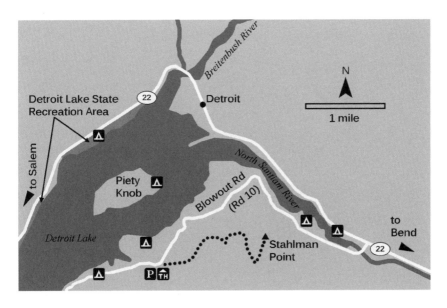

DUFFY LAKE TRAIL, MOUNT JEFFERSON WILDERNESS

This sometimes-rocky trail ascends gently through a mature forest of fir and hemlock, crosses the North Santiam River near its source, and ends at an alpine lake.

To get there: From Salem, take Hwy 22 east for 75 miles. Pass milepost 75, cross the North Santiam River bridge, and make an immediate left turn from the passing lane onto Big Meadows Rd (Rd 2267). (If you can't do this safely, pull off onto a forest road to the right opposite Big Meadows Rd and let traffic pass before attempting the turn.) Drive for 3 miles, staying right at the first turnoff to the Big Meadows Horse Camp and going left at the next fork, where the pavement turns to gravel for the last 0.4 mile to a parking loop. Take either fork at the loop to reach the trailhead kiosk.

DIFFICULTY AND LENGTH: Moderate, 6.6 miles round-trip with 800 feet elevation gain. **FACILITIES:** Vault toilet, picnic table at trailhead. **FEES AND REGULATIONS:** Northwest Forest Pass or day-use fee required for parking; self-issue wilderness permit required for the hike. Dogs and horses allowed; no bikes or motorized vehicles. Campfires must be at least 100 feet from any water or trail. **BEST MONTHS:** June to November. Mosquitoes thrive here in early to mid-summer, and the trail is closed by snow in winter. **MANAGING AGENCY:** US Forest Service, Detroit Ranger District.

The 111,177-acre Mount Jefferson Wilderness encompasses 163 miles of trails (including a 40-mile stretch of the Pacific Crest Trail), five glaciers, and more than 150 lakes, along with steep talus slopes, rock outcrops, and alpine meadows. At 10,495 feet, Mount Jefferson is the second highest peak in Oregon and is the dominant feature of this High Cascades area, along with Three Fingered Jack at 7,841 feet. Snow blankets the higher peaks and ridges from October through May.

Lungwort © Wendy C. Thompson

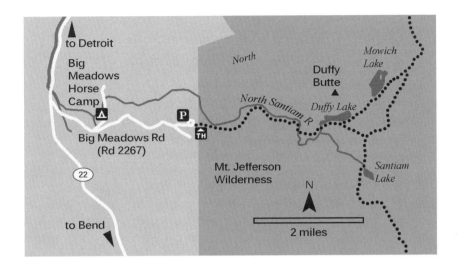

Duffy Lake (elevation 4,795 feet) is one of many alpine lakes that dot the wilderness between Mount Jefferson and Three Fingered Jack. The trail to the lake is one of the most popular access routes into the wilderness because the ascent is fairly gentle and the lake offers campsites along with swimming and fishing. The trail roughly follows the course of the North Santiam River. In the few stretches where the river comes into view, it's more a creek than a river this close to its source as snowmelt on the rocky slopes above Santiam Lake.

From the trailhead, begin the gentle ascent. At the Eight Lakes Basin sign a quarter of a mile in, ignore the trail splitting off to the left to Big Meadows Horse Camp. Traverse the quiet forest, cross three or four tributary streams, and skirt a couple of talus slopes before the Turpentine Trail splits off to the left at 1.5 miles. The North Santiam River with some inviting pools comes into view down a rocky embankment on the left.

In another 1.1 miles, the trail crosses the river. During the late summer and early fall before the rains start, the river is shallow and easy to cross on stepping-stones or on a downed log that spans the width. However, in early summer and late fall, the rushing water can be 30 feet wide and the log crossing can be underwater. It might be easier to don appropriate footgear and wade if this is the case.

At 0.4 mile past the crossing, ignore the trail splitting off to the right at the Maxwell Trailhead sign. Continue another 0.3 mile to a junction at the west end of Duffy Lake. Take one of the lesser-used trails directly behind the Duffy Lake sign to reach the west shore of the lake and see craggy, rugged Duffy Butte above the lake's northern shore. Bear right to stay on

WILDFIRE IN WILDERNESS AREAS

The so-called B&B Complex fires (Bear Butte and Booth fires) burned nearly 40,500 acres in Mount Jefferson Wilderness in 2003, including the area north and east of Duffy Lake, in the largest wildfire since 1934. You can see the burn scars on Duffy Butte and past Mowich Lake if you hike in that direction. Wildfire suppression is allowed in wilderness areas but timber harvest and reforestation are not, giving the public and scientists a chance to witness how a forest recovers from this natural event.

Wildfires happen periodically in forests and are nature's way of clearing out diseases and insects. Although they can devastate plant and animal populations, they also make nutrients in the soil readily available for use by regenerating plants, and they increase food and nesting sites for birds. As browse and cover grow back, large mammals (deer and elk) and their predators (bears and cougars) return.

With climate change, wildfires in the Cascades are expected to become more frequent and more intense. The recovery process can take many years, and during this time, the changes to the landscape have a definite impact on recreational uses of the wilderness area.

the main trail if you want to go on to Mowich Lake or Santiam Lake and Santiam Pass.

Options: To reach the less-crowded Mowich Lake, which has a small sandy beach at the southern end and a large forested island, continue along the main trail another 1.1 miles, taking the route signed Eight Lakes. To reach Santiam Lake on a trail that passes by small open meadows full of wildflowers, split off to the right from the Duffy Lake Trail 0.2 mile past Duffy Lake's outlet and follow the signs to Santiam Pass.

BIKING THE NORTH SANTIAM WATERSHED

In the North Santiam watershed, the Willamette National Forest offers miles and miles of mountain biking opportunities. Pick small roads or fire trails and ride as far as you're comfortable. Shellburg Falls Recreation Area just north of Mehama offers Freeride Mountain Bike Areas 1 and 2, maintained by the Mountain Street Dirt Crew and accessible by way of Shellburg Road. For road bikes, Stayton is a good starting point.

COVERED BRIDGE LOOP FROM STAYTON

This loop southeast from Pioneer Park in Stayton winds over hilly country roads past historic barns and covered bridges.

Distance and climb: 22.5 miles round trip, 603 feet total ascent. **Road surface:** Paved, with shoulders of variable widths. **Start/end point:** Pioneer Park at 7th Ave and Marion St in Stayton. **Facilities:** Restrooms at Pioneer Park.

This ride gives close-up views of three covered bridges: Jordan Covered Bridge in Pioneer Park, Hannah Covered Bridge over Thomas Creek, and Shimanek Covered Bridge over Thomas Creek (the longest span in Linn County). For the most part, this is a pleasant ride with long vistas and a stretch along Thomas Creek, which offers a swimming hole under Hannah Bridge, but be forewarned that there is a 5-mile climb at the beginning on

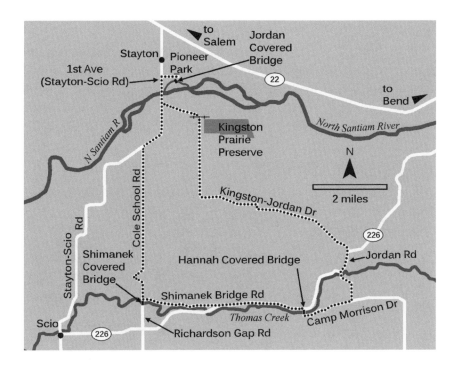

Kingston-Jordan Drive and that the hills on Jordan Road and Cole School Road are punishing.

Turn-by-turn directions: Exit the park on Marion St and turn left onto 1st Ave (Stayton-Scio Rd). Cross the North Santiam River and at mile 1 turn left onto Kingston-Jordan Dr. After the stop at the railroad tracks, continue straight on Kingston-Jordan Dr. Continue on this road until you reach Hwy 226 at mile 8.5, and turn right. After just a half mile, turn left onto Jordan Rd, cross Thomas Creek, and make a right onto Camp Morrison Dr. At mile 11.5, cross the Hannah Covered Bridge and turn left to get back onto Hwy 226. At mile 13.7, bear right onto Shimanek Bridge Rd. At mile 15.8, where you can view the Shimanek Covered Bridge, turn right onto Richardson Gap Rd. Go straight onto Cole School Rd at mile 16.8. At mile 20, go right onto Stayton-Scio Rd, cross the North Santiam River, and go right onto Marion St to return to Pioneer Park.

PADDLING THE NORTH SANTIAM RIVER

The North Santiam is runnable above Detroit Lake and from Big Cliff Dam down to the mouth. However, the stretches above Packsaddle Park are best left to experienced boaters. This river can be very tricky with many challenging rapids and hazards, particularly in the early season. For class 3, 4, and 5 kayaking, Opal Creek and the Little North Santiam are local favorites because of their great rapids, crystal-clear water, and gorgeous scenery.

According to Pete Giordano on his website oregonpaddling.north-west-rivers.com, "The Packsaddle stretch of the North Santiam is one of the primary beginner runs in the mid-Willamette Valley. Packed with forgiving rapids, lots of practice spots, and consistent year-round flows, Packsaddle is the perfect place to learn to boat or brush up on skills."

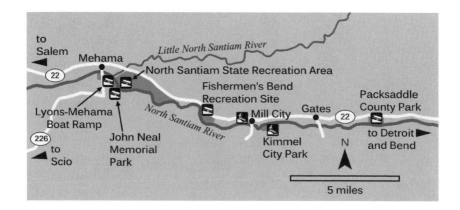

MINTO FISH COLLECTION FACILITY

If you stand at the Packsaddle County Park boat ramp in the fall, you can see large salmon holding and jostling so thickly that their backs stick up out of the shallow water. Just barely visible upstream, the Minto Fish Collection Facility and its 12-foot barrier dam is part of the Army Corps of Engineers' ongoing efforts to restore Upper Willamette River spring chinook salmon and steelhead. The original facility, built in 1951, collected brood fish for the Marion Forks Hatchery about 30 miles upstream in order to compensate for the impact of Detroit and Big Cliff Dams on the fishes' journey upstream to spawn.

The facility had become decrepit and was rebuilt beginning in 2011, closing the river to boaters at that point for a couple of years. It re-opened in April 2013 to support the hatchery program as well as to trap adult fish that are then hauled upstream of the dams and to the Little North Santiam, where they are released to spawn naturally. The new facility also serves as a holding and acclimation site for juvenile summer steelhead and spring chinook before their release and supports the movement of hatchery summer steelhead downstream for anglers.

River flow depends on how much water is released from the Detroit and Big Cliff Dams; water is held back to fill Detroit Reservoir in the summer so the flow gets too low for rafts and drift boats. To reach the put-in points for the following two trips, head east on Highway 22 from I-5 just south of Salem.

PACKSADDLE PARK TO FISHERMEN'S BEND

This popular run offers playful class 2 and 3 rapids, feelings of isolation (a good thing on the river), and plenty of wildlife.

Skill level: Intermediate (class 2–3, class 4 in high water). **Duration:** 3 or 4 hours. **River miles:** 8.5 miles. **Put-in point:** Packsaddle County Park (34.2 miles east of I-5 on Hwy 22). **Take-out point:** BLM Fishermen's Bend Recreation Site (27 miles east of I-5 on Hwy 22). **Facilities:** Cement boat ramp, ADA vault toilet, and picnic table at Packsaddle Park; cement boat ramp, flush toilets, showers, and campsites at Fishermen's Bend. **Season:** Year-round for small craft such as canoes and kayaks; September to June for rafts and drift boats.

This reach of the North Santiam River takes you through numerous class-2 rapids and two notable class-3 rapids: Spencer's Hole and Mill City Falls. The first class-2 rapid, about 0.8 mile downstream from the put-in, is called the Swirlies and is a popular play spot for kayaks. The series of rapids with fake Spencer's Hole (class 2) and real Spencer's Hole (class 3) begins about

0.5 mile past the bridge at Gates. To scout these two rapids on the way to the put-in, turn west (right) on Central Street in Gates and go 0.7 mile to a hard-to-see trail on the left side of the road.

About 0.2 mile below Spencer's Hole, Carnivore (class 2+) is easily avoidable by going around the right side of an island. If you choose to run Carnivore on the left side of the island, enter on the left and do a quick dogleg right and left as you drop over this pour-over. Before you reach Mill City, you'll run through a fun class-2 rapid. Then the river takes a sharp left turn and the bridges at Mill City come into view. Mill City Falls (class 3) is just upstream of the first bridge. You can scout it on the way to the put-in by parking on the north end of the bridge and walking out onto the bridge.

The standard way to run the falls is to look for the rooster tail of water when you are upstream of the falls. It should be about a third of the way from the left bank. You want to drop through the falls just to the left of that rooster tail. Below Mill City Falls is the most technical rapid, a class-2 rock garden. The simplest route is to hug the left bank and pick your way through. The Fishermen's Bend boat ramp is about 1.5 miles downstream from Mill City.

FISHERMEN'S BEND TO MEHAMA

This stretch of the North Santiam River has smaller rapids than upstream and is perfect for inflatable kayaks and white-water canoes; it can be combined with the upstream paddle to make a nice long day.

Skill level: Beginning/intermediate (class 2). **Duration:** 1.5 or 2 hours. **River miles:** 6.4 miles. **Put-in point:** BLM Fishermen's Bend Recreation Site (27 miles east of I-5 on Hwy 22). **Take-out point:** Lyons-Mehama Boat Ramp just upstream of the Mehama city bridge. Cross the bridge on Hwy 226 and turn right on Kapok St and then right on Locust St. Park along Locust to reduce the chance of vandalism. **Facilities:** Cement boat ramp, flush toilets, showers, and tent sites at Fishermen's Bend; asphalt ramp and portable toilet, removed during the winter months, at the Lyons-Mehama Boat Ramp. **Season:** Year-round for small craft such as canoes and kayaks; September to June for rafts and drift boats.

After departing from the concrete boat ramp at BLM Fishermen's Bend Recreation Site, you encounter the first of five class-2 rapids. These rapids are best run, for the most part, straight forward down the V. (When reading the river, you can see an upside-down V where the water is funneled between two obstructions.)

At mile 2.5 you arrive at the upstream end of North Santiam State Recreation Area on the right bank. You can see picnic tables and, often, people fishing. After about a mile, the park's boat landing comes into view. There is a restroom here, but it is a 0.2-mile hike from the boat ramp.

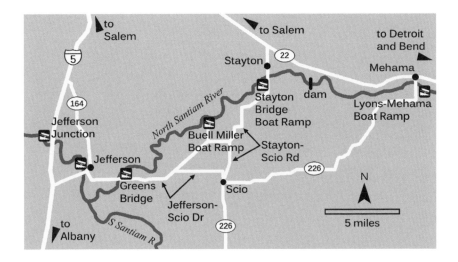

Two more miles down the river, you encounter John Neal Memorial County Park on the left bank, which has an asphalt boat ramp open only in the summer. Finally, you pass the Little North Santiam River emptying into its big sister on the right. Linn County's Lyons-Mehama Boat Ramp is 0.5 mile beyond on the left, on the upstream side of the bridge on Highway 226 between Lyons and Mehama.

Options: Of course, you can always continue downstream. For the most part, the water is class 1, moving slowly with a few riffles through quiet farmlands, but you should always keep a watch out for hazards such as logjams. Just upstream of Stayton (10 miles downstream) is a diversion dam that you will have to portage. You can also float 5.3 miles from the Linn County boat ramp at Stayton Bridge (on the left bank where Stayton-Scio Road crosses the river) to Linn County's Buell Miller Boat Ramp (on the left bank where Hess Road ends). From Buell Miller you can float 11 miles downstream to the confluence of the North and South Santiam and then another 2.3 miles to the Jefferson boat ramp on the right bank under the Jefferson Highway bridge.

Or you can float about 8 miles from Green's Bridge to I-5. Put in where Jefferson-Scio Drive crosses the North Santiam, float to the confluence with the South Santiam, and proceed down the Santiam River to the Jefferson Junction boat ramp, a concrete boat ramp on the right bank at the Santiam Rest Area on I-5 (exit 241). This trip is near enough to Ankeny Wildlife Refuge that you can expect to see thousands of birds at close range.

MIDDLE WILLAMETTE
WATERSHED

Between the points where the Santiam and Molalla Rivers empty into the Willamette, a number of parks and natural areas drain more or less directly into the Willamette River. Most of these have river frontage; two are national wildlife refuges that are hotspots for observing birds. The riverside parks

THE EVER-CHANGING WILLAMETTE RIVER

Rivers are dynamic systems that are always changing. A free-flowing river is a complex system of side channels, sloughs, oxbow lakes, and islands. During periods of normal flow, the outer bank erodes and rocks and soil deposit on the inner bank. Over time, the forces of bank erosion and sediment deposition cause the river to meander, or curve back and forth, and eventually to form a U shape, or oxbow. During floods or periods of high water, the river may jump its banks and cut a new channel that's a more direct route from point A to point B.

The largest flood in the recorded history of the Willamette River occurred in December 1861 and changed the river's course in several places. The floodwaters at their peak covered more than 350,000 acres. The high water washed away the cities of Champoeg (near Newberg), Orleans (opposite Corvallis), and the lower half of Wheatland (at the west dock of the Wheatland Ferry). When the waters receded, former oxbows were left stranded as lakes or sloughs that are now part of Minto-Brown Island Park and Willamette Mission State Park. We aren't likely to experience another flood like 1861 because dams for flood control now block many main tributaries, including the McKenzie, the Middle Fork of the Willamette, and the North and South Santiam Rivers.

are popular in summer, but winter visitors get a clearer view of the river and its full power. These sites contain floodplain forests with enormous cottonwoods and tell stories of human settlement disrupted by floodwater.

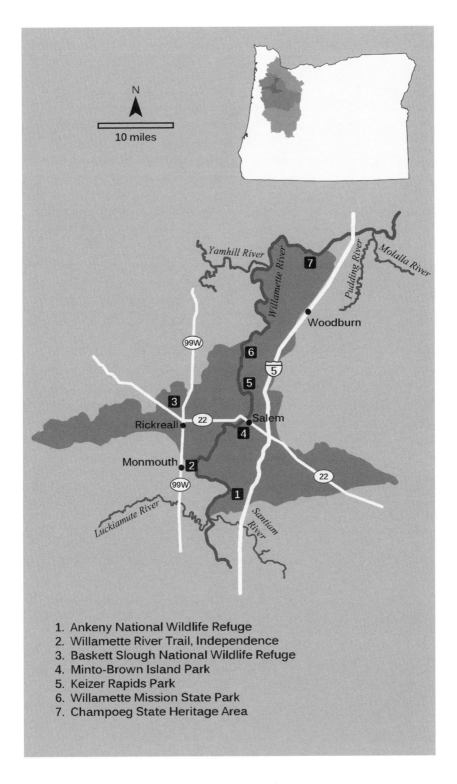

1. Ankeny National Wildlife Refuge
2. Willamette River Trail, Independence
3. Baskett Slough National Wildlife Refuge
4. Minto-Brown Island Park
5. Keizer Rapids Park
6. Willamette Mission State Park
7. Champoeg State Heritage Area

Canada geese © Wendy C. Thompson

Birds of the Mid-Willamette Valley
LISA MILLBANK AND DON BOUCHER

Whether your home is an apartment downtown or a farm in the country, birds are your neighbors. Birds are everywhere in the mid-Willamette Valley, in every season. And while each bird plays a role in the ecology of our region, birds also enrich our lives in intangible ways. Perhaps no other element of the natural world sparks human curiosity and wonder the way birds do. Birds inspire us to explore, to slow down enough to look and listen, to care deeply about the natural world as a whole.

Although some birders make it their goal to learn the most subtle features of bird sounds and plumage, you can enjoy birding at any level of skill or involvement. Birding doesn't necessarily mean going to extremes to find rare species or making lists of birds. Many birders look forward to visiting wildlife refuges that teem with birds, but sitting quietly by a hummingbird feeder or just bringing binoculars on a lunch-hour walk also counts as birding.

Here in the mid-Willamette Valley, an experienced birder can spot 150 bird species in one year just by sampling the diverse habitats that surround us and being aware of the seasonal patterns of migration and breeding. Each habitat—whether a wetland or a forest, an agricultural field or an urban yard—holds a unique collection of birds. As the seasons change, so too do the birds in each habitat.

It may surprise you to learn that winter is one of the best times to go birding in our area. Vast numbers of ducks, geese, and swans spend the summer in far northern latitudes, but the tundra wetlands freeze solid through the winter. The climate of the Willamette Valley is mild enough to provide a winter home for hundreds of thousands of these birds. You can see marshes packed with incredible concentrations of these overwintering waterfowl at William L. Finley, Baskett Slough, and Ankeny National Wildlife Refuges.

But the waterfowl are never alone. Sharp-eyed hunters watch over the marshes and flooded fields. It's not uncommon to see several bald eagles on a winter day, and in fact, birders have counted up to 130 bald eagles roosting in a line of black cottonwood trees along the Calapooia River in the mid-valley in the winter. Bald eagles and peregrine falcons provoke ducks and geese into flight in order to single out a victim, often a sick or injured bird. Ten thousand panicked waterfowl may fill the sky when one of these raptors is on the hunt, and the roar of their beating wings and their calls of alarm drown out all other sounds. Despite the pressure they face from predators, waterfowl are relatively safe within the massive flocks.

Cackling geese are the most abundant of all our winter waterfowl, and loose skeins of these small geese fly over the valley daily. They're not migrating in January—they're simply shuttling between resting and feeding locations. Although they're superficially similar to Canada geese, cackling geese have short necks and high-pitched voices. Most "cacklers" are only a little larger than a mallard.

Winter is also the time to watch stately great blue herons and dazzling white great egrets stalking agricultural fields in search of voles. Swirling, bounding flocks of American goldfinches and pine siskins will brighten your winter days if you have a bird feeder.

As days gradually lengthen, male songbirds begin to sing more often as their hormone levels change to prepare them for the spring breeding season. While song sparrows and Bewick's wrens will pipe up with a song or two on any winter day, by February they're spending a few hours singing each morning. Black-capped chickadees join in with their whistled songs (in a dialect unique to northwest Oregon). By March, spotted towhees, brown creepers, white-breasted nuthatches, and American robins have added their voices to the morning's chorus.

At about that time, birders are eagerly awaiting the return of a harbinger of spring. With its characteristic tippy flight, silver-lined underwings, and wings held in a shallow V shape, the turkey vulture rides on the turbulent southwest winds of spring as it makes its way north. Hardy rufous hummingbirds and tree swallows aren't far behind.

The stamina and navigational accuracy of migrating birds are almost beyond belief. Migrating birds may be guided by the sun's position, memorized landmarks, constellations in the night sky, the earth's magnetic field, and even odors. Though turkey vultures, swallows, and hummingbirds migrate during the day, most songbirds feed and rest during the day and depart at dusk. Flycatchers, thrushes, warblers, and other songbirds fill the night sky as we sleep. On calm, clear nights at the peak of migration, the birds are detected by weather radar stations and may be visible to birders as fleeting silhouettes passing in front of the full moon.

Nocturnal migrants land right around sunrise, and they are ravenous. In April, birders can spot dozens of orange-crowned, black-throated, gray and yellow-rumped warblers swarming through a single blooming bigleaf maple tree, searching for caterpillars. Some warblers will even take nectar from flowers in their search for enough calories to make it through the next night's flight.

In May and June, early-rising birders have the opportunity to listen to the dawn chorus at its peak. For some, it's a rewarding challenge to identify each species among the layers of musical songs and calls. For the birds themselves, this is a time of constant activity, as they defend breeding territories, court potential mates, and raise their young. From the first light of dawn until after sunset, both parents constantly search for food for their nestlings. When they leave the nest, young songbirds are practically the same size as their parents, but sometimes their plumage and calls are so different that they can be difficult to identify. Many songbirds attempt to raise two or more broods throughout the spring and summer, so singing and breeding activity continues into early summer.

By early August, parent birds may still be tending the last broods of fledglings, but most young birds are on their own. With all of the youngsters around, there are three or four times more birds than there were back in June, but they're quiet and inconspicuous. Adult males are no longer singing to defend territories or attract mates. The frantic search for enough food for growing babies is over.

During this quiet time, you may notice that birds look a little disheveled. Right after the breeding season is over, most adult birds molt, shedding and replacing their worn feathers in a gradual process. And since feathers account for 5 to 12 percent of their body weight, birds require a large amount of food to replace them. Ducks undergo the most dramatic transformation during their molt, since they lose all of their flight feathers at once. They endure a flightless month, quietly slinking around in dense wetland vegetation, and the males briefly lose their bright colors and resemble females.

The first wave of the southbound migration alleviates the summer lull in bird activity. By mid-July, birders are scanning the mudflats around drying marshes and wetlands for shorebirds that are already returning from their Arctic nesting grounds. Throughout August and September, sandpipers, plovers, and phalaropes stop to rest and refuel at local wetlands before continuing to Central and South America.

While shorebirds continue to pass through the mid-Willamette Valley, other subtle changes are taking place. Male rufous hummingbirds, black-headed grosbeaks, and lazuli buntings leave the valley quite early. By August, Wilson's warblers and western tanagers are beginning to leave the upland forests where they bred and turn up in neighborhoods like they did upon their arrival in the spring.

Migration begins to pick up as fall approaches. In the first weeks of September, birders listen for the soft calls of many hundreds of Swainson's thrushes flying southward on calm nights. And beginning in September, birders stake out certain chimneys in the evening, waiting for Vaux's swifts. These small, unusual, insect-eating birds can't perch like most birds but must cling to a vertical surface to roost. In Corvallis, a swirling vortex of up to one thousand swifts forms above the chimneys of the Whiteside Theater and OSU's Wiegand Hall before the birds finally drop in, and the Lebanon Hotel offers a similar show on the east side of the valley.

When the Vaux's swifts and Swainson's thrushes are all but gone, cackling geese and thousands of other waterfowl start filling the wetlands. Birders watch flocks of golden-crowned, fox, and Lincoln's sparrows scampering around hedgerows and thickets. Ruby-crowned kinglets and Townsend's warblers flit through trees in suburban yards, while elegant varied thrushes hop in lawns alongside American robins. By the end of October, most overwintering migrants have arrived. Most of them will wait out the long, rainy winter in the same general area until April, when the lengthening, warming days call them north once again.

No matter the season or habitat, the mid-Willamette Valley offers abundant birds. With the area's excellent wildlife refuges and local parks, not to mention your own backyard, birding adventures are never far away.

Extensive agricultural fields and seasonal and permanent wetlands combined with viewing platforms and boardwalks make this refuge a migratory birding hotspot.

To get there: From I-5 between Albany and Salem, take exit 243 for Ankeny Hill. Turn west onto Ankeny Hill Rd and drive about 1.5 miles to the Ankeny Overlook information kiosk and viewing area. To get to the Rail Trail, continue straight after the exit onto Wintel Rd for 2.1 miles. Turn left into the Rail Trail parking area.

Like the William L. Finley and Baskett Slough refuges, Ankeny National Wildlife Refuge was established in 1964 to provide overwintering habitat for the dusky Canada goose and other migratory waterfowl. The refuge's extensive croplands are maintained to provide winter forage for geese, which reduces depredation on surrounding private fields. The 2,796-acre refuge also provides wetlands and riparian woodland sanctuary for migratory and resident wildlife.

ACTIVITIES: Hiking, wildlife watching. **FACILITIES:** Vault toilets, viewing blinds, photography blind. **FEES AND REGULATIONS:** No fee. Boardwalks and kiosks are open dawn until dusk year-round, but all other trails are closed from October 1 through March 31 to provide sanctuary for wintering waterfowl. Watch for restricted access signs while on the trails. Leashed dogs permitted in parking areas only. No jogging, biking, horseback riding, hunting, fishing, or dogs permitted on the refuge trails. No removal of plant, animal, or mineral specimens. **BEST MONTHS:** Fall and spring to view migratory birds; winter to view overwintering waterfowl. **MANAGING AGENCY:** US Fish and Wildlife Service.

The refuge offers miles of boardwalk and dirt trails. The Eagle Marsh is a popular birding spot for families as the sheltered kiosk provides uninterrupted views of this key stopover point for migratory shorebirds and other water birds such as American white pelicans and great egrets. The Pintail and Egret Marsh boardwalk and the Rail Trail boardwalk feature viewing blinds where you might catch a glimpse of shy wood ducks and Virginia rail. A photography blind, available by reservation during the winter sanctuary season, overlooks Frog Pond.

The easy, level Rail Trail offers five different loops and extensions weaving through riparian ash swales, oak woodland, and wetlands. From the Rail Trail parking lot, follow the gravel trail through a shady riparian zone. Turn right onto the boardwalk to head through a seasonally flooded ash swale. Stop along the way to listen for Bewick's wren and black-capped chickadees and look for downy woodpeckers among the branches above. From the observation blind on Wood Duck Pond, look for wood ducks and hooded mergansers alongside egrets and herons. From here the boardwalk wraps around Wood Duck Pond before ending at a dike where the seasonal loop portions of the trail begin.

From here you can either turn left to follow the dike for the Dunlin Pond Loop and other wetland trails, or you can head straight down into a riparian woodland habitat rich with willow, oak, and Nootka rose for

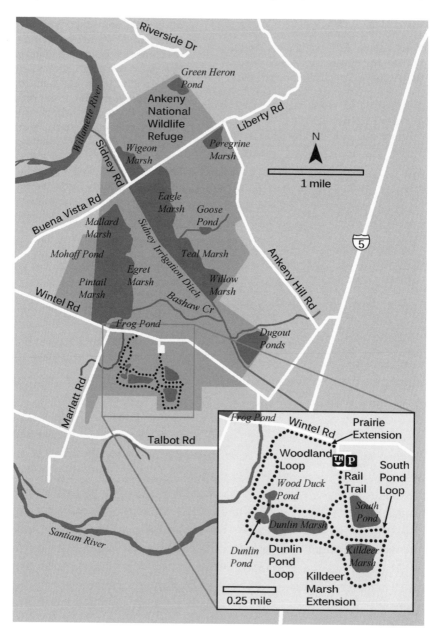

the 0.5-mile Woodland Loop. The Woodland Loop skirts Bashaw Creek for 0.25 mile before coming to a junction. Here you can turn right to complete the Woodland Loop and follow the dike back to the boardwalk junction, or you can turn left for the 0.5-mile Prairie Extension and follow a mown trail skirting wet prairie and grassland habitat along a hedgerow to return to the Rail Trail parking lot.

For the wetland loop options, turn left at the boardwalk junction where the trail wraps around Dunlin Pond for the 0.75-mile Dunlin Pond Loop. At the first trail fork, either take the left fork to complete the Dunlin Pond Loop or detour to the right for the 0.45-mile Killdeer Marsh Extension, which circles Killdeer Marsh before meeting up with the 0.5-mile South Pond Loop. The wetland loops provide great opportunities to spot marsh wrens building nests along the trail edges, dragonflies and damselflies zipping through the cattails, and northern harriers swooping low over the fields.

This community-created path loops north along the river through a riparian forest from Independence Riverview Park to Independence Sports Park, offering views of river and wildlife.

To get there: From Salem, take Hwy 22 west for 5.5 miles and turn left onto Hwy 51 / Independence Hwy. Drive 6.3 miles, turn left onto C St, and park in the lot at the end. From Corvallis, take Hwy 99W north for 20.2 miles and in Monmouth turn right onto Main St / Hwy 51. Drive 2.4 miles to Independence and turn left onto Main St / Hwy 51. Take the first right onto C St and park in the lot at the end. Trail access parking is also available at Independence Community Dog Park on Grand St and at Independence Sports Park on DeAnn Dr.

DIFFICULTY AND LENGTH: Easy, mostly level, 2.4 miles round-trip. **FACILITIES:** Restrooms at Riverview Park, portable toilet at Independence Community Dog Park, vault toilets at Independence Sports Park. **FEES AND REGULATIONS:** No fee. Riverview Park open a half hour before sunrise to a half hour after sunset. Dogs allowed on leash. **BEST MONTHS:** March through October. Trail can be muddy or even under-water in places in the rainy season. **MANAGING AGENCY:** City of Independence.

In Independence Riverview Park, an amphitheater with a fountain hosts the River's Edge summer movie and concert series. Envisioned by a group of local runners and built largely by community volunteers, the Willamette River Trail, completed in 2012, extends north from the park.

The trail begins on the north side of Riverview Park and crosses a concrete footbridge over Ash Creek. Just past the dog park at mile 0.25, the trail enters a 0.1-mile easement through private property and jogs sharply right toward the river. After you pass through the easement section, look for a spur trail to the right that takes you into the thick of the riparian forest along the river. Massive hundred-year-old cottonwood trees and ancient forked Douglas-firs cluster densely along the trail. Stay on this riparian segment for as long as you can, about 0.4 mile, before the trail heads into the open again just before reaching Independence Sports Park (also known as North Riverside Park).

Past the boat ramp, the trail curves left around an open field and passes between a concrete-block retaining wall and a wetland restoration area planted with yellow twig dogwood and other moisture-tolerant species. This wide-open 1-mile loop crosses a pair of gravel roads before reconnecting with the main route.

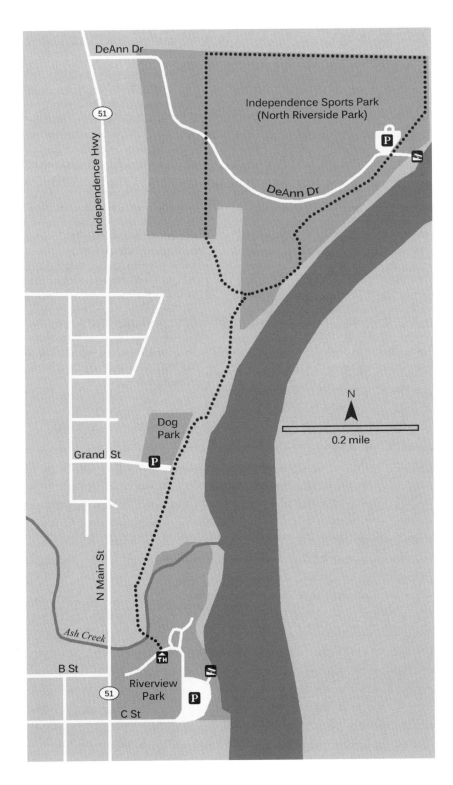

BASKETT SLOUGH NATIONAL WILDLIFE REFUGE

Hiking trails provide views of migratory and resident wildlife, farmed fields, rolling oak-covered hills, and shallow wetlands.

To get there: From Salem, cross the Marion Street Bridge and take Hwy 22 west 13 miles to Hwy 99W. Travel 2.5 more miles west on Hwy 22 for a pull-off wildlife viewing area with interpretive panels and spotting scope. For trailheads, turn north onto Hwy 99W. To reach the Baskett Butte trailhead, go 1.9 miles and turn left onto gravel Coville Rd, then drive 1.5 miles to the trailhead parking lot on the right. For the Morgan Lake trailhead, travel 1.3 miles beyond Coville Rd on Hwy 99, turn left onto Smithfield Rd, and drive 2.4 miles to the trailhead parking lot on the left just before Livermore Rd.

ACTIVITIES: Hiking, wildlife watching. **FACILITIES:** Vault toilet and picnic table at trailhead on Coville Rd. **FEES AND REGULATIONS:** No fee. The loop trail to the observation platform on Baskett Butte is open dawn until dusk year-round, but all other trails are closed from October 1 through March 31 to provide sanctuary for wintering waterfowl. Leashed dogs permitted in parking areas only. No jogging, biking, horseback riding, hunting, fishing, or dogs permitted on the refuge trails. No removal of plant, animal, or mineral specimens. Stay on the trail to avoid poison oak. **BEST MONTHS:** Fall and spring to view migratory birds; winter to view overwintering waterfowl. **MANAGING AGENCY:** US Fish and Wildlife Service.

Like the Ankeny and William L. Finley refuges, Baskett Slough was established in 1964 to provide overwintering habitat for the dusky Canada goose and other migratory waterfowl. The 2,492-acre refuge is the most northerly of the three, and thus dusky Canada geese usually appear here first in the fall and leave here last in the spring as they head back to their nesting grounds on Alaska's Copper River delta. The low area that is now Baskett Slough was formed by the main channel of the Willamette River, which had been pushed to the west by volcanic flows from the Cascades. The main stem eventually found its way back to the east, but the wetlands remain.

For an expansive view of the refuge, take the Baskett Butte/Rich Guadagno Memorial National Recreation Trail from the Coville Road trailhead. The trail was renamed in 2007 to honor the memory of Rich Guadagno, manager of the Baskett Slough and Ankeny refuges from 1990 to 1998, who died on September 11, 2001, aboard United flight 93 in Pennsylvania. The first 0.4 mile of the trail gains 160 feet in elevation as it climbs through oak savanna and upland prairie to the top of Baskett Butte (formerly known as Mount Baldy). Stay left at the first junction, at mile 0.2, to reach the viewing platform. Watch for bald eagles and red-tailed hawks.

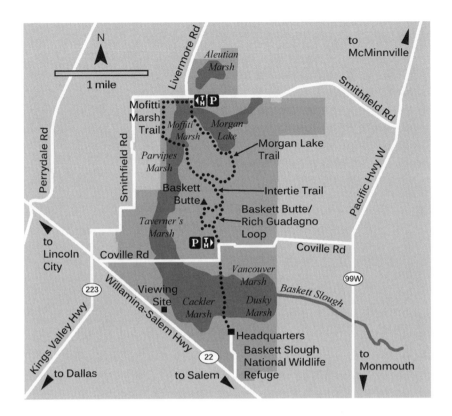

You can return the way you came, or you can continue the 1.4-mile Rich Guadagno loop trail by backtracking 0.1 mile on the gravel path from the viewing platform and then taking the mowed grass path that heads north. Travel through oak woodlands and turn right onto the mowed grass path on the east side to complete the loop. If you turn left onto the path at that point, you'll be on the seasonal 0.6-mile Intertie Trail, which gives you a wide view of the north side of the refuge and meets up with the Morgan Lake and Moffitti Marsh Trails.

The Moffitti Marsh Trail heads west and then north from the Intertie Trail junction on a gravel road for nearly a mile to Smithfield Road, giving you close-up views of red-winged blackbirds, marsh wrens, teals, and mallards, among other birds. The indistinct Morgan Lake Trail heads east from the Intertie Trail junction and skirts a farm field and the west shore of Morgan Lake before reaching Smithfield Road in nearly a mile; in early spring this trail can be mucky and dotted with goose droppings. You can also visit Morgan Lake and its bird life by parking at the Smithfield Road trailhead and making the short walk on the gravel path to the shore of the lake.

FENDER'S BLUE BUTTERFLY

Baskett Slough is home to one of the largest populations of the little butterfly known as Fender's blue, which lives only in the Willamette Valley. The butterfly was first collected by entomologist Kenneth Fender of McMinnville in 1929 and identified as a new subspecies of *Icaricia icarioides*. Between 1937 and 1989, the butterfly was thought to be extinct, until it was rediscovered at Baskett Butte. At one stage in its life cycle, Fender's blue is totally dependent upon a few lupine species, most notably Kincaid's lupine (*Lupinus sulphureus* var. *kincaidii*), an upland prairie plant that had all but disappeared from the Willamette Valley. This lupine lives in the hilly meadows

Fender's blue butterfly © Wendy C. Thompson

of Baskett Slough, so the preservation of the refuge also provided just what the butterfly requires.

Both Kincaid's lupine and the butterfly have been federally protected under the Endangered Species Act since 2000 and have been making a comeback. The blue butterfly, which is about the size of a quarter, emerges in mid-May through early June to dine on lupine nectar. The trail to Baskett Butte goes through prime lupine and butterfly territory and can offer glimpses of the two if you're there at the right time. (Note, though, that nearly all the lupine on the butte is spurred lupine, *Lupinus arbustus*, and if you see a blue butterfly in late April and early May, it's most likely a silvery blue butterfly, a nearly identical but less specialized and more prolific species.)

This 1,205-acre park on the Willamette River encompasses farm fields, orchards, sloughs, ponds, creeks, and wooded areas, offering a variety of recreational possibilities.

To get there: From downtown Salem, drive south on Commercial St SE for about a mile and turn right onto Owens Rd, which becomes River Rd. Turn right onto Minto Island Rd to enter the park. From Independence, take River Rd off of E Main St and drive 9.6 miles to a stoplight at Minto Island Rd. Turn left there to enter the park.

Despite its name, Salem's largest park isn't located on an island but is actually made up of two former islands the Willamette River once flowed between. Minto Island on the east was purchased by John Minto in 1867 and

ACTIVITIES: Walking, biking, dog walking, roller blading, skateboarding, fishing, boating, picnicking, bird-watching. **FACILITIES:** Restrooms, picnic tables, large playground, dog park, fishing docks and observation platforms, small-boat ramps, shelter with BBQ pit (to reserve, call 503-588-6261). **FEES AND REGULATIONS:** No fee. Park open 5 a.m. to midnight. Dogs must be on leash except for off-leash area. Bikes, roller blades, skateboards, and scooters must alert pedestrians before passing. **BEST MONTHS:** Year-round, but parking can be hard to find on sunny weekends and sections of the park are subject to flooding during the rainy season (call 503-588-6336 for closure information). **MANAGING AGENCY:** City of Salem.

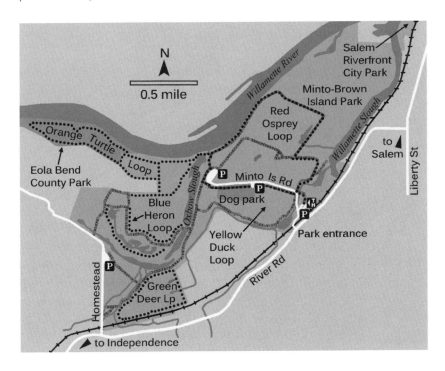

cleared of dense brush and flood debris to become productive farmland, and Brown's Island on the west was settled by Isaac "Whiskey" Brown, who arrived in 1857 to raise livestock, produce, and tobacco. The massive flood of December 1861 changed the course of the river to its present location; only a slough remains to mark the old riverbed. The City of Salem purchased 308 acres here for a city park in 1970, Marion County deeded another portion to the city in 1979, and over the years smaller purchases and donations have added up to the present acreage.

Today the farm fields are leased to farmers who rotate crops of wheat, corn, beans, potatoes, and other produce. The lease agreement stipulates that a portion of the crops must remain unharvested to provide food for waterfowl and wildlife in the park. A couple of major restoration projects have been undertaken in Minto-Brown in recent years. In spring 2001, more than 750 volunteers planted a buffer of ten thousand trees in the park to allow natural filtration of farm field runoff, prevent erosion, and improve wildlife habitat. In 2010, native trees and grasses were planted on 166 acres to protect floodplain and restore native habitats.

Minto-Brown has about 19 miles of trails, which can be combined and traversed any number of ways. If you're new to the park, it's a good idea to print out a copy of the map from the park's website (via cityofsalem. net) to take with you, as the trails are not well marked and can be confusing. There are paved paths and soft-surface trails, including a number of color-coded loop trails. There's even a compass course, with instructions on the park website.

For a 6.6-mile walk or bike ride that skirts a couple of farm fields before running along a low bluff above the Willamette River with many unobstructed river views, park in the first lot off the access road (Lot 1), cross a bridge, and follow the park's paved 5-Kilometer Loop northeast along a farm field and then along the Willamette River for 0.7 mile. Split off

EOLA BEND COUNTY PARK

The Orange Turtle Loop trail from Minto-Brown provides the only access to Eola Bend County Park. This 60-acre park, tucked between the Willamette River and the old Brown's Island landfill, was created in the year 2000 from badly eroded cropland. Hundreds of volunteers planted more than forty-five thousand native trees and shrubs on the land to control erosion, reduce flood damage, and provide critical habitat along the river. The park offers picnic tables with river views and is a great place to see osprey, bald eagles, herons, and other river dwellers.

WILLAMETTE VALLEY PONDEROSA PINE

When white settlement of the Willamette Valley began, ponderosa pine grew in abundance in scattered pure stands or mixed in groves with Douglas-fir, ash, and oak. Willamette Valley ponderosa pines are genetically different from the ponderosa that grow on the east side of the Cascades and are adapted to the weather and pest conditions here. Concern about the dwindling supply of native Willamette Valley ponderosa pines, and the realization that the local source could not be replaced with eastside sources, led to the formation of the Willamette Valley Ponderosa Pine Conservation Association in 1996. The group seeks to restore ponderosa pine to the Willamette Valley through research, education, and increased availability of seed from the local race of pines. For more information: westernforestry.org/wvppca/.

onto the dirt trail to begin the Orange Turtle Loop. The packed-dirt path proceeds through an alley of cottonwood trees very close to the river for another 0.7 mile before reaching Eola Bend County Park, where the path widens and becomes gravel over a bed of recycled asphalt grindings; it loops through an area of small trees planted in 2000, including Willamette Valley ponderosa pine, grand fir, and giant sequoia. Return to your starting point by way of the 5-Kilometer Loop.

The City of Salem has long been working toward connecting three major urban parks, including Minto-Brown, via two pedestrian bridges over the Willamette River. In 2009 the historic Union Street Railroad Bridge was renovated to connect Wallace Marine Park with Riverfront Park. In 2016 the Peter Courtney Minto Island Bridge and an adjoining multimodal trail through Minto-Brown Park will connect Minto-Brown and Riverfront Parks.

Wooded trails and river access are offered by this newer community park held in a curve of the Willamette River where early settlers crossed.

To get there: From I-5 north of Salem, take exit 260 (if heading north) or 260B (if heading south) and go west on Chemawa Rd. In about 0.5 mile, Chemawa Rd turns slightly left and becomes Lockhaven Dr. Follow Lockhaven Dr about a mile and take a left onto River Rd (Hwy 219). In about 0.5 mile, go right onto Chemawa Rd. Drive 1.5 miles and turn left at the sign into the park on Walsh Wy to reach the boat ramp, amphitheater parking, and paved trails. The turnoff to the dog park is just beyond this on Chemawa Rd. For the disc golf course parking area, continue straight on Chemawa Rd until it turns to gravel and immediately turn left onto a gravel road. You can also follow gravel Chemewa Rd to the end for two more gravel parking areas at trailheads for soft-surface trails into the woods.

ACTIVITIES: Hiking, bike riding, dog walking, picnicking, fishing, boating, disc golf, volleyball. **FACILITIES:** Vault and portable toilets, picnic tables, dog park, reservable amphitheater (call 503-856-3440), boat ramp, kayak and canoe rack, bike rack, disc golf course, sand volleyball court, boat-in campsite. **FEES AND REGULATIONS:** No fee. Open sunrise to sunset. Dogs on leash except in dog park. **BEST MONTHS:** Year-round; gravel bar area can be flooded in winter. **MANAGING AGENCY:** City of Keizer Parks Division.

Keizer Rapids is a spot on the Willamette River where a gravel bar and a few larger rocks on the river's west bank create riffles and minor rapids. Although it posed a navigational obstacle to steamboats that moved cargo and passengers up and down the river in the 1880s, it earlier provided the shallow east-to-west crossing for a wagon train led by Thomas Dove Keizur, fresh off the Oregon Trail in the autumn of 1843. Keizur decided he liked the east bank better and staked his land claim there. Today this is the site of 120-acre Keizer Rapids Park, the result of a significant community effort. The City of Keizer is leasing the land from the Oregon Parks and Recreation Department and developing it into a local and regional park.

Much of the acreage is floodplain land supporting Pacific willow and black cottonwood, but there is also upland fir forest and a wetland area. Paved and unpaved walking trails weave through the property and give access to a disc golf course (download a map from keizer.org/Rapids/DiscGolfCourse.pdf). A free summer concert and movie series is offered at the Keizer Rotary Amphitheater at the park; see kraorg.com/ for info.

For an easy loop of about a mile sampling riparian area and woods, take the paved trail to the right of the boat ramp and follow it along the

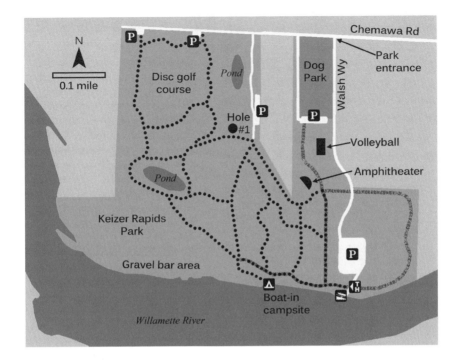

river. At a three-way intersection, you can access the gravel bar area by heading toward the river. To return, go right here onto a gravel road through the woods and then make another right at the first intersection onto a soft-surface path that takes you back to the parking area.

WILLAMETTE MISSION STATE PARK

This park hugging a bend of the Willamette River offers 15 miles of trails along with gallery forest, two oxbow lakes, historic orchards, working farmland, and ghost outlines of long-gone Willamette Mission.

To get there: From I-5 north of Salem, take exit 263 (Brooks) and go west on Brooklake Rd. Travel 1.7 miles and turn right onto Wheatland Rd. In 2.4 miles, turn left at the sign into the park and proceed to the pay station to purchase a day-use permit and pick up a park map. To reach the Wheatland Boat Ramp on the Willamette River and a north parking lot for the park at the Wheatland Ferry, take Wheatland Rd north from the park entrance and turn left onto Matheny Rd. Make the first right turn for the boat ramp, or continue to the river for the ferry parking lot.

Set in rich bottomland along the Willamette River, the 1,600-acre

ACTIVITIES: Hiking, jogging, bicycling, horseback riding, bird-watching, boating, picnicking, fishing, tent camping, gathering filberts and walnuts from the picnic area grounds in fall. **FACILITIES:** Restrooms, pet exercise area, picnic tables, volleyball courts, horseshoe pits, picnic shelters, tent camping sites for bicyclists and large groups, multiuse equestrian trails and overnight horse camps, boat ramp on Mission Lake, fishing docks, wildlife blinds. **FEES AND REGULATIONS:** Fee for camping and day-use parking (for current fees, see oregonstateparks.org). Open 7 a.m. to sunset for day use. Dogs allowed on leash. **BEST MONTHS:** Year-round. Horse trails are open when flooding subsides May through September. **MANAGING AGENCY:** Oregon Parks and Recreation Department.

Willamette Mission State Park encompasses two lakes (Mission and Goose) that are remnants of the old river channel; a gallery forest of conifer, hardwood, and deciduous trees; and 200 acres of leased farmland. Old walnut and filbert orchards and the Wheatland Ferry at the park's northern boundary remind visitors what it was like to live close to the land with the river as the primary transportation route. Now bicyclists riding the 132-mile Willamette Valley Scenic Bikeway often camp here, just 19 miles south of the route's northern end at Champoeg State Heritage Area.

In 1834, Methodists led by Jason Lee, a Canadian who had trained to be a minister in Massachusetts, built a mission here on the banks of the Willamette River to educate the native Kalapuyan people. But by 1841 the missionaries had had little success; when the main mission building was flooded, they moved the operation to Chemeketa (now Salem). Lee went on to found the first school for white Americans west of Missouri, the Oregon Institute, which eventually became Willamette University, and was instrumental in establishing the early foundation

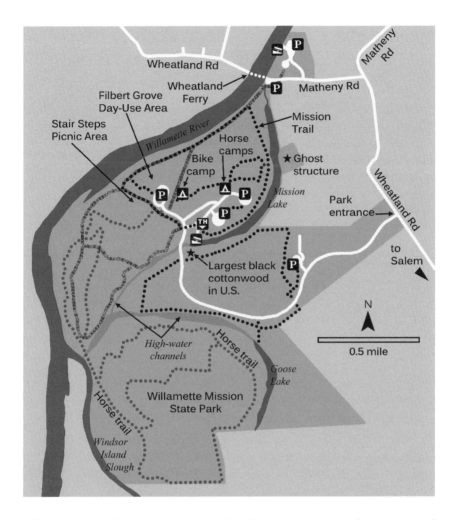

Map labels (clockwise / as positioned):

Wheatland Rd

Matheny Rd

Wheatland Ferry

Filbert Grove Day-Use Area

Stair Steps Picnic Area

Mission Trail

Willamette River

Horse camps

Bike camp

★ Ghost structure

Mission Lake

Park entrance→

★ Largest black cottonwood in U.S.

to Salem

N

0.5 mile

High-water channels

Horse trail

Goose Lake

Willamette Mission State Park

Horse trail

Windsor Island Slough

Matheny Rd

Wheatland Rd

---

of a provisional government in the Oregon Territory; he is one of the two Oregonians commemorated with a statue in Statuary Hall in Washington, DC.

Ghost outlines of the original structures bring the missionaries' efforts to life. Ironically, the ghost mission structure is no longer on the main stem of the Willamette River but on Mission Lake, an oxbow lake formed when the river changed course in the great flood of 1861. For an easy, nearly level 2.5-mile loop with views of the ghost buildings and the Willamette River, start at the Mission Lake Boat Ramp parking area and walk the Mission Trail to its junction with the bicycle path. (Be sure to take in the view of the nation's largest black cottonwood, the Willamette Mission Cottonwood, registered as an Oregon Heritage Tree, which probably began growing in about 1735.) Go left on the paved bike path, pass the Filbert Grove Day-Use Area, and turn left to take the bike path past the Stair Steps Picnic Area and back to the main road.

Bald eagle © David Wagner

Stretching along the Willamette River for more than 3 miles, this state park with shaded river trails and forest paths preserves a historic townsite and the birthplace of American government in Oregon.

To get there: From I-5 midway between Portland and Salem, take exit 278 (Donald/Aurora). Follow the park signs 6 miles west to the park entrance.

In a contentious outdoor vote pitting fur trappers against early settlers, the first provisional government in the Northwest was established in 1843 on the banks of the Willamette River. The site is now marked by a stone obelisk (sometimes called the Plymouth Rock of the West) in a plaza beside Pioneer Memorial Building, which served as the visitor center for 600-acre Champoeg (sham-POO-ee) State Heritage Area until 1977. The park also encompasses the townsite of Champoeg, swept away in the 1861 flood, whose level is marked on the

ACTIVITIES: Hiking, jogging, bicycling, dog walking, picnicking, fishing, boating, RV and tent camping, bird-watching, ranger tours, historic reenactments and celebrations. **FACILITIES:** Visitor center, restrooms, historic buildings and townsite markers, museums, picnic tables, pet exercise area, disc golf course, boating/fishing dock, campground with showers (A loop open April 1 to October 31; B loop open year-round), walk-in tent sites, yurts, cabins (some accessible to campers with disabilities), reservable picnic shelter and pavilion (for all reservations, call 800-452-5687). **FEES AND REGULATIONS:** Fee for camping and day-use parking (see champoeg.org for current fees). Open 7 a.m. to sunset for day use. Separate entrance fee for museums (newellhouse.com). Dogs allowed on leash. **BEST MONTHS:** Year-round, but the history museums are closed November through February; visit in the summer for historic reenactments and the historic Butteville Store. **MANAGING AGENCY:** Oregon Parks and Recreation Department.

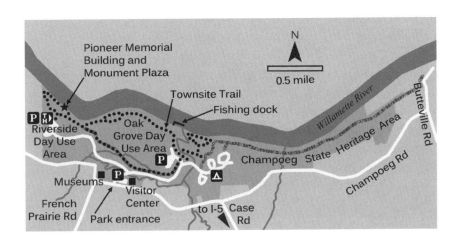

YAMPAH

Before Europeans arrived, members of the Kalapuya tribe lived where Champoeg State Heritage Area is today and subsisted on the roots of camas and yampah, hazelnuts, berries, tarweed seeds, wapato, salmon, trout, eels, birds, small game, deer, bear, and elk. The name *Champoeg* probably comes from the Kalapuya word *tchampuick*, "the place of yampah." Fur trappers who first visited the place in 1811 called it Champooick, a pronunciation corrupted to cham-POH-eg (with a "ch" sound) by the settlers of the town.

Oregon yampah (*Perideridia oregano*), a member of the parsley family, probably grew across the river on Parrett Mountain, not in the park. The plants look like tall grass and are invisible in a prairie until they flower with umbels resembling Queen Anne's lace. Their roots are about the size of a large peanut shell. When baked or steamed, the roots are highly nutritious and resemble water chestnuts in texture and flavor.

wall of Pioneer Memorial Building. Wooden posts engraved with street names now mark where intersections used to be, and archeological work is ongoing. A museum complex in the park at the corner of Champoeg and French Prairie Roads displays items owned by Oregon pioneers and recreates a nice home from Champoeg's heyday.

Stop at the visitor center to pick up a park map and activity guide. Near the visitor center, volunteers in costume tend a pioneer kitchen garden and an apple orchard at the Manson farmstead in July and August. From early spring until December, the park offers celebrations such as Pioneer Farmstead Day and the Apple Harvest Festival; visit champoeg.org for an event calendar. The park has a paved bicycle trail running nearly 4 miles from one end of the park to the other, as well as three short no-bicycle trails with river views. The Riverside and Oak Grove Day-Use Areas are both good places to begin a hike or bike ride.

For an easy, nearly level 3-mile loop hike offering a sample of Champoeg's history and habitats, start at the Riverside area parking lot and walk up to the Pioneer Memorial Building and Monument Plaza; then take the stairs down to the trail by the river and head right. The trail soon reaches the bicycle trail; go left through the parking lot and stay on the bicycle trail for a mile until you pass the Oak Grove area. Go left on the Townsite Trail and follow it back along the river to the Riverside area.

BIKING THE MIDDLE WILLAMETTE WATERSHED

Champoeg State Heritage Area is the start of the 132-mile Willamette Valley Scenic Bikeway, the first designated scenic bikeway in the United States. The section between here and Albany takes riders past the state capitol building and through charming small towns, with views of Cascade Range volcanoes and the Willamette River. The first leg to Salem (31 miles) is mostly flat; the second leg to Albany (49.5 miles) has several short grades and ascends about 450 feet overall. Each turn on the route is clearly marked. Plan your route and download maps at oregon-scenicbikeways.org. Links to exportable GPS files and cue sheets are also available on rideoregonride.com.

INDEPENDENCE TO ANKENY NATIONAL WILDLIFE REFUGE

This easy loop ride traverses country roads on either bank of the Willamette River, with views of croplands, vineyards, nurseries, and a wildlife sanctuary.

Distance and climb: 26.2 miles round-trip, 146 feet total ascent. **Road surface:** Well-maintained asphalt with narrow shoulder. **Start/end point:** Independence Riverview Park. **Facilities:** Restrooms and water at Riverview Park, vault toilets at Ankeny NWR.

Traffic is light on this route, but use caution because of the narrow shoulder. Parts of the route and the Buena Vista Ferry are closed occasionally by high

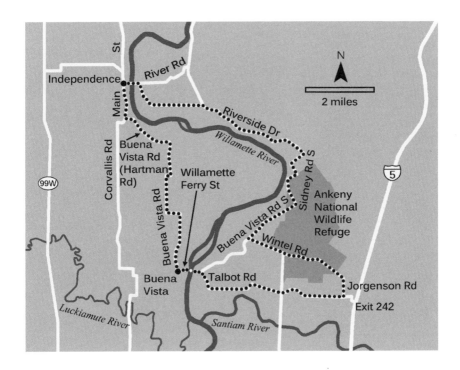

water, so make this ride during fair weather. You begin in the Independence National Historic District and roll along Main Street, passing buildings dating from the 1880s when the city was a transportation hub. You then pass farmlands as you head to the brief crossing of the Willamette on the Buena Vista Ferry (open 7 a.m. to 7 p.m. every day except Thanksgiving and Christmas; call 503-588-7979 for recorded information). After the ferry, you wander the floodplain between the Santiam and Willamette Rivers and transect Ankeny National Wildlife Refuge. Then you ride a shady stretch of Riverside Drive, part of the Willamette Valley Scenic Bikeway, bracketed by a friendly vineyard and an interesting example of nursery stock production, leaving a short jaunt back to Independence.

Turn-by-turn directions: Head south on Main St, which soon becomes Corvallis Rd. At mile 1.5, turn left onto Buena Vista Rd (Hartman Rd). At mile 7.2, turn left onto Willamette Ferry St and descend to the Buena Vista Ferry at mile 7.5. Cross the Willamette River on the ferry and continue on Buena Vista Rd S. At mile 7.9, turn right onto Talbot Rd. At mile 12.5, turn left onto Jorgenson Rd. Keep left at mile 13 onto Wintel Rd. At mile 16, turn right onto Buena Vista Rd S. At mile 17.7, turn left onto Sidney Rd S, then left at mile 19.6 onto Riverside Dr. At mile 25.2, pass under River Rd, climb the cloverleaf, and turn right onto River Rd. Cross the Willamette River and at mile 25.6 turn right onto Main St to return to your starting point.

Options: You can shorten the ride to 19.5 miles by continuing on Buena Vista Rd to Sidney Rd instead of turning onto Talbot Rd at mile 7.9.

YAMHILL RIVER WATERSHED

The Yamhill River watershed is bordered by the Coast Range on the west, the Chehalem Mountains to the northeast, and the rolling Eola and Amity Hills along with the Red Hills of Dundee to the east. Dozens of small creeks stitch together to supply three subbasins: the North Yamhill, the South Yamhill, and the Yamhill River main stem. McMinnville is the largest city in the region, which is mostly rural. The South Yamhill loops past the east side of McMinnville and comes together with the North Yamhill about 3 miles east of town. The 11-mile main stem meanders east from there past the small agricultural town of Dayton before spilling into the Willamette River south of Dundee.

The landscape of the Yamhill River watershed is diverse, due in part to its varied elevations, ranging from 3,423 feet at Trask Mountain in the Coast Range to 60 feet at the Willamette River confluence. Steep forestlands in the western two-thirds of the watershed give way to the gently sloping valley bottomlands that dominate the southern and eastern third. The two sides are also distinctly different in terms of rainfall, with 80 to 100 inches falling annually in the west compared to 40 to 60 inches on the lower, eastern side.

The indigenous people of the Yamhill River basin were the Che-ahm-ill, a subgroup of the Kalapuyan people. Since the time of white settlement in the mid-to-late 1800s, the oak savanna and woodlands and the upland and wet prairies that were once the dominant land-scapes have all but disappeared. Nevertheless, Yamhill County has the largest concentration of Oregon white oak remaining in the Willamette Valley. Rich sedimentary soil, laid down by the Missoula floods some fifteen thousand years ago, supports a vibrant agriculture and nursery stock industry. Grass seed, grain, row crops, berries, and wine grapes grow here in abundance. With more than 225 vineyards and 89 wineries, Yamhill County has, since 2005, emerged as a major wine-growing region in the Northwest.

In addition to agriculture, the watershed includes forestland held by the Confederated Tribes of the Grande Ronde. Some 440,000 acres of the watershed are private land, while nearly 53,000 acres are federally owned. Like the landscape itself, recreation opportunities are varied. You can stop by one (or several) of the many artisan wineries that dot the Yamhill Valley and sip an exceptional pinot noir. You may opt to fish for steelhead in the Yamhill River, splash in Mill or Willamina Creek on a hot summer day, or brave the 26-mile Muddy Valley bike ride.

OREGON'S DWINDLING WHITE OAKS

Oregon white oaks hold a significant place in the human and natural history of the Willamette Valley. At one time, forests of conifers and hardwood stretched from Canada to central California. Oak woodlands, in particular, provided food and meeting places for native tribes. The white oak's large acorns mature in one season, ripening from late August to November, and the Molalla and Kalapuya tribes gathered and processed them into meal or mush. The white oak provides food and shelter for a variety of wildlife beneath its open canopy. The acorn woodpecker, white-breasted nuthatch, western bluebird, and western gray squirrel are dependent on the white oak for habitat.

Today less than 1 percent of the historic Willamette Valley white oak population still exists. The remaining trees are two hundred to four hundred years old. The Oregon Department of Fish and Wildlife has identified oak woodlands and oak savannas as Strategy Habitats (habitats that are considered important to conserve and restore) for the Willamette Valley and has listed the three bird and one squirrel species dependent on the white oaks as Vulnerable Sensitive Species (species facing one or more threats to their populations and/or habitats).

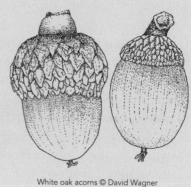

White oak acorns © David Wagner

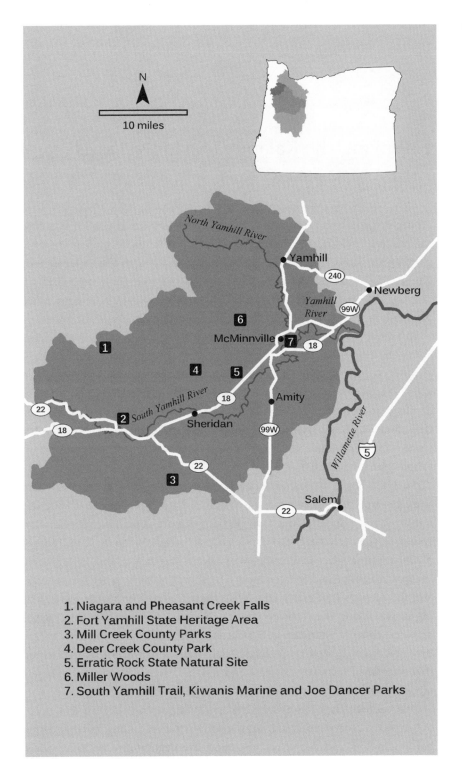

1. Niagara and Pheasant Creek Falls
2. Fort Yamhill State Heritage Area
3. Mill Creek County Parks
4. Deer Creek County Park
5. Erratic Rock State Natural Site
6. Miller Woods
7. South Yamhill Trail, Kiwanis Marine and Joe Dancer Parks

Following the Kalapuya Shadow Trails
LAURA McMASTERS

As this gentle storm drops moisture into my watershed, the soft hiss of falling rain is a background for my thoughts. Rain clouds develop as westerly winds travel across the broad Pacific and meet up with the Oregon Coast Range. This water is headed for the Yamhill River system. It is June 24, 68 degrees, and wet. Vegetation in the little creekside valley below my home is a verdant tangle, a lush scramble, a kaleidoscope in shades of green.

In spring 1944 I was brought home to live in a little house perched above the Cozine, a slow-moving flatland creek in prairie country in the shadow of the Coast Range. Growing up I realized that my family was not the first to have made this place a home. In our clay soil we found pieces of obsidian and jasper. Occasionally we uncovered perfect arrowheads. One summer while playing in the warm mud of our creek, we found a big stone tool. Our parents could only tell us that it had been very important to someone long, long ago.

Slowly I began to realize a deep connection to the "people who had come before," a people called the Yamhills. Later I realized that they did not grow yams in hills and that perhaps a more accurate pronunciation would be *yamel* or *cheahmill*, which means "people of the ford" or "people of the stepping-stones." They were one band of the thousands of Kalapuya Indians who once had thrived along the shores of lakes, creeks, and rivers and in the lush foothills of the Willamette Valley. The rivers were their highways. Along the twisting path of the south fork of the Yamhill River between today's Sheridan and Dayton, they built large mounds where they lived and buried their dead. Their trade and travel routes bisected this watershed from west to east and north to south. Today many of our modern roads follow the shadow traces of those original trails.

The Salmon River Highway (Oregon 18) follows an old trail that drops out of steep canyons through long narrow valleys, rolling hills, and rich bottomlands. Roadsides of early summer are decorated with blue camas, shocking white and sweet-smelling mock orange, and pastels of spirea, checker mallow, and sweet pea. Miniature cascades of fluffy ocean spray dangle in breezes. Later in the year, patches of vegetation above the roadsides turn bright yellow and orange and give off tangy medicinal scents. All of these colorful plants were essential to the Yamels, who lived here in cooperation with their natural world.

One overland trail between the coast and inland Oregon passed by small Hebo, North, and South Lakes in the Coast Range. By the early 1900s sections had simply disappeared in the lush coastal vegetation, but in the 1980s we learned that BLM and tribal workers had restored the trail. It was now possible to hike from a trailhead above Grand Ronde all the way to Hebo Lake. Right away our family set out to find the Coast Creek end of the trail. To our chagrin, three hours later we ended back where we had started, having accomplished a full circle without locating the trailhead. Clear-cuts and landslides and logging roads can totally change the landscape of these mountains. We did better on the next attempt.

Even before the first waves of settlers reached here, diseases had killed many Indians. Little-used trails became overgrown. Soggy lowland pathways were torn up by horses, wagons, and stagecoaches. Like their ancient trails, the native people were disappearing, beaten down by disease and pressure on their food sources. By 1850 only about 150 speakers of the Yamel and Altfalati-Kalapuyan languages remained. Survivors did not have the strength to resist when pushed to move onto a reserve of land. Native people from throughout the Willamette Valley were eventually brought to Grand Ronde in a forced march we now know as Oregon's own Trail of Tears.

Tears did not stop when the people reached the reservation. Fort Yamhill was built along the Indian trail passing above the south fork of the Yamhill. When people from distant bands tried to return to their native lands, soldiers forcibly marched them back to the reservation. Abuse and deprivation continued throughout the next hundred years. As native numbers decreased, federal recognition of the Confederated Tribes of Grand Ronde was terminated in 1954 and reservation lands shrank from thousands of acres to the size of the reservation's cemetery, a total of less than 3 acres.

Then in 1983 things began to change. The few remaining descendants were successful in forcing restoration of federal recognition of the Confederated Tribes. A casino named for Spirit Mountain, a small peak near the reservation, began to bring in money. Tribal council member

Kathryn Harrison proudly told a small group at Linfield College that for the first time the council had been able to give each member $100. Since then they have bought hundreds of acres, given hundreds of thousands of dollars to the larger community, and built a beautiful community with a hospital, schools, parks, and a traditional longhouse. Although they still do not own Spirit Mountain itself, they now hold powwows on land where their ancestors were formerly forced to live under the shadow of the fort.

As I pulled up the hill to Fort Yamhill, my windshield wipers swept at a steady autumn rain. A few cars were parked on the gravel at the powwow grounds. Heavy clouds hung snagged on the forest trees. There were no visitors at the kiosk, no sign of the park ranger. I had come here to walk a short section of a pioneer road where carved ruts tore deeply into the original Indian path. Here, I felt the weight of history. Halfway up the shadow trail I realized that I was hearing the slow beat of big drums. The sound came up through the wet, dark forest below where a slow procession of warmly clad visitors was entering the new longhouse. The only other sound was that of water dripping through high branches of the old forest trees.

Ancient trails dropped to the floodplains below where slowing water becomes golden brown with silt. The Yamels crossed rivers and creeks where basalt lava provides firm footing, the stepping-stones after which they were named. The Indian villages developed at these crossings were succeeded by towns like Sheridan, Willamina, Lafayette, and Carlton. These towns and the twisting contours of the river can be seen from high spots such as the Dundee and Eola Hills. My favorite overlook is Erratic Rock State Natural Site.

I had arranged to meet schoolchildren at the top of the park. As I stood waiting near the huge argilite boulder, I saw movement in the tall grasses and realized I was looking at a female bobcat. She did not see me as she lazed her way across the open meadow. Then the wind shifted, and I could almost read her eyes as she decided that there was something besides the boulder perched on the bare hillside. She quickened her pace, slipped over the fence, and melted into the security of the forest, leaving me with a great story for the kids who were soon tromping noisily up the path.

The short hike to the top offers a cardiovascular challenge and a terrific view of the valley. In addition, this upland meadow provides an opportunity to admire a small sunflower that was an important food plant of the Kalapuyan people. This sweet-smelling plant formerly covered hundreds of acres. In autumns of the ancient past, the view below would often have been obstructed by plumes of racing fires set by the Kalapuya to stimulate seed germination and burn off a sticky coating. The edible seeds were then easily knocked off into burden baskets. Settlers gave this pretty little sunflower the unappealing name of tarweed. Trouble came when the "tar" caused mats and sores on the legs of livestock. Soldiers soon forbade the Kalapuya to burn their land. As a result, valley underbrush grew rapidly. Native oak savanna flora and fauna such as the Willamette Valley daisy, Fender's blue butterfly, native earthworms, and even the native rattle-snake began to disappear.

Through this altered landscape winds the Willamette River, ultimate destination of many of the old Indian trails. Paths skirted around wetlands and reached the wide river at several locations. It was the freeway, the fastest way from village to village. In several places the river slows as it maneuvers around low gravel bar islands and allows for a relatively safe crossing, and here settlers built ferryboat landings. At the ghost town of Wheatland, the ferry still runs as it has since 1844. The original ferry was a flat boat built of old-growth planks, caulked with pitch and religious tracts from the abandoned Methodist mission across the river.

The wide gravel bar at the crossing is a favorite winter haunt of mine. As I drove in and parked, the shiny new Matheny IV ferry crouched, waiting for its next load. My grandson and I were there to stroll the beach in search of treasures. The Kalapuya came to gravel bars to get supplies of rock for making tools and arrow points. These days the crossing is dredged and a new supply of jasper, agate, and petrified wood regularly ends up on the beach. As we strolled, we saw that a recent flood had uprooted a big willow. There, snared in its upturned roots, was our treasure—a large, shiny, river-worn cobble of dark jasper.

Later, as we sat watching the river run, we considered our options. The journey did not need to end here. We could hop the ferry and travel into yet another Willamette Valley watershed.

NIAGARA AND PHEASANT CREEK FALLS

A short trail switchbacks down through Douglas-fir forest to a pair of hundred-foot waterfalls in the north Coast Range.

To get there: From Salem, take Hwy 22 west about 26 miles to its intersection with Hwy 18. From there go right at the sign for Willamina, which puts you on Business 18 / Main St. Take this road 2 miles to the center of Willamina and turn left at the sign for Willamina Creek Rd, which starts as NW Main St. Drive 6 miles and bear left onto Coast Creek Rd. In 1.3 miles,

DIFFICULTY AND LENGTH: Easy/moderate, 2.5 miles round-trip with 515 feet elevation gain. **FACILITIES:** No restrooms. Picnic table at Pheasant Creek Falls. **FEES AND REGULATIONS:** No fee. Dogs allowed on leash. **BEST MONTHS:** Year-round; the water flow peaks in early spring, but the road in and the trail are muddy in spots during the rainy season. **MANAGING AGENCY:** US Forest Service, Siuslaw Ranger District.

bear right on the paved road as it turns into Gilbert Creek Rd. Continue 3.2 more miles and go left at the Bible Cr Rd / Niagara Falls / To Hwy 101 sign. In 1.4 miles, turn left at the sign for Niagara Falls. The road becomes gravel here. Stay right at the first fork and, ignoring all spurs and watching for oncoming traffic, drive 3.5 miles to a T. Following the signs to Niagara Falls, go right here onto Rd 8533 and after 0.9 mile go left at the signed fork. Drive another 0.7 mile on Rd 8533-131 to the parking area and trailhead on the left. On the way out, be sure to retrace your steps exactly as it's easy to get lost in the maze of roads.

Niagara and Pheasant Creek Falls lie within the Nestucca River watershed but are included here because the road in takes you past Willamina and Coast Creeks, two of three major tributaries of the Yamhill River (Mill Creek being the other). The trail descends along an unnamed creek nestled into lush coastal forest and takes you across a couple of footbridges to a simultaneous view of the two waterfalls (whose names are often switched in guidebooks). On your left, Niagara Falls, on an unnamed creek draining from Niagara Point, cascades down 122 feet; on your right, Pheasant Creek Falls, on Pheasant Creek, drops 112 feet straight down.

BLACKWELL COUNTY PARK

Your drive to the trailhead of Niagara and Pheasant Creek Falls takes you past Blackwell County Park, 4.5 miles up Willamina Creek Road. In this 6-acre park, Willamina Creek bends around a shady grove of Oregon white oak before cascading over sculpted bedrock formations. Pools invite swimming and wading in the warm summer months. Fishing is also good, and there are picnic tables, barbecue pits, and a vault toilet.

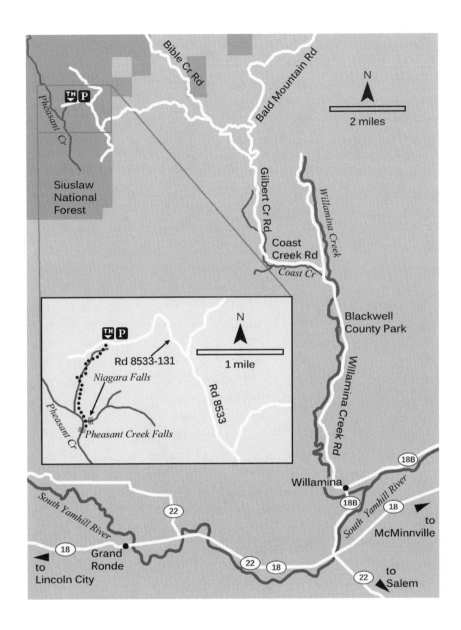

N

2 miles

Bible Cr Rd

Bald Mountain Rd

Pheasant Cr

Siuslaw
National
Forest

Gilbert Cr Rd

Willamina Creek

Coast
Creek Rd

Coast Cr

Blackwell
County Park

TH P

Rd 8533-131

N

Niagara Falls

1 mile

Rd 8533

Pheasant Cr

Pheasant Creek Falls

Willamina Creek Rd

Willamina

18B

South Yamhill River

22

18B

South Yamhill River

18

to
McMinnville

18

to
Lincoln City

Grand
Ronde

22

18

22

to
Salem

FORT YAMHILL STATE HERITAGE AREA

A quiet white oak savanna hilltop with views of the Grande Ronde Valley offers a glimpse of an important chapter in Oregon's history.

To get there: From Salem, take Hwy 22 west about 32 miles, bear right where it splits off from Hwy 18, and in another mile turn right at the sign for the park. Drive past the Confederated Tribes powwow grounds and longhouse to the parking area near the top of the hill.

ACTIVITIES: Hiking, picnicking. **FACILITIES:** ADA vault toilets, picnic tables. **FEES AND REGULATIONS:** No fee. Open daily 7 a.m. to 5 p.m. Dogs allowed on leash. **BEST MONTHS:** April and May, September and October. **MANAGING AGENCY:** Oregon Parks and Recreation Department.

Built in 1856 to regulate the eastern border of the Grand Ronde Indian Reservation, Fort Yamhill served to control traffic and to ease tension between settlers and natives, as Fort Hoskins did for the coastal Siletz Indian Reservation. The fort closed in 1866 and the property was auctioned off to families who farmed the land until Oregon Parks and Recreation bought it in 1988; it was opened to the public in 2006. Visiting Fort Yamhill today offers insight into the physical and emotional hardships of that time period. Interpretive signage provided in partnership with the Confederated Tribes of the Grand Ronde presents a balanced view of native and white experiences and feelings. Ongoing archeological excavation by Oregon State University researchers is uncovering structures and artifacts to help better understand the history. The one remaining building on the land, which once served as officer quarters, is being restored; the original blockhouse survives in a city park in Dayton, Oregon.

A 0.6-mile walking trail winds up the hillside past interpretive signage describing fort history and descends again to the parking area on a soft trail through mixed woods. The first 0.4 mile of the trail is wheelchair-accessible gravel and boardwalk. The soft trail traces a small portion of

---

HIKING AND CAMPING ON THE GRAND RONDE RESERVATION

The South Yamhill River goes through the Grand Ronde Reservation in the western part of its watershed. The Confederated Tribes of Grand Ronde maintain hiking trails and campgrounds for everyone to enjoy. Hiking trail maps and free camping permits are available at the Natural Resources Office at 47010 SW Hebo Road, open 8–12 and 1–5 Monday through Friday. For further information, call 503-879-2424.

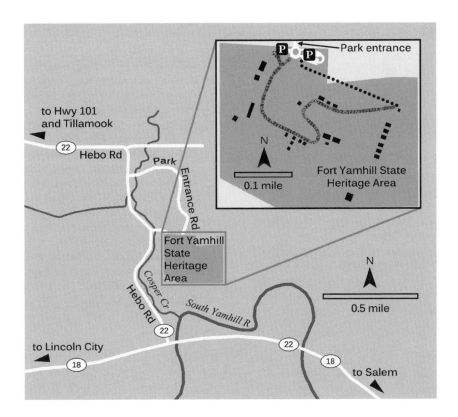

the old Killimuck Trail, a path used by the native people to travel from the coast to the Cascades.

MILL CREEK COUNTY PARKS

A string of three county parks along cold, clear Mill Creek offer shady, grassy picnic areas and places to splash in the water, along with hiking and horseback riding on BLM land surrounding the upper two parks.

To get there: From downtown Salem, take Hwy 22 west for 23 miles to Mill Creek Rd. To reach Mill Creek and BLM Upper Mill Creek Parks, turn left onto Mill Creek Rd. Drive 2.3 miles to Mill Creek Park on the left and 0.3 mile beyond this to BLM Upper Mill Creek Park on the right. For Buell County Park, turn right onto Mill Creek Rd off of Hwy 22 and drive 0.2 mile to the park on the right.

ACTIVITIES: Picnicking, wading, swimming, inner tubing, skipping stones, fishing, hiking, horseback riding. **FACILITIES:** ADA vault toilets, picnic tables, fire pits, horseshoe pits. **FEES AND REGULATIONS:** No fee. Day use only, from sunrise to one half hour after sunset. Dogs allowed on leash. **BEST MONTHS:** Open May 1 to September 30, weather permitting. Before and after those dates, you can still visit even though the toilets are locked. Parks can be crowded on warm summer days. **MANAGING AGENCY:** Polk County Parks and Recreation.

Mill Creek, a major tributary of the South Yamhill River, is a popular place to cool off in the summer. In the early days of logging, the creek was blocked with a splash dam that allowed sudden release of water to transport logs to the mill; this practice scoured the creek down to basalt bedrock from the Siletz volcanic flows of forty million years ago. The clear waters of the creek tumble over and around chunks of rock, creating some fine swimming holes accessible from BLM Upper Mill Creek, Mill Creek, and Buell County Parks.

Buell County Park, which has a children's playground, is set along an especially family-friendly stretch of the creek, where the shallow waters rush over a smooth rock bottom and a network of gravel paths leads down to pebbly beaches. A popular adventure on hot summer days is to inner tube from this park about 4 miles downstream to Yamhill County's Stuart Grenfell Park, which is alongside Highway 18 on Harmony Road. The creek meanders gently and harbors crawdads and fossils to investigate.

The upper two parks are surrounded by BLM land open and accessible to the public by way of a gravel road. To walk or ride horses there, park at the locked white metal gate on the gravel road off Mill Creek Road at the upper end of Mill Creek Park.

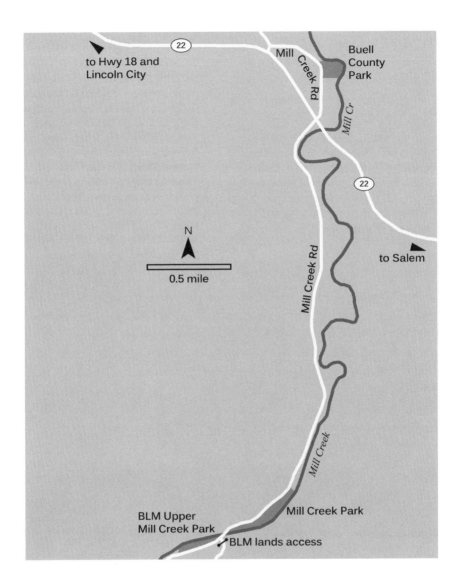

to Hwy 18 and
Lincoln City

22

Mill Creek Rd

Buell
County
Park

Mill Cr

22

N

0.5 mile

Mill Creek Rd

to Salem

Mill Creek

BLM Upper
Mill Creek Park

Mill Creek Park

BLM lands access

DEER CREEK COUNTY PARK

This quiet and secluded park in the foothills of the Coast Range contains the largest remnant wet prairie in the Willamette Valley.

To get there: From Hwy 99 in McMinnville, drive 9.7 miles southwest on Hwy 18 to Gopher Valley Rd. At the sign to Deer Creek Park, turn right onto Gopher Valley Rd and continue for 5.4 miles to Deer Creek Park Rd. Turn left onto this gravel road and continue a short way to the parking lot.

ACTIVITIES: Walking, picnicking, bird-watching. **FACILITIES:** ADA vault toilet, picnic tables, barbecue pit. **FEES AND REGULATIONS:** No fee. Day use only, from one hour before sunrise to one hour after sunset. Dogs allowed on leash. The wet prairie section is closed to public access during its restoration; for information, call 503-474-1047. **BEST MONTHS:** Year-round. **MANAGING AGENCY:** Yamhill County Parks and Recreation.

At the confluence of Cronin and Deer Creeks, Deer Creek County Park invites you to imagine a time before the land was drained and farmed. Before white settlement, the native Kalapuya periodically burned such landscapes to maintain open hunting and gathering ground. Efforts by early white settlers in the middle 1800s to drain the wetland for farming are still evident in ditches and dikes that mark the landscape. Farmers abandoned attempts to cultivate this wet prairie in the 1950s, and in 1962 local farmers Cecil and Delores Gross donated 6 acres along the creek for a park. In 1978 the county purchased additional acreage to bring the total to around 30 acres.

Wild rose © Wendy C. Thompson

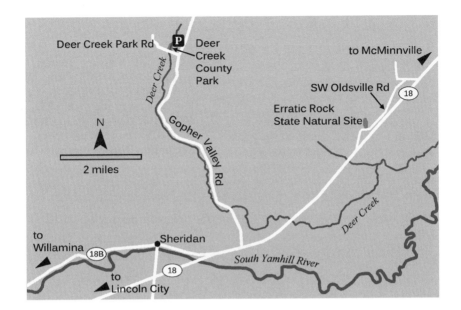

In the 1990s a botany class from nearby Linfield College found Kincaid's lupine, host plant for the endangered Fender's blue butterfly. Since that time various agencies have made contributions to study, preserve, and restore this remarkable wild space. A controlled burn in 1998 began the restoration efforts. The picnic area, shaded by hundred-year-old ash trees, is mowed after blooming season to preserve wildflowers such as Nelson's checkermallow. From here, a short gravel walking trail offers creekside views.

YAMHILL OAKS PRESERVE

West of McMinnville in rural Yamhill County, the Nature Conservancy's 630-acre Yamhill Oaks Preserve protects a remnant of Oregon's once-extensive native habitats. In addition to oak woodland and prairie, the preserve includes 1.5 miles of stream habitats important to fish and wildlife in the headwaters of Deer Creek, a tributary to the Yamhill River. It is also the northern Willamette Valley's first protected area for the endangered Fender's blue butterfly. The preserve is not presently open to the public; Conservancy ecologists and volunteers are conducting biological inventories and developing a management plan.

ERRATIC ROCK STATE NATURAL SITE

A peripatetic rock perched high on a hill in the middle of Oregon wine country reveals a dramatic chapter in the history of the Willamette Valley.

To get there: From Hwy 99W in McMinnville, head south on Hwy 18 for 3.8 miles. Turn right onto SW Oldsville Rd at the Glacial Erratic sign

ACTIVITIES: Walking, geology watching. **FACILITIES:** Picnic table. **FEES AND REGULATIONS:** No fee. Be kind to the rock. **BEST MONTHS:** Year-round. **MANAGING AGENCY:** Oregon Parks and Recreation Department.

and bear left to stay on Oldsville Rd when the road forks. Drive 1.9 miles to the Glacial Erratic Rock sign and park at the wide spot on the left.

Erratic Rock State Natural Site is a unique wayside dedicated to a rock with a very unusual life story. You can walk up a 0.3-mile paved trail that gains around 100 feet of elevation to get a close look at this 90-ton rock with a strange pedigree and name: a glacial erratic. According to geologists, an erratic is a rock that differs in size, composition, or origin from surrounding rocks and has been transported by some mechanism often involving glacial processes. In front of you is a wandering rock that probably began its life around six hundred million years ago as part of a muddy sea floor somewhere near what is now British Columbia. Compressed into rock by burial and pressure and uplifted into a piece of a towering mountain range, this rock's journey had just begun. Perhaps twenty thousand years ago, the rock was scraped off, captured, and transported by a huge continental glacier to near what is now Missoula, Montana. There it sat, encased in ice, part of a huge dam that impounded the waters of the Clark Fork River into a lake half the volume of Lake Michigan.

But then the dam broke, not once but many times, releasing floods of almost inconceivable size, power, and intensity (now known as the Missoula floods). Floodwaters swept over eastern Washington, stripping the soil down to bedrock, carving the Grand Coulee, spilling over the tops of the mountains surrounding the Columbia River, and charging up the Columbia's tributaries as a roaring wall of water.

Imagine standing here fifteen thousand years ago, as the first humans in this area might have done, watching the waters race south, filling the valley as far as the eye can see (you would actually have been underwater during some of the largest floods), and rafting in tremendous icebergs (remnants of the former dam) the size of cruise ships carrying rocks like the one you see in front of you. Picture the bucolic Willamette Valley filled with water from the Coast Range to the Cascades, as far south as Eugene, a brown, fetid, churning cauldron on which floated immense rafts of logs and uprooted trees, blue-white icebergs, and dead mastodons. Watch as the wind blows an iceberg with its load of rocky debris toward the hill where you stand; see the iceberg shudder to a halt against the shore. Then, if you have the patience, watch the iceberg melt away under the summer sun, dropping this tremendous rock into the muddy receding lakebed.

Here it lies, a mute testimonial to the great geologic drama that filled the valley with rich soil, presenting the first pioneers with fertile farmland high out of reach of the modern river and setting the stage for the fields of grass and grapes, hops and hazelnuts to come. And the only price the farmers paid for this bounty was when their plows hit the occasional erratic lying in wait just below their furrows. Fortunately this rock, the largest glacial erratic in the Willamette Valley, lies aboveground.

MILLER WOODS

A network of trails takes you past oak savanna, open pasture, and ponds and streams, and into quiet and peaceful woods.

To get there: From Hwy 99W in McMinnville, turn north onto Baker Creek Rd. Go 2.9 miles and as Baker Creek Rd bears left, stay straight to go onto NW Pheasant Hill Rd. At the stop sign turn right onto NW Orchard View Rd. Drive another 1.8 miles and after passing NW Blacktail Ln, turn right into the tree-lined gravel entrance to Miller Woods. Proceed through the gate and down the gravel road to a large gravel parking area to the right.

ACTIVITIES: Hiking, picnicking, photographing, nature education. **FACILITIES:** Portable toilets, picnic tables. **FEES AND REGULATIONS:** Day-use fee is $3 per person. Open dawn through dusk. No dogs, horses, bikes, skateboards, roller blades, or motorized vehicles allowed. Stay on trails. Group activities require a fee and must be scheduled with the Yamhill Soil and Water Conservation District, 503-472-6403. **BEST MONTHS:** Year-round. The trails might be muddy in places in the rainy season. **MANAGING AGENCY:** Yamhill Soil and Water Conservation District.

Miller Woods encompasses 94 acres of forest and 36 acres of pasture and hay land. This property was owned by K. T. and Frieda Miller from 1968 until Frieda's death in 2004, when she bequeathed it to the Yamhill Soil and Water Conservation District. The couple had no children and were determined to save the land from becoming a subdivision; they took out many logs but planted replacements, left some old-growth giants, and encouraged wildlife. The site

Blue-eyed darner and
wild bleeding heart © Wendy C. Thompson

© Wendy Thompson

YAMHILL RIVER WATERSHED

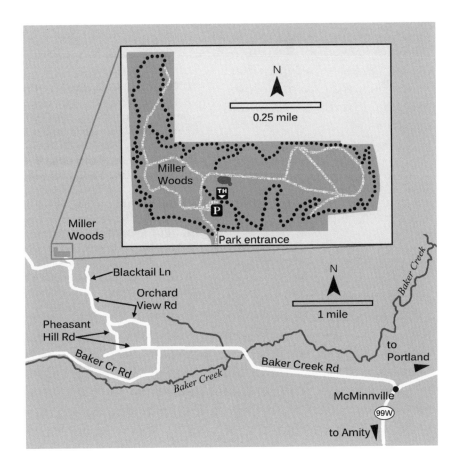

is maintained primarily as an educational venue and is used by the McMinnville School District as the basis of its nature education program. Volunteers care for and work on improving the site with such projects as installing bird boxes and planting native species.

You can self-register, pay your fee, and pick up a trail map at the visitor kiosk at the bottom of the parking area. The start of the trail system is marked by a sign to the right of the kiosk. The 4-mile outer loop trail, which you can follow in either direction, takes you around the mostly wooded perimeter of the property with a few easy ups and downs, while service roads and connecting trails offer many options for shortening the trip. A 0.7-mile education station trail takes you past the pond, pasture, and forested areas. Numbered posts with directional arrows that correspond to the trail map help you know where you are at all times.

SOUTH YAMHILL TRAIL, KIWANIS MARINE AND JOE DANCER PARKS

A short forested trail along the South Yamhill River offers glimpses of bird drama and a garden of wildflowers in the spring.

To get there: From Hwy 99W in McMinnville, take NE 3rd St east for less than a mile and turn left onto Brooks St and immediately right into the parking lot for Kiwanis Marine Park at 1400 NE Brooks.

Kiwanis Marine Park is a 4.6-acre park that once offered McMinnville's only boat ramp on the South Yamhill River and may once again, if flood damage to the ramp can be repaired. It's

DIFFICULTY AND LENGTH: Easy, 2.4 miles round-trip with insignificant elevation change. FACILITIES: Portable toilets, picnic tables, sports fields. FEES AND REGULATIONS: No fee. Parks open dawn to dusk. Leashed dogs allowed on forest trails. Joe Dancer Park is closed to field use and vehicular traffic from November 1 to March 1. BEST MONTHS: March through November; often closed by high water in winter. MANAGING AGENCY: City of McMinnville Parks and Recreation.

nestled against the river at the west entry to 100-acre Joe Dancer Park (named for McMinnville's first city manager), encompassing a complex of baseball and soccer fields and a skateboard park. A forested trail on the bank above the river runs from Kiwanis Marine to the far end of adjoining Joe Dancer. The trail has some spurs down to the river and offers glimpses of the water through the vegetation. In springtime the east end of the trail blooms with Indian plum, red osier dogwood, western trilliums, and fawn lilies. Red-tailed hawks, bald eagles, and osprey can be seen along the river. In Joe Dancer Park the trail skirts the playing fields. Go to the end and turn around for the return trip.

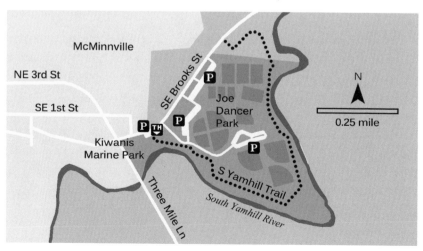

BIKING THE YAMHILL WATERSHED

The Yamhill Valley offers cyclists plenty of country roads threading together fields and vineyards, as well as peak and creek climbs for those wanting a more strenuous workout. For a number of routes of varying lengths and degrees of challenge recommended by Tommy's Bicycle Shop and starting mostly in McMinnville, go to tommysbicycle.net/ride-routes/. Be aware that traffic is always heavier on Memorial Day and Thanksgiving weekends, when the wineries celebrate their new releases.

FARMLAND LOOP FROM AMITY

This rolling ride past lush farm fields features views of the Coast Range and Cascades, a midroute picnic stop at Ballston County Park, and the option to sample chocolate at the Briggitine monastery.

Distance and climb: 16.6 miles round-trip (18.4 with optional side trip to the monastery), 158 feet total ascent. **Road surface:** Well-maintained asphalt with no shoulder, gravel on the side trip to the monastery. **Start/end point:** Amity City Park (from Hwy 99W, turn west on 5th St and look for the park a couple of blocks ahead on the right). **Facilities:** Restrooms and water at Amity City Park, restrooms and water at the Brigittine monastery, vault toilet at Ballston County Park.

This low-traffic loop crosses the South Yamhill River a couple of times and passes by vineyards, hazelnut orchards, cornfields, old barns, and llama ranches. It offers the option of a short (1.8 mile total) side trip to sample the famous fudge and truffles made by the Brigittine monks at the Priory of Our Lady of Consolation (brigittine.org). Ballston County Park, with its 1855 Ballston School building, picnic tables, and swings, makes a perfect lunch

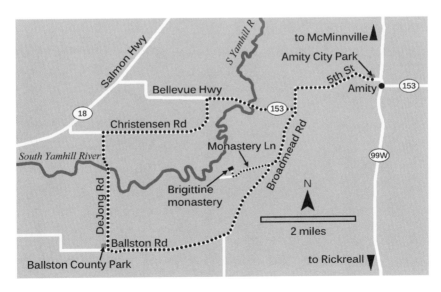

stop. On a clear day, you'll have a view of Mount Hood across the fields on your way back. You'll also pass by a large, ground-mounted solar array put in by a savvy farmer to sell power to Portland General Electric.

Turn-by-turn directions: Turn right onto 5th St to head out of the park, cross the bridge over Salt Creek, and follow the road as it becomes the Bellevue Hwy. At mile 2.1 go straight onto Broadmead Rd. At mile 3.4 you can make a right onto gravel Monastery Ln and travel 0.9 mile through hazelnut orchards to the Brigittine monastery. Back on Broadmead, at mile 5.2 bear right onto Ballston Rd. Go straight across DeJong Rd at mile 7.6 to make a rest stop at Ballston County Park. Then go north on DeJong Rd, cross the South Yamhill River at mile 9.2, and at mile 10 turn right onto Christensen Rd. At mile 12.7, just past the solar array farm, turn right onto the Bellevue Hwy, cross the South Yamhill River again, and return to your starting point.

PADDLING THE YAMHILL RIVER AND ITS TRIBUTARIES

The undammed South Fork Yamhill River winds through farmland and, with its low gradient, offers some good rainy season floats for beginning and advanced beginning paddlers. Muddy and embedded in the Willamette plain, the river offers cottonwood-willow habitat, a surprisingly remote feel, and a long canoeable reach of slow water. A couple of tributaries, Mill and Willamina Creeks, also have stretches that can be kayaked or navigated in a white-water canoe after a few days of heavy rain. The

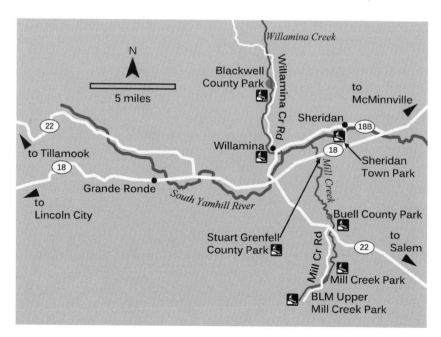

main stem can be paddled in either direction from Dayton; in 1900 it was dredged and scoured of logs for navigation up to McMinnville, and though entrenchment damage remains, the river has reverted to a green corridor of forest and undergrowth.

According to *Paddling Oregon*, the South Yamhill is canoeable at high water (700 cfs at Willamina) for 29 riffling miles, from Sheridan to McMinnville. Sizable ledges are encountered above Sheridan, and the 15 miles from Grand Ronde to Sheridan offer class-2 and -3 rapids that should not be attempted by novice boaters. The run from Sheridan to Highway 153 is 11 miles of class-1 riffles. Put in at the Sheridan town park, on the south side of the Highway 18 bridge. Downstream at the Highway 153 bridge, a path reaches the river on the river-right, upstream side.

Soggy Sneakers reports that the 5 miles from Blackwell County Park on Willamina Creek to the Yamhill River is a mostly class-1 run with some class-3 water that makes the run unsuitable for beginners. Clear, cold Mill Creek is the other Yamhill tributary that can be kayaked. The 5.5-mile section between Upper Bridge and Mill Creek County Park offers continuous white water with a few technical class-3 and -4 drops and is for experienced boaters only. The lower section from Buell County Park out to the South Yamhill and down to Sheridan, for a total of 10 miles, offers continuous class-2 white water with many fun play waves after a few days of heavy rain. Although wood often blocks the main channel, the

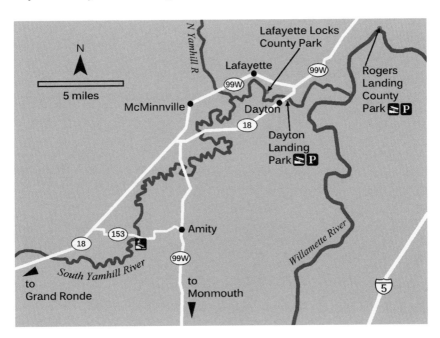

LAFAYETTE LOCKS COUNTY PARK

The county park on Locks Road south of Lafayette offers a vantage point from which to view a long concrete monolith, all that remains of a grand scheme to bring steamboats to McMinnville. The locks extended the navigable waterway so commodities such as wheat and lumber could be shipped out to mills. Operated from 1900 until 1954, the locks were eventually sold to Yamhill County for $10. In 1964 the county decided to dynamite the dam and remove the lock doors as they were obstructing fish passage. Today the park offers restrooms and shady picnic tables by the river.

current is slow enough that boaters should have no problem finding an eddy to turn out into. You can avoid the last 3 miles on the South Yamhill by taking out at Stuart Grenfell County Park just before the confluence.

To paddle the lazy, secluded main stem Yamhill River, put in at Dayton. Walk or drive down Ferry Street to Dayton Landing Park, a 1.4-acre county park with a small boat ramp and ample parking located 5 miles upstream from the Willamette River at the confluence of the Yamhill and Palmer Creek. From there you can paddle about 3 miles upriver to the remnants of the Yamhill Locks (also known as the Lafayette Locks), just downstream from Lafayette. This section of the river is very peaceful, with the exception of the Highway 18 crossing and an occasional irrigation pump. You can also paddle downstream from Dayton 5 miles to the Willamette River, then paddle 5 more miles downstream to take out at Rogers Landing County Park in Newberg.

PUDDING RIVER WATERSHED

A traveler heading toward Silverton from I-5 follows Highway 213 through the eastern fringes of Salem and out into the countryside. The road gently dips and climbs until it clears one last rise and the land opens up before it. The valley of the Pudding-Molalla watershed spreads out to the south and north, and eastward to the looming edge of the Cascades. The grounds of Mount Angel Abbey north of Silverton provide a central perspective; views from those 420-foot heights take in a patchwork of fields on all sides marked by a canopy of oaks, cottonwoods, and other trees bordering the streams that thread their way across the landscape.

The Pudding River first emerges from the curve of the Waldo Hills as a small stream beginning its journey northward through the heart of some of Oregon's richest farmland. Soon it is joined by one after another of the creeks that arise along the timbered lower slopes of the Cascades beneath 4,280-foot Panther Rock Ridge and then tumble over basalt rocks and small waterfalls. As the river follows the relatively flat benches on the east side of the valley, it cuts through silts deposited long ago during the Missoula floods—silts that give the lower river its somewhat muddy appearance. After irrigating and draining thousands of acres filled with crops and livestock along its slow, serpentine course, it arrives at its juncture with the Molalla River, which then joins the main stem Willamette at an altitude of just 66 feet.

More than 92 percent of the land in the Pudding River watershed is privately owned. Thus, particularly in the lowlands, not many places can be found where the public can readily enter and enjoy the natural world. On the upper reaches, however, where private timberland is interspersed with state and federal holdings,

PANTHER ROCK RIDGE

Panther Rock Ridge, on the western slope of the Cascades, is the source of many creeks and rivers that provide abundant fresh water to the Pudding River watershed below. It occupies a central position in a swath of mostly public land that includes parts of Mount Hood National Forest, Table Rock Wilderness, Santiam State Forest, and Silver Falls State Park. Interspersed with a patchwork of private land and Bureau of Land Management properties as well, the ridge and its environs include uncommon mid- and upper-elevation wetlands along with shallow lakes and associated plant and animal communities. Like other mid-elevation areas, this sensitive environment is at risk due to both human activity and climate change. Lacking the glaciers of the High Cascades, the ridge has a limited snowpack, subjecting its fragile, varied, transitional ecosystems to the vagaries of climate conditions.

there are a number of public access points in and along the complex of creeks that feed the river. Three of those creeks—Butte, Abiqua, and Silver—offer woodland trails along their banks or close by and feature stunning waterfalls.

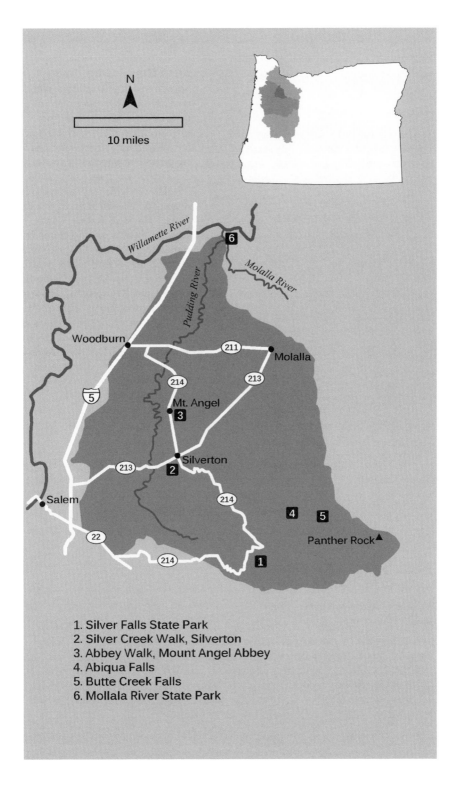

N

10 miles

Willamette River

Pudding River

Molalla River

6

Woodburn

5

211

Molalla

214

213

Mt. Angel

3

213

Silverton

2

214

Salem

213

22

4

5

214

Panther Rock▲

214

1

1. Silver Falls State Park
2. Silver Creek Walk, Silverton
3. Abbey Walk, Mount Angel Abbey
4. Abiqua Falls
5. Butte Creek Falls
6. Mollala River State Park

Huge fir trees and plunging water-falls, hiking trails and bike paths, and a unique facilities history make this a popular destination.

To get there: From Salem, take Hwy 22 east about 10 miles. Take exit 9 toward Aumsville and follow signs to Hwy 214 and Silver Falls State Park.

Silver Creek flows over ledges of ancient basalt, resulting in a spec-tacular series of waterfalls. Truly one of Oregon's gems, Silver Falls State Park, which opened in 1933, now covers more than 9,000 acres and is our larg-est state park. To many out-of-state visitors, this park is the quintessential Oregon landscape—a temperate rain forest with huge fir trees, plunging wa-terfalls (ten of them, ranging from 27 to 177 feet high), steep terrain, forest wildflowers dripping with moisture, abundant wildlife, and cool glades that are dark green year-round.

ACTIVITIES: Hiking, biking, horseback riding, wildlife watching, picnicking, swimming, camping. **FACILITIES:** ADA restrooms, playgrounds, historic buildings and displays, nature/visitor center, range of campgrounds and camp-ing facilities/types. **FEES AND REGULATIONS:** Day-use permits required. Open 7 a.m. to 9 p.m. June 1 through August 31; 8 a.m. to various closing times for remaining months. Dogs allowed in camping and off-leash areas and on some trails. **BEST MONTHS:** Year-round. The park is a cool and popular getaway in the summer, but the waterfalls are fuller and the park is less crowded in the winter and spring. **MANAGING AGENCY:** Oregon Parks and Recreation Department.

The park has more than 22 miles of multiuse trails as well as a 4-mile paved bike path. The multiuse trails, open to horses, hikers, and bicy-clists, are a combination of old logging roads and narrower footpaths. Abundant links and cutoffs make it possible to create your own hike to suit your time, fitness level, and interest.

TRAIL OF TEN FALLS

An up-and-down trek takes you to ten different waterfalls and lets you walk behind curtains of falling water.

Difficulty and length: Easy/moderate, 8.7 miles round-trip with 900 feet elevation gain (if you complete the full hike; shorter segments possible). **Regulations:** No dogs or bikes allowed on this trail. **To get there:** This trail can be hiked from the north or the south; to hike it from the south (the more common way to do it), park at the South Falls parking area, as close as you can get to the end of Picnic Area C. Follow the paved path toward the lodge.

The South Falls Lodge was built by the Civilian Conservation Corps during the 1930s using raw materials from the park itself. The workers quarried

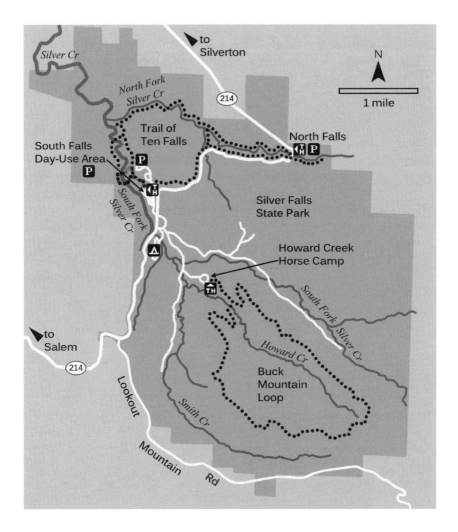

twenty-six-million-year-old sandstone from the park's oldest precincts to build the historic stone shelter near the lodge, where seashells in the stone are visible evidence of a time when this was the Oregon coast. The CCC actually laid the trail to the falls using hand tools. It's now a nationally recognized trail, and the lodge and other areas are listed on the National Register of Historic Places.

Leaving the lodge, continue down the path to the overlook for 177-foot South Falls. Take the paved trail on the right to hike down a series of switchbacks to the falls, and then walk *behind* the falls. This is the first of four falls on this trail where you can walk directly behind the curtains of falling water.

Leaving South Falls, you soon come to a footbridge. Crossing it puts you on a path back up to the top where you parked. To continue the hike, take the unpaved path that follows the creek. After about a mile, you come to

LAVA FLOWS AND WATERFALLS

Butte Creek Falls, Abiqua Falls, and the waterfalls at Silver Falls State Park are all part of the same geological formation. Twenty-six million years ago, the land where the lower Pudding now flows was a sea. The sandstone in the lower edges of Silver Falls State Park is a remnant of that era. As the area rose and the seafloor receded between about 15 and 16.6 million years ago, a series of basaltic lava flows erupted again and again from great fissures in the ground of what is now central and eastern Oregon and Washington. Between flows, forests grew and ancient waters ran upon old flows, only to be covered by the next outburst.

Much of the upper Pudding watershed is located on the western edge of the plateau formed by these flows, and the streams we see today are cutting down through the flow basalts. The caverns behind Upper Butte Creek Falls and several falls on Silver Creek were formed by stream erosion of the softer rock that once was a buried riverbed or forest floor.

Lower South Falls, where you drop down 185 steps and, again, walk behind the falls.

Here is another opportunity to return to the top, by taking a right fork. To continue, head straight on for a little more than a mile to Lower North Falls. Shortly thereafter, you come to the tallest waterfall in the park, Double Falls, which drops over two ledges for a total of 178 feet. By contrast, the next waterfall, Drake, is the shortest in the park, 27 feet. (It's named after June Drake, a Silverton photographer whose photos of the park's beauties brought prominence to the area.) Middle North Falls is next, a 106-foot cascade and yet another opportunity to enter the cavern behind the water, via a short separate trail.

When you come to the Winter Falls junction, you have three choices. You can take the right trail about 0.5 mile to 134-foot Winter Falls—it relies on winter runoff and is said to be at its best in (surprise!) winter or early spring—and continue on this trail back to South Falls, completing a 5.1-mile loop. Or you can hike up to Winter Falls and then return to the main trail to continue on for the full hike.

Next you arrive at Twin Falls, where the water splits over the rocks and descends in two cascades. Over the next mile, you start to see North Falls at a number of places along the trail. When you finally arrive there, walk down 77 steps and behind this spectacular 136-foot waterfall. In the amphitheater, look up to see round holes in the ceiling, remnants of a forest that once grew in a period between lava flows. When the lava resumed flowing, the trees were incinerated and their charred trunks either decayed or became petrified within the wells formed by their temporary resistance to the lava.

Beyond North Falls, don't miss the final sight: take a short trek under the highway bridge to see Upper North Falls drop 65 feet into a gleaming, silent pool. Return to the trail junction above North Falls to pick up the trail back to the parking lot. It runs along the canyon rim as far as the highway pullout at Winter Falls and then parallels the highway most of the way back to the lot entrance.

BUCK MOUNTAIN LOOP

A mostly rolling loop trail through a dense forest of fir, hemlock, and cedar allows you to enjoy the quieter side of Silver Falls State Park.

Difficulty and length: Moderate, 7 miles round-trip with 890 feet elevation change. **Regulations**: Horses and bikes allowed; dogs allowed on leash. **Best months**: Summer and fall; can be muddy and slippery during winter and spring. **To get there**: Once inside Silver Falls State Park on Hwy 214, go right at the sign for Overnight Facilities / Conference Center. Proceed to the registration booth to get your day-use permit and trail map, and follow the signs for Overnight Facilities / Conference Center. Turn left at the sign for Howard Creek Horse Camp about a mile from the main road. Park in the day-use lot near the Howard Creek Trailhead kiosk.

To reach the Buck Mountain Loop, walk past the "Trails" sign and follow the signs for Howard Creek Loop / Buck Mountain Loop at each junction until you reach the start of the Buck Mountain Loop in 0.5 mile. Go left to take the loop clockwise. There are several intersections on the trail but all are clearly marked with large maps on posts to help you find your way and mark your progress.

Even on a day when the South Falls parking lot is swarming with cars and people, this part of the park is likely to be uncrowded and peaceful. The trail circles Buck Mountain and is fairly gentle aside from a couple of short steeper stretches where rocks and roots demand close attention to your footing. You'll pass a few massive four-hundred-year-old trees and cross a couple of streams on footbridges. Howard Creek flows under the trail by culvert toward the end of the loop.

SILVER CREEK WALK, SILVERTON

A short walk from Town Square Park crosses Silver Creek twice and follows it upstream through wooded Coolidge-McClaine Park.

To get there: Entering Silverton on Hwy 213 from the west, turn left onto Main St and in half a block turn right onto Fiske St and immediately left into the parking lot for Town Square Park.

DIFFICULTY AND LENGTH: Easy, 0.6 mile round-trip. **FACILITIES:** Restrooms in both parks. **FEES AND REGULATIONS:** None. **BEST MONTHS:** Year-round. **MANAGING AGENCY:** City of Silverton Parks and Recreation.

Silver Creek flows northwest from Silver Falls State Park and soon enters the town of Silverton. Like most Oregon towns built on streams, Silverton made heavy industrial use of the creek for more than a century and diverted it for drinking water as well. Today, while the city still gets its water from a reservoir above town, Silver Creek runs clear and free through parks in the middle of town. In a matter of minutes you can walk right out of downtown along the creek through the woods.

Cross Silver Creek by way of the covered footbridge and head to the right up Water Street (Highway 214) past historic City Hall (built in 1925) and the Silver Falls Library. Just before the Information and Visitors Center, turn right at the sign pointing to Coolidge-McClaine Park. Bear left when the paved path forks and then go right to cross the footbridge

---

THE OREGON GARDEN

The 80-acre Oregon Garden in Silverton is a showcase for Oregon plants. The Oregon Garden partnered with the city of Silverton to create a wetland area using the city's treated wastewater, and it reuses that water to irrigate all of its gardens. Gardens include the Conifer Collection, one of the nation's largest collections of dwarf and miniature conifers; the Lewis and Clark Garden, featuring many of the native plants the explorers documented on their 1804–06 journey to the Pacific Ocean; and the Native Oak Grove, a remnant of the mighty white-oak forest that once blanketed the Willamette Valley, featuring the massive Signature Oak, 100 feet tall and four hundred years old.

The Oregon Garden is also home to the only Frank Lloyd Wright–designed house in Oregon and the only one in the Pacific Northwest open to the public. The Gordon House was designed by Wright in 1957 and moved in 2001 from its original setting on the south side of the Willamette River near the Charbonneau District in Wilsonville. Call 503-874-6006 to reserve a spot on the guided tour.

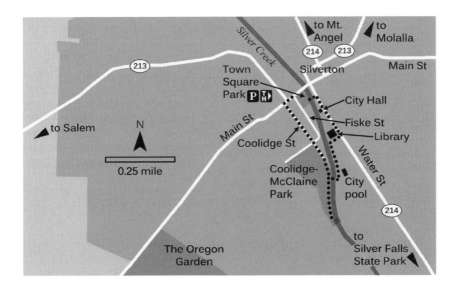

into 9-acre Coolidge-McLaine Park. (You could also continue straight up the East Bank Trail another quarter mile to the Salamander Island Overlook and then return to cross the bridge.) Take the unpaved path to the left through a tall stand of Douglas-firs and uphill along the west bank of the creek. The rapids below increase along with the stream gradient, ending in a 5-foot waterfall formed by the remnants of an old dam. Here the trail's end is marked by a small boulder in the path.

Retrace your steps as far as the footbridge, but for a different return route continue straight into the park. Amble under its Oregon white oaks and take Coolidge Street straight ahead through the historic Coolidge-McLaine neighborhood (built 1890–1912). Turn right onto Main Street to return to the parking lot.

Oak galls and woolly bear © Wendy C. Thompson

ABBEY WALK, MOUNT ANGEL ABBEY

A paved path winds upward through a cathedral of mixed conifers, offering extensive views of the valley along with Mount Hood and Mount Saint Helens.

To get there: From Salem, follow Hwy 213 north to Silverton, then take Hwy 214 north to Mount Angel. Head east on Church St. It becomes E College St after passing Saint Mary's Catholic Church. Continue up the hill for about 0.5 mile and turn left at Towers Ln. (The street to the right at this intersection is Humpert Ln.) Park at the curb on Towers Ln and walk back across E College St to the southeast corner of the intersection. Take the paved walkway uphill toward the signed entrance to Mount Angel Abbey.

DIFFICULTY AND LENGTH: Easy, 1.5 miles round-trip with 200 feet elevation change. **FACILITIES:** Restrooms in the Abbey Guest House. **FEES AND REGULATIONS:** No fee. Dogs allowed on leash if you clean up after them. Please respect the quietude that prevails on the abbey grounds. **BEST MONTHS:** Year-round. **MANAGING AGENCY:** Mount Angel Abbey.

A visit to Mount Angel Abbey takes the mind back to a slower, simpler time. This place was of sacred importance to the Native Americans, who called it *Tap-a-Lam-a-Ho*, meaning Mount of Communion. Surveyor Timothy Davenport witnessed these first inhabitants in 1851 as they sat silently in prayer on stone seats facing west, overlooking the *Chek-ta* ("beautiful and enchanting") plain. Benedictine monks from Engelberg, Switzerland, who first arrived at the mount in 1882, were drawn to its fertile soil and beautiful view that reminded them of their homeland. Today the butte is an island of mature Douglas-fir, remnant Oregon white oak, and grassland rising from a valley floor dominated by intensive agriculture. The monastic community maintains a warm welcome for those wanting to experience this sublimely peaceful place.

A paved path paralleling Abbey Drive winds up the northwest slope through a grove of tall mixed conifers dominated by Douglas-fir, some of which were here before settlers arrived. Dotted along the path are the fourteen Stations of the Cross—glass-cased dioramas depicting Christ carrying the cross to his crucifixion. The statuary is from Munich and dates back to 1889. Along the trail are young native trees and shrubs planted and tended by the Benedictine fathers. A fence inside the grove encloses an area where goats and sheep browse on invasive plants such as Himalayan blackberry, Scotch broom, and English ivy. They are part of the abbey's effort to restore open habitat while reducing the risk of fire.

Once the path crosses Abbey Drive, it leads in a clockwise direction to the top of the mount. Passing beneath a few remnant Oregon white

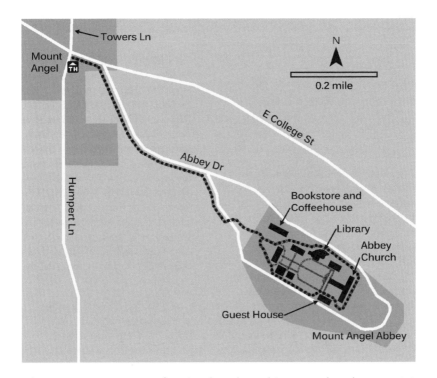

oaks, you see a grotto of native basalt and imported rocks containing a statue of Mother Mary. Proceed up the hill past the bookstore and coffeehouse (open 9 a.m. to 4:30 p.m. Tuesday through Saturday) to reach the long, expansive courtyard of grass and pavers at the heart of the abbey and seminary buildings. Continue clockwise past Mount Angel Abbey Library, designed by Finnish architect Alvar Aälto, one of only two buildings of his in North America. Toward the east end of the butte, the path leads to another mountain viewpoint just above the historic abbey bells. Continue on the path past the abbey church and rose gardens. In the garden area between the church and the Abbey Guest House (which contains public restrooms and a visitor hospitality center where you can get an abbey walking tour brochure) is the Guardian Angel statue, which survived a catastrophic 1926 fire and was later moved to this spot. The path winds past several large sequoia trees before completing the circuit around the top of the mount.

Notice the wall beneath the trees on the south side of the butte, built from local basalt to keep balls from rolling downhill when the grassy area was a ball field. Looking southeast from the wall, just past the series of greenhouses, you can see Abiqua Creek a mile and a half away bordered by a thin row of trees.

ABIQUA FALLS

A short but steep and sometimes slip-pery scramble takes you to a stunning 92-foot waterfall held within curving walls of columnar basalt painted rusty red and spring green by lichens and moss.

To get there: From Salem, take Hwy 213 north through Silverton. About 4.8 miles past Silverton, turn right onto Mount Angel–Scotts Mills Rd and drive a couple of miles to Scotts Mills. Continue through town, and just before the bridge over Butte Creek, turn right onto Crooked Finger Rd. Follow this road approximately 9.6 miles to where the pavement ends and continue on the potholed gravel road for another 1.3 miles. Turn right on one-lane gravel CF300 Rd and head downhill, ignoring all spurs. After about 0.9 mile you'll see a large ATV staging area to the right. The road down from here is rough and steep in places but is easily driveable by vehicles with good clearance. If you have a low-clearance vehicle, you may want to park here and walk the remaining 1.6 miles of gravel road to the trailhead. Otherwise, continue to follow this road downhill, ignoring all spurs, to where it ends at a locked gate, and park without blocking the gate. Walk about 60 feet back up the road and take an unmarked trail that leads downhill past a white Abbey Foundation of Oregon sign on a maple tree.

DIFFICULTY AND LENGTH: Moderate/difficult, 1 mile round-trip with 200 feet elevation change. **FACILITIES:** None. **FEES AND REGULATIONS:** None, but show courtesy and respect, as this is private property owned by the Abbey Foundation of Oregon. Be cautious and exercise extreme care. Use at your own risk. **BEST MONTHS:** Year-round. Rain makes the trail slick and muddy; high water can temporarily make the base of the falls inaccessible. **MANAGING AGENCY:** Mount Angel Abbey.

WINTER STEELHEAD

Steelhead (*Oncorhyncus mykiss*) are large rainbow trout that spend part of their lives in the ocean before returning to freshwater to spawn (making them anadromous). Unlike salmon, steelhead don't die after spawning but return to the Pacific Ocean and can spawn multiple times. They spend from one to four years at sea before reentering fresh water. There are two runs—winter and summer.

Winter steelhead begin migrating up rivers in late fall and early winter and spawn shortly after entering their native stream. The steelhead you may see in Abiqua Creek are usually late-migrating fish, entering the streams in March and April, but some may migrate as early as December. Steelhead fishing is very popular in Oregon, although the upper Willamette steelhead are listed as threatened under the federal Endangered Species Act, with the risk of becoming endangered in the foreseeable future.

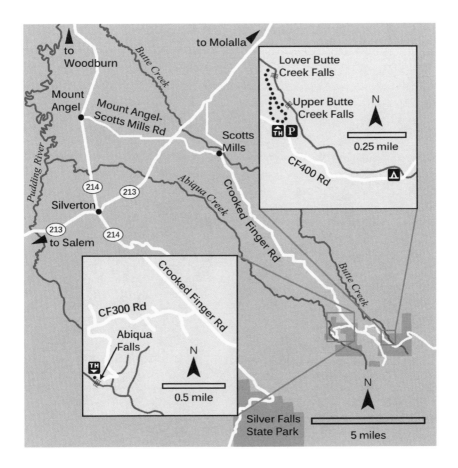

With its fast-flowing cool water, pools, and cobbled bed, Abiqua Creek harbors the largest winter steelhead run in the Pudding River basin. The upstream journey of the steelhead from the Willamette to the Pudding and then to their natal stream ends at Abiqua Falls, located about 14 miles southeast of Mount Angel Abbey as the crow flies. Abiqua Falls lies on land owned by the abbey, a remnant of a much larger landholding originally homesteaded by the Benedictines in the 1890s as a dairy farm. The creek and base of the falls offer clear, cold, deep swimming holes that draw many visitors in the hottest months.

The hike to Abiqua Falls requires scrambling down a steep canyon to the edge of a fast-moving stream, clambering over craggy rocks and downed trees, and ending in a cobble field at the base of an awe-inspiring 92-foot waterfall. Though it is definitely not an easy hike, it is relatively short. From the trailhead, the path descends steeply 0.2 mile to the creek, with a rope strung between trees to hang onto in the steepest parts, and then turns upstream and ambles over and around rocks and logs for another 0.3 mile to the falls. While the path and direction are never in question, there are some tricky areas to negotiate. Sturdy boots or tennis shoes with well-gripping soles are a must.

Winter steelhead © M. L. Herring

BUTTE CREEK FALLS

A short loop hike traversing a ferny Douglas-fir and hemlock forest offers hikers close views of two dramatic waterfalls.

To get there: From Salem, take Hwy 213 north through Silverton. About 4.8 miles past Silverton, turn right onto Mount Angel–Scotts Mills Rd and drive a couple of miles to Scotts Mills. Continue through town, and just before the bridge over Butte Creek, turn right on Crooked Finger Rd. Follow this road 9.6 miles to where the pavement ends. Continue on the potholed gravel road for another 2.1 miles. Turn left on one-lane gravel CF400 Rd (may not be signed) and head downhill 2 miles to the trailhead parking area.

DIFFICULTY AND LENGTH: Easy/moderate, 1.1 miles round-trip with 300 feet elevation gain. **FACILITIES:** Vault toilet. **FEES AND REGULATIONS:** No fee. Day use only. Dogs allowed on leash. **BEST MONTHS:** Year-round. **MANAGING AGENCY:** Oregon Department of Forestry.

Butte Creek, one of the larger tributaries of the Pudding River, arises in the Santiam State Forest and serves as the boundary between Marion

NURSE LOGS

About halfway between the two falls, the trail is bordered by a prominent nurse log supporting a colonnade of mountain hemlock. Nurse logs are common in temperate rain forests, and this one is an especially good example. It illustrates how giant trees regenerate themselves and dead material leads to new life in the endless recycling that takes place on a forest floor.

This dead tree came crashing down when its roots had decayed to the point where they could no longer support it. Lying on the moist earth, it was invaded by worms, beetles, fungus, and microbes, which over the years broke down the upper surface of the log into rich soil. Moss blanketed the log, and ferns and mushrooms rooted in it. A squirrel perched on the log and dropped seeds while breaking apart a hemlock cone.

These seeds found a perfect place to grow, a platform raised above the forest floor and its competing undergrowth, complete with a patch of sunlight created by the hole in the canopy where the tree fell. The roots of the new trees pushed deep into the softening wood and took up water and nutrients from the old tree. The new trees will continue feeding on the nurse log for several decades and sending their roots into the deeper soil under the log until the log has decayed to the point where it loses its definition. For now, the log provides a bench to rest on while contemplating the cycles of life and death in nature.

and Clackamas Counties for much of its course. It flows through and alongside Scotts Mills, where it once powered a flour mill, the remnants of which can now be found in the 13-acre Scotts Mills County Park. Farther upstream, lava flows created surface conditions for the formation of two dramatic waterfalls.

From the parking area, take the trail downhill to the right. After roughly 0.2 mile, an unmarked trail to the right allows you to descend a short distance via a couple of switchbacks to Upper Butte Creek Falls, where the creek drops 26 feet over a broad rocky shelf. Depending on the time of year, it may be possible to walk behind the falls, where the water has cut a fairly sizable cavern.

After returning to the main trail, turn right and continue heading downstream. The trail comes out on a rocky bluff 150 feet above the creek, where multistage Butte Creek Falls drops 78 feet into a deep, cold pool. Heading back up the trail, take a right at the sign pointing to the trailhead to loop back to the parking area.

Home to one of the largest heron rookeries in the Willamette Valley, this state park offers forest, wetland, and river confluence.

To get there: From I-5 in Woodburn, take Hwy 211/214 east a couple of miles and then take 99E north about a dozen miles to Canby. In Canby, turn north onto N Ivy St, left onto 9th St, and right onto Holly St. Stay on Holly all the way to 40th; then turn left to enter the park. The Canby Ferry (for information: 503-650-3030) crosses the Willamette a quarter mile downstream.

ACTIVITIES: Boating, fishing, hiking, wildlife viewing, bird-watching, picnicking. **FACILITIES**: Restrooms, picnic tables, boat ramp, pet exercise area. **FEES AND REGULATIONS**: No fee for day use, unless reserving for large groups; then the fee is $50 for the first fifty people. **BEST MONTHS**: Spring and fall; can be very crowded on summer weekends. **MANAGING AGENCY**: Oregon Parks and Recreation Department.

This park encompasses two river confluences: that of the Pudding and the Molalla, and that of the Molalla and the Willamette. The Pudding River used to flow directly into the Willamette, according to maps from the 1930s. The historic 1964 flood of the entire Willamette system caused

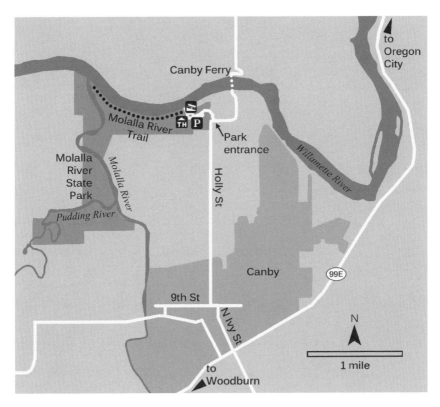

widespread channel changes, and these days, the Pudding flows into the Molalla River. Much of the associated floodplain is actually within the state park, where it's home to one of the largest heron rookeries in the Willamette Valley. Other frequent visitors include ospreys in the spring and summer, mallards and cinnamon teal in the winter, and pileated woodpeckers.

The easy Molalla River Trail is a 1-mile round-trip ramble along fields and through woods, best done in the dry season. The trail begins near the boat ramp and heads off upstream, following the Willamette River. Where the trail enters the woods and drops down into an active channel shelf of the Willamette, it's prone to flooding in the winter, so the trail from here on is not maintained. Enough people use it during the dry season to keep it viable, though. The path eventually arrives at the Molalla, shortly upstream from its confluence with the bigger river.

BIKING THE PUDDING WATERSHED

Silverton makes a great starting point for a variety of loop rides. The ambitious can ride to Silver Falls State Park and back. Those up for a more relaxing ride can put together any number of different loops on local roads through farmland.

FARMLAND LOOP FROM SILVERTON

A ride through farmland surrounding Silverton offers interesting barns, views of the Cascades, and a roller coaster experience toward the end.

Distance and climb: 18.6 miles, 230 feet total ascent. **Road surface**: Paved, some loose gravel from driveways. **Start/end point**: Town Square Park, corner of Main St and Fiske St, Silverton. **Facilities**: Restrooms at Town Square Park and at Rogers Wayside County Park, mile 17.3.

This ride makes a rough square to the west and then to the south of Silverton, passing the Oregon Garden near the end of the ride. Silverton's roads provide only a small shoulder for cyclists and the traffic can be heavy depending on the time of year, but the traffic lightens as the loop takes off into farmland. Straight roads and spacious views give way to hills and curves as you reach Sunnyview Road; Cascade Highway offers lots of rolling hills and substantially more car traffic but also broader shoulders for cyclists.

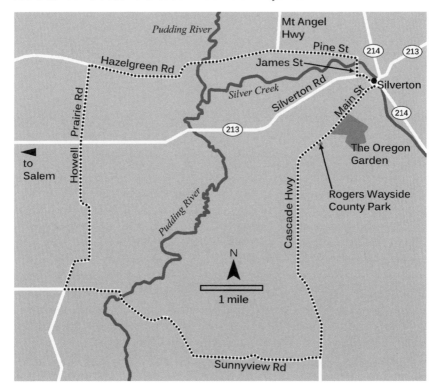

Turn-by-turn directions: From Town Square Park, turn left onto Main St (Hwy 213). Turn right onto McClaine St to continue on Hwy 213. Turn right onto James St. Turn left onto Pine St. At mile 2, go straight across Mount Angel Hwy; Pine St becomes Hazelgreen Rd. Cross the Pudding River at mile 3.3. At mile 5.1, turn left onto Howell Prairie Rd. Cross Hwy 213 (Silverton Rd) at mile 6.3. At mile 9, turn left onto Sunnyview Rd. Cross the Pudding River at mile 10. At mile 13.6, turn left onto Cascade Hwy. Pass the Oregon Garden at mile 17.9. End at Town Square Park.

PADDLING THE PUDDING RIVER

In its lower reaches, the summer and fall Pudding is sluggish, slow, and muddy, sometimes almost a trickle; the winter Pudding is a different creature entirely. Every winter when storms bring exceptionally heavy rains to the Willamette Valley, the Pudding River is one of the first rivers for which flood warnings are issued—and one of the rivers most frequently named in flood warnings.

LOWER PUDDING TO THE WILLAMETTE

This easy paddle trip takes you on a long, lazy drift as the river meanders through farmland on its gradual path down to the Molalla and then into the Willamette.

Skill level: Beginning (class 1). **Duration**: 4 to 5 hours. **River miles**: 9 miles. **Put-in point**: Anderson Rd near Aurora, under the railroad bridge next to Hwy 99E. **Take-out point**: Molalla River State Park boat ramp on the Willamette. **Facilities**: Restrooms in Molalla River State Park. **Season**: Dry season.

This is a peaceful trip for the most part, with birds chattering and swooping in and out of the trees and bushes along the banks. Because it's in the lower

---

FLOODPLAIN IN ACTION

After a spell of heavy rains, when the flood warnings start to go out, drive about 2.3 miles east of Hubbard on Whiskey Hill Road. (Take the Broadacres Road exit from I-5 and drive east until it turns into Whiskey Hill Road in Hubbard, or take Highway 99E to Hubbard and go east on Whiskey Hill Road.) Roughly 100 or 200 yards before you reach the river, pull over and check out the farm field on the right. When the river is running high, the field is a floodplain in action, a dramatic demonstration of how river hydrology works. The field accommodates some of the extra volume of water the river carries while swollen from heavy rains, helping to keep it within its banks elsewhere and forestall flooding that would otherwise occur downstream.

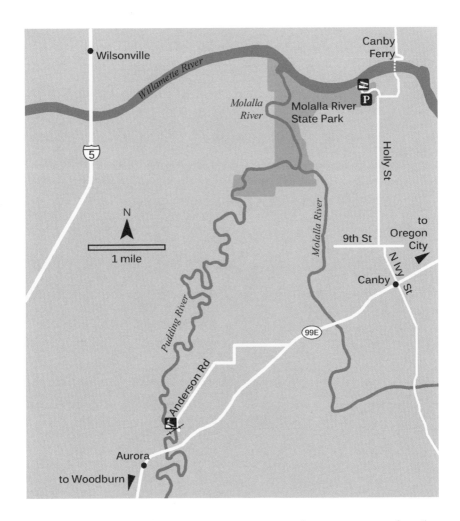

reaches of a river that floods almost every winter, keep an eye out for piles of debris and logs, especially early in the year. Sometimes there are little sandy or gravel beaches along the way where you can pull off for a break, and sometimes not. The tree cover increases as you continue downstream, and so does the bird life.

After the Pudding enters the Molalla, you find yourself traveling in a much wider waterway. Try to stay to the middle, or wherever the channel is deepest. Look for the heron rookery on the right bank; eagles and osprey are also common sights. The later in the dry season you make this trip, the more likely you are to find convenient beaches—and inconvenient sand or gravel bars where you may have to walk your canoe or kayak to continue. Once you enter the Willamette, keep to the right side and a half mile downstream look for the boat ramp at Molalla River State Park.

Appendix A
Best Outings

BEST FOR THE ALTER-ABLED

Abbey Walk (Mount Angel Abbey)
Ankeny National Wildlife Refuge
Bald Hill Natural Area
Cascadia State Park
Champoeg State Heritage Area
E. E. Wilson Wildlife Area
Homer Campbell Boardwalk Trail (William L. Finley National Wildlife Refuge)
Jackson-Frazier Wetland
John Neal Memorial County Park
Minto-Brown Island Park
North Santiam State Recreation Area
North Shore Trail (Cheadle Lake Park)
Peavy Arboretum (McDonald Forest)
River Bend County Park
Talking Water Gardens (City of Albany Trails)
Thompson's Mills State Heritage Site
Waterloo County Park
Willamette Mission State Park
Willamette Park

BEST FOR BIRD-WATCHING

Ankeny National Wildlife Refuge
Baskett Slough National Wildlife Refuge
Champoeg State Heritage Area
Jackson-Frazier Wetland
Kingston Prairie Preserve
Snag Boat Bend Unit, William L. Finley National Wildlife Refuge
Talking Water Gardens (City of Albany Trails)
William L. Finley National Wildlife Refuge

BEST HIKES WITH CHILDREN

Anderson Loop Trail (North Santiam State Recreation Area)
Deer Creek County Park
Jackson-Frazier Wetland
John Neal Memorial County Park
McDowell Creek Falls County Park
Meadow Edge Loop Trail (Marys Peak)
Miller Woods
North Shore Trail (Cheadle Lake Park)
Old Growth Trail and Quarry Loop (McDonald Forest)
Powder House Trail (Niagara County Park)
River Bend County Park, loop trail
Santiam Wagon Road, Mountain House to House Rock
Takena Landing Trail (City of Albany Trails)
Thompson's Mills State Heritage Site
Waterloo County Park, loop trail
Woodpecker Loop (William L. Finley National Wildlife Refuge)

BEST FOR HISTORY

Champoeg State Heritage Area
Fort Hoskins Historic Park
Fort Yamhill State Heritage Area
Niagara County Park
Opal Creek Loop (Opal Creek Wilderness and Scenic Recreation Area)
Willamette Mission State Park

BEST FOR PEAK BAGGERS

Dan's Trail to Dimple Hill (McDonald Forest)
North Ridge and Summit Trails (Marys Peak)
Soap Creek Valley to McCulloch Peak Loop (McDonald Forest)
Tidbits Mountain Trail
Stahlman Point Trail
Trout Creek to Rooster Rock (Menagerie Wilderness)

BEST SWIMMING HOLES

Abiqua Falls
Cascadia State Park
Chimney Peak Trail to the Middle Santiam River
Little North Santiam Recreation Area
McKercher County Park
Mill Creek county parks
Opal Pool Loop (Opal Creek Wilderness and Scenic Recreation Area)
Santiam Wagon Road, House Rock area

Shellburg Falls Recreation Area
Three Pools Day-Use Area (Opal Creek Wilderness and Scenic Recreation Area)
Yellowbottom Recreation Site

BEST FOR TURTLE WATCHING

Cheadle Lake Park
Luckiamute Landing State Natural Area, south tract
Snagboat Bend Unit, William L. Finley National Wildlife Refuge
William L. Finley National Wildlife Refuge

BEST WATERFALLS

Abiqua Falls
Butte Creek Falls
Henline Falls (Opal Creek Wilderness and Scenic Recreation Area)
McDowell Creek Falls
Niagara and Pheasant Creek Falls
Shellburg Falls
Trail of Ten Falls (Silver Falls State Park)

BEST FOR WILDFLOWERS

Bald Hill Natural Area
Deer Creek County Park
Homestead Loop (McDonald Forest)
Kingston Prairie Preserve
Meadow Edge Loop Trail (Marys Peak)
South Yamhill Trail (Kiwanis Marine and Joe Dancer Parks)

BEST WILLAMETTE RIVER VIEWS

Champoeg State Heritage Area
Luckiamute Landing State Natural Area
Minto-Brown Island Park
Keizer Rapids Park
Simpson Park Trail (City of Albany Trails)
Takena Landing Trail (City of Albany Trails)
Willamette Mission State Park
Willamette Park
Willamette River Trail, Independence

Appendix B
Who to Contact

Albany Parks and Recreation Department
333 Broadalbin St SW
Albany, OR 97321
541-917-7777
cityofalbany.net/departments/parks-and-recreation

Benton County Natural Areas and Parks Department
360 SW Avery Ave
Corvallis, OR 97333
541-766-6871
co.benton.or.us/parks/

BLM Salem District Office
1717 Fabry Rd SE
Salem, OR 97306
503-375-5646
or.blm.gov/salem

City of Independence
555 S Main St
Independence, OR 97351
503-838-1212
ci.independence.or.us

City of Keizer Parks Division
930 Chemawa Rd NE
Keizer, OR 97303
503-856-3569
keizer.org

City of Lebanon Parks
925 Main St
Lebanon, OR 97355
541-258-4917
ci.lebanon.or.us/index.aspx?page=37

City of Salem
555 Liberty St SE
Salem, OR 97301
503-588-6211
cityofsalem.net/Residents/Parks/

City of Silverton Parks and Recreation
830 McClaine St
Silverton, OR 97381
503-873-6359
silverton.or.us/index.aspx?nid=159

Corvallis Parks and Recreation Department
1310 SW Avery Park Dr
Corvallis, OR 97330
541-766-6918
corvallisoregon.gov/index.aspx?page=56

Greenbelt Land Trust
101 SW Western Blvd, Ste 111
Corvallis, OR 97333
541-752-9609
greenbeltlandtrust.org

Linn County Parks and Recreation
3010 Ferry St SW
Albany, OR 97321
541-967-3917
linnparks.com

Marion County Parks
5155 Silverton Rd NE
Salem, OR 97305
503-588-5036
co.marion.or.us/PW/Parks

Mount Angel Abby
One Abbey Dr
St. Benedict, OR 97373
503-845-3030
mountangelabbey.org

The Nature Conservancy in Oregon
821 SE 14th Ave
Portland, OR 97214
503-802-8100
oregon@tnc.org

Oregon Department of Forestry
Santiam State Forest
22965 North Fork Rd SE
Lyons, OR 97358
503-859-2151
oregon.gov/ODF/northcascade/pages/santiamstateforest.aspx

Oregon Parks and Recreation Department
725 Summer St NE
Salem, OR 97301
80-551-6949
oregon.gov/oprd

Oregon State University College of Forestry
140 Peavy Hall
3100 SW Jefferson Wy
Corvallis, OR 97331
541-737-2004
forestry.oregonstate.edu

Polk County Parks and Recreation
850 Main St
Dallas, OR 97338
503-623-8172
co.polk.or.us/ms/polk-county-parks

US Fish and Wildlife Service
Pacific Region
911 NE 11th Ave
Portland, OR 97232
503-231-6120
fws.gov/pacific/

US Forest Service, Detroit Ranger District
44125 North Santiam Hwy SE
Detroit, OR 97342
503-854-3366
fs.usda.gov/willamette

US Forest Service, Siuslaw Ranger District
3200 SW Jefferson Wy
Corvallis, OR 97331
541-750-7000
fs.usda.gov/siuslaw

US Forest Service, Sweet Home Ranger District
4431 Hwy 20
Sweet Home, OR 97386
541-367-5168
fs.usda.gov/willamette

Yamhill County Parks and Recreation
615 E Sixth St
McMinnville, OR 97128
503-434-7463
co.yamhill.or.us/content/about-yamhill-county-parks-recreation

Yamhill Soil and Water Conservation District
2200 SW 2nd St
McMinnville, OR 97128
503-472-6403
yamhillswcd.org

Appendix C
Further Resources

NATURE IN THE MID-VALLEY

The Right Trail website (therighttrail.org) is a comprehensive, interactive resource for trails of all kinds (hiking, biking, paddling, equestrian) in Benton County, Oregon. It lets you search by your favorite ways to go and things to see.

Neighborhood Naturalist (neighborhood-naturalist.com) has published a quarterly newsletter (free to e-mail subscribers, small fee to receive by mail) since 2003 spotlighting the plant and animal life of the mid-Willamette Valley. Authors Don Boucher and Lisa Millbank have also produced DVDs and CDs focused on nature sights and sounds in the mid-valley, and they lead monthly Neighborhood Naturalist adventures.

Mid-Valley Nature (groups.google.com/group/mid-valley-nature) is a free Google Group for those who want to share field observations of plants, birds, mammals, insects, aquatic life, and other natural features of the mid-Willamette Valley.

A team of botanists at the Oregon Flora Project at Oregon State University has created an app on Oregon wildflowers to make it easy to identify plants in the field, available at highcountryapps.com.

HIKING TRAILS

Corvallis Area Trails is an excellent trail map from Sky Island Graphics. The map is sold at Peak Sports, Grass Roots Books and Music, and the First Alternative Co-op in Corvallis as well as other local businesses.

EveryTrail is a website (everytrail.com) that lets hikers share write-ups of trails. You can find an abundance of trails in the mid-Willamette Valley (and anywhere in the United States) just by entering a location.

Two of the best hiking guides to our area are *Corvallis Trails: Exploring the Heart of the Valley* by Margie C. Powell (OSU Press, 2006) and *100 Hikes in the Central Oregon Cascades* by William L. Sullivan (Navillus Press, 4th edition 2012). *Kaleidoscope: An Introductory Guide to the Yamhill River Watershed* by Laura McMasters and Wendy Thompson (2008) is a collection of guided road trips to parks and walking trails.

Wheelchairs in the Wild (wheelchairwild.com) is a website that gives detailed information about accessibility of various trails for those with physical challenges.

BIKING TRAILS

You can pick up bicycle maps at most local bike shops, city hall, or the Chamber of Commerce office. In addition, the City of Corvallis website offers bike maps of Corvallis and Benton County at corvallisoregon.gov under Engineering and Transportation > Bike and Pedestrian Programs.

The Mid-Willamette Valley Bicycle and Pedestrian Map at co.linn.or.us/webmap/bikewv/main.html maps more than fifty bike and walking routes from Springfield to Keizer and lets you sort according to difficulty or distance.

The Mid-Valley Bicycle Club, centered in Corvallis, offers several ride options every Saturday morning for members to tour the valley and the coast mountains. The club's website (mvbc.com/) has a Routes page that provides links to route sheets for nearly seventy different local rides.

Santiam Spokes (santiamspokes.org), a bicycle club based in Lebanon, offers a number of group rides every week.

The Ride Oregon website (rideoregonride.com) provides a wealth of information and inspiration about mountain biking trails, road routes, and Oregon Scenic Bikeway tours.

BIRDING TRAILS

The Willamette Valley Birding Trail Guide at oregonbirdingtrails.org/wvtrailguide.htm offers pdf downloads of guides to a dozen driving loops that cover the Willamette Valley. These guides give information about the best sites for watching birds as well as a birding checklist.

WATER TRAILS

The Willamette River Water Trail website (willamettewatertrail.org/) aids in trip planning and offers updated river hazard information and more. The project has published two waterproof guides to the river—one for the upper reaches and one for the lower reaches, with the midpoint being the Buena Vista Ferry.

The Willamette River Field Guide by Travis Williams (Timber Press, 2009) describes the Willamette River stretch by stretch and gives an abundance of natural history information.

Field Guide to Oregon Rivers by Tim Palmer (OSU Press, 2014) is a comprehensive guide to rivers all over the state.

Willamette River Recreation Guide (oregon.gov/osmb/library/docs/willametteriverguidepdf.pdf), a December 2007 booklet from Oregon's State Marine Board and its Parks and Recreation Department, gives helpful information about boating on the river, plant and animal life, and popular destinations, as well as detailed maps.

Useful paddling guides include *Soggy Sneakers: A Paddler's Guide to Oregon's Rivers* by Pete Giordano and the Willamette Kayak and Canoe Club (Mountaineers Books, 4th edition 2004), *Paddling Oregon* by Robb Keller (Falcon Guides, 1998), *Canoe and Kayak Routes of Northwest Oregon* by Philip N. Jones (Mountaineers Books, 3rd edition 2007), and *Oregon River Tours* by John Garren (Garren Publications, 2nd edition 1991).

Aimed at more advanced and adventurous kayakers, oregonkayaking.net is a nonprofit, independent website offering information about paddling and preserving Oregon rivers and creeks.

The Willamette Kayak and Canoe Club (wkcc.org), based in the mid-Willamette Valley, organizes outings for its members and helps conserve and protect local free-flowing rivers.

Pat Welch of Corvallis maintains a useful kayaking and whitewater information page at levels.wkcc.org/kayak.html. For Oregon river levels, see levels.wkcc.org/?P=Oregon.html.

American Whitewater also maintains a page showing gauges for Oregon rivers at americanwhitewater.org/content/Gauge2/view/state/OR/. And the National Water Information System gives current water data for Oregon at waterdata.usgs.gov/or/nwis/rt.

CAMPING

For camping destinations, visit the Oregon State Parks website (oregonstateparks. org), the Willamette National Forest Camping and Cabins page (fs.usda.gov/activity/willamette/recreation/camping-cabins), the Siuslaw National Forest Camping and Cabins page (fs.usda.gov/activity/siuslaw/recreation/camping-cabins), the Campgrounds on the Santiam State Forest page (oregon.gov/odf/northcascade/pages/campgrounds.aspx), the Linn County Parks and Recreation website (linnparks.com), and the North Santiam Chamber of Commerce Parks and Campgrounds page (nschamber.org/parks-campgrounds/).

FISHING

Visit the Oregon Department of Fish and Wildlife website (dfw.state.or.us/resources/fishing/) for fishing resources and regulations.

WATERSHED COUNCILS

Marys River Watershed Council
P. O. Box 1041
Corvallis, OR 97339
541-758-7597
mrwc.org

Calapooia Watershed Council
P. O. Box 844
Brownsville, OR 97327
541-466-3493
calapooia.org

Luckiamute Watershed Council
226 South Main Street, Suite L
Independence, OR 97351
503-837-0237
luckiamutelwc.org

South Santiam Watershed Council
4431 Highway 20
Sweet Home, OR
541-367-5564
sswc.org

North Santiam Watershed Council
284 E. Water Street
Stayton, OR 97383
503-930-8202
northsantiam.org

Greater Yamhill Watershed Council
237 NE Ford Street, Suite 9
McMinnville, OR 97128
503-474-1047
yamhillwatershedcouncil.org

Pudding River Watershed Council
c/o Woodburn Public Works Building
190 Garfield Street
Woodburn, OR 97071
puddingriver.org

Acknowledgments

This book was first conceived by Gail Achterman, Karyle Butcher, and Trish Daniels. It was coaxed into being by a small committee—consisting of Karyle, Trish, Kent Daniels, and Jessica McDonald, with early input from Kathleen Dean Moore and Charles Goodrich—that met over a period of years to supervise and raise funds. Nearly three dozen volunteers as well as professional writers fanned out across the mid-Willamette Valley with pens and notebooks in hand to do the groundwork without which this book would not exist. M. L. Herring, Wendy C. Thompson, and David Wagner generously donated drawings to decorate the book.

Thanks go to M. J. Cody, Mike Houck, and Bob Sallinger for helpful conversations about developing the book based on their experience with *Wild in the City*. The mid-valley watershed councils—the Marys, Calapooia, Luckiamute, South Santiam, North Santiam, Pudding, and Yamhill—gave insight and direction to the list of outings. Liz Redon and Wendy Hudson of the Oregon Watershed Enhancement Board provided important early contact information for the Pudding and Santiam watersheds.

Valuable expertise and help with fact checking were provided by Peter Adams, Bureau of Land Management; Dick Brainerd, *Carex* Working Group; Brian Carroll, director of Linn County Parks; Jamison Cavallero, Cascadia Watershed Planners; Jim Cook; Holly Crosson, director of Benton Soil and Water Conservation District; Sean Daniels; Pat Dunn, volunteer with the Lebanon Genealogical Society; Jude Geist, parks operations supervisor, Corvallis Parks and Recreation; Jason Gottgetreu, planner for the City of Silverton; Shawn Irvine, development director of the City of Independence; Nadene LeCheminant, communications manager, Mount Angel Abbey; Bruce Marbin and Jana Zvibleman, on access for the alter-abled; Tim Palmer, author of *Field Guide to Oregon Rivers* (timpalmer.org); Whitey Recknor; Jackie Rochefort, parks planner, Corvallis Parks and Recreation; Tina Schweickert; Rod Sell, president of Build Lebanon Trails; Rachel Wray and Dennis Hahn; and Alan van Zuuk.

Ideas and background information were gleaned from *Boots and Bikes: Hiking, Biking, and Cycling in the Mid-Willamette Valley* by Lokahi Enterprise; *Canoe and Kayak Routes of Northwest Oregon* by Philip N. Jones; *Corvallis Trails* by Margie C. Powell; *Kaleidoscope: An Introductory Guide to the Yamhill River*

Watershed by Laura McMasters and Wendy Thompson; *Paddling Oregon* by Robb Keller; *100 Hikes in the Central Oregon Cascades* by William L. Sullivan; and *Soggy Sneakers: A Paddler's Guide to Oregon's Rivers* by Pete Giordano and the Willamette Kayak and Canoe Club.

The editors thank Cascade Pacific RC&D for managing the book's finances, as well as Stoel Rives LLP, the Network of Oregon Watershed Councils, the Spring Creek Project, the Institute for Natural Resources, and Greenbelt Land Trust for helping to drum up money and spread the word about the book. The Oregon Community Foundation facilitated Gail Achterman's estate funding as a grant in support of this project.

Last, but certainly not least, the generosity of these donors made the production of the book possible: Christopher A. and Virginia A. Achterman, Daniel J. R. and Rebecca R. Achterman, Gail Achterman Fund of the Oregon Community Foundation, Margaret E. Achterman, Thomas W. and Patty C. Achterman, Virginia M. Burdick, Scott F. and Glenda M. Burns, Karyle Butcher, Deborah A. Coleman Trust, Kimberly Cooper, The Gun and Tom Denhart Family Fund, Jerry R. Fish, Beth S. Ginsberg and Annette L. Hayes, Nancy L. Golden, Susan Hammer Fund of the Oregon Community Foundation, Craig Hanneman, Sonja L. Haugen, Carolyn Hennion, Christopher R. Hermann, The Richard Karl Hermann Trust, Joanne Jene MD, Marie Lamfrom Charitable Foundation, Gregory Macpherson, Michael and Krista McIntyre, Meyer Memorial Trust, John D. Miller, J. Mark and Marjory Morford, Patricia L. Moss, Oregon State University Institute of Natural Resources, OSU Printing and Mailing Services, Owls Roost Enterprise LLP, William F. Paulus, Gretchen N. Pierce, Nancy A. Rangila, Sharon V. Robbins, The Roundhouse Foundation, Lynne H. Saxton, Barbara J. Sloop Trust, Patricia Smullin, Stoel Rives LLP, Jean Tate, Geoffrey Tichenor and Stephanie Engelsman, Philip S. Van Der Weele and Joan P. Snyder, Christine Vernier, Mary D. Wilcox, Deborah J. Wilson, and Marcia Johnston Wood, PhD, and Thomas Wood.

ACKNOWLEDGMENTS

Contributors

CHRIS ACHTERMAN, MD ("Welcome to Our Valley"), is an orthopedic surgeon at Randall Children's Hospital in Portland who enjoys the outdoors and has a special interest in water and regional development.

LORRAINE ANDERSON is a freelance environmental editor whose previous books include *Sisters of the Earth, Literature and the Environment*, and *Cooking with Sunshine*. She has lived in Corvallis since 2005 and blogs at earth-and-eros.blogspot.com.

JESSICA BEAUCHEMIN (Marys Peak, North Ridge Trail; Section 36/ Powder House Loop Trail; Cascadia State Park; Duffy Lake Trail; Stahlman Point Trail; Willamette Park / Kendall Natural Area; Pheasant and Niagara Falls) is a personal trainer, yoga instructor, and business owner who has been blogging about hiking in the Pacific Northwest for almost a decade on portlandhikers.org and her own site, jessB.org.

DON BOUCHER and LISA MILLBANK ("Birding in the Mid-Willamette Valley") of Corvallis are birders and naturalists who promote the study of nature on a local scale through field trips, classes, photography, videos, and their Neighborhood Naturalist program (neighborhood-naturalist.com).

KIM BRASEL (Fitton Green Natural Area; McDowell Creek County Park) has a degree in journalism and has written for newspapers and magazines on a variety of subjects, including one of her favorite pastimes: being in the outdoors.

JESSICA BROTHERS (Opal Creek Wilderness and Scenic Recreation Area; Opal Pool Loop; Henline Falls Trail; Little North Santiam Trail) enjoys writing about local trails and hikes on her blog (thebrightnessofbeing.com), as well as photographing the beautiful places of the Pacific Northwest.

JO BRUNO (Minto-Brown Island Park) has an associate of arts in journalism from Los Medanos College in Pittsburg, California, and a bachelor's in anthropology from Western Oregon University and enjoys bicycling, writing novels, gardening, and making connections with people.

KELLY BURNETT, PhD (splash dams sidebar), is a river ecologist, emeritus researcher with the USFS Pacific Northwest Research Station, and courtesy assistant professor in the Department of Fisheries and Wildlife at Oregon State University.

JOHN CAMPBELL ("Vision Begins: On Dixon Creek"), a writing teacher at Western Oregon University, is an award-winning poet and essayist (johnrobertcampbell.com) and author of *Absence and Light: Meditations from the Klamath Marshes*.

JOHN DANIEL ("Opal Creek") is the author of eight books of poetry, essays, and memoir and the recipient of two Oregon Book Awards for Literary Nonfiction and the Pacific Northwest Booksellers Association Award.

PATRICIA DANIELS (introduction to Pudding River Watershed; Silver Falls State Park; Silver Creek Walk, Silverton; Butte Creek Falls; Molalla River State Park) is a writer and editor who lives in Corvallis and has been exploring the nearby natural world with her husband, Kent, since 1980.

STEPHAN DEGOEY (Luckiamute Landing State Natural Area) is the park ranger at Luckiamute Landing State Natural Area.

KENNETH DICKSON-SELF (Cheadle Lake Park; Waterloo County Park) has hiked trails abroad and in all four corners of the United States, in addition to working in high tech and the Army infantry.

BARBARA DRAKE (Champoeg State Heritage Area; Deer Creek County Park) is the author of numerous works, including *Morning Light: Wildflowers, Night Skies, and Other Ordinary Joys of Oregon Country Life*; *Peace at Heart: An Oregon Country Life*; and *Writing Poetry*, a widely used college textbook.

MONICA DROST (all maps except Willamette Basin; Packsaddle Park to Fishermen's Bend paddle trip; Fishermen's Bend to John Neal Memorial Park paddle trip) earned a master's in geography from Oregon State University and has lived in the Willamette Valley, where she met her husband and raised four children, since 1979.

DAVID ECKERT ("Watersheds of the Mid-Willamette Valley") of Willamette Watershed Productions has produced numerous films about local water issues that have played a key role in inspiring local clean water action throughout the United States.

JOEL GEIER (E. E. Wilson Wildlife Area) is a hydrogeologist (groundwater guy) who has contributed to the Oregon Cascades and Oregon Coast guides for the Oregon Birding Trail project (oregonbirdingtrails.org) and coordinated the development and production of the Willamette Valley Birding Trail guide (willamettebirding.org).

JENNIFER GERVAIS (Bald Hill Loop Trail; Mulkey Creek Trail; Homestead Trail; sidebars on banana slugs and great horned owls) is a courtesy assistant professor in OSU's Department of Fish and Wildlife, where she researches ecotoxicology, population-level ecological risk assessment, and conservation in agricultural systems.

CHARLES GOODRICH ("Reinhabiting the Valley: A Field Guide to Being Here"), director of the Spring Creek Project for Ideas, Nature, and the Written Word at Oregon State University, is the author of three volumes of poems (*Insects of South Corvallis, Going to Seed: Dispatches from the Garden*, and *A Scripture of Crows*) and a collection of essays (*The Practice of Home*).

GORDON GRANT (Erratic Rock State Natural Site) is a research hydrologist with the US Forest Service at the Pacific Northwest Research Station in Corvallis as well as a courtesy professor in the College of Earth, Ocean, and Atmospheric Sciences at Oregon State University.

KEVIN GRANT (sidebar on sustainable travel to natural areas; Soap Creek Valley to McCulloch Peak Loop; and Biking McDonald Forest) is a Willamette Valley native and an avid cyclist who enjoys cruising the city, exploring rural roads, and rolling fat tires in the nearby forest.

BENNETT HALL (introduction to the Marys River Watershed) is the special projects editor for the Corvallis *Gazette-Times* and reports frequently on environmental issues affecting the mid-Willamette Valley.

M. L. HERRING (illustrations of great horned owl, northern spotted owl, salmon, steelhead, and osprey) is an award-winning science writer, illustrator, and professor of communications who leads communications at Oregon State University's College of Agricultural Sciences.

HENRY HUGHES ("Salmon on the Santiam"; Paddling the Luckiamute River), professor of English at Western Oregon University and winner of the 2004 Oregon Book Award in Poetry, is a poet, essayist, and editor of the Everyman's Library anthologies *The Art of Angling: Poems about Fishing* and *Fishing Stories*.

DONALD LYON (Paddling the Calapooia River; McClun Wayside to McKercher County Park paddle trip; McKercher County Park to Brownsville paddle trip) traveled the world as a photographic tour guide for thirty-five years and is delighted to be settling down on a small piece of land on the edge of the Calapooia River in Brownsville.

KATRINA MAGGIULLI (Finley National Wildlife Refuge; Ankeny National Wildlife Refuge; Baskett Slough National Wildlife Refuge), a Willamette Valley native, has worked as the visitor services intern for the Willamette Valley

National Wildlife Refuge Complex and holds a degree in English and writing from Oregon State University.

BRUCE MARBIN and JANA ZVIBLEMAN (sidebar on trail access for the alter-abled) are partners in Aha Educational Consulting and mobility advocates who curate the website Wheelchairs in the Wild (wheelchairwild.com). They have been exploring the world with Bruce's wheelchair since 2007.

JESSIE McCARTNEY (Jackson-Frazier Wetland) is a 2013 graduate of Oregon State University (master's in applied physics) who enjoys exploring her neighborhood's open spaces and natural areas.

LAURA McMASTERS ("Following the Kalapuya Shadow Trails") comes from a family of scientists and naturalists (her father, Kenneth Fender, was an entomologist for whom Fender's blue butterfly is named, and her mother is an oligochaetologist who specializes in Pacific Northwest native earthworms) and teaches children's nature classes in McMinnville.

JONATHAN MEIER (Chimney Peak Trail to the Middle Santiam River) has worked as a recreation planner for the US Forest Service, Sweet Home Ranger District, and enjoys trail running, mountain biking, and spending time with his toddler son.

ABBY PHILLIPS METZGER ("Story Mapping") grew up near the Willamette River in Corvallis and is the author of *Meander Scars: Reflections on Healing the Willamette River*.

KATHLEEN DEAN MOORE ("Foreword: The Blessed Truth"), former Distinguished Professor of Philosophy at Oregon State University, is the award-winning author of *Riverwalking, Holdfast, The Pine Island Paradox*, and *Wild Comfort*, as well as co-editor of *Moral Ground*, which collects testimony from the world's moral leaders about our obligations to the future.

RUBY HANSEN MURRAY (Willamette Mission State Park), a writer and photographer (rubyhansenmurray.com) living on Puget Island in the lower Columbia River estuary, is an enrolled member of the Osage Nation and has been featured on National Public Radio and in *The Lake Rises, The Salal Review*, and *Oregon Humanities* magazine.

GAIL OBERST (introduction to Luckiamute River Watershed) publishes a monthly beer magazine and serves on the Luckiamute Watershed Council.

JIM O'CONNOR (Erratic Rock State Natural Site), PhD in geological sciences, is a Pacific Northwest native who has spent the past twenty-plus years focused on fluvial geomorphology and quaternary geology in western North America, mostly with the US Geological Survey Oregon Water Science Center in Portland.

MARIE OLIVER (Simpson Park Trail; Talking Water Gardens) is a professional writer / editor (claritywriting.com) and native Oregonian who enjoys hiking, camping, organic gardening, and blogging at riahamilton.com.

JENNIFER PARKE (Dan's Trail to Dimple Hill; Old-Growth Trail and Quarry Loop; sidebars on false brome and Jory soil) is an outdoor enthusiast/natural historian/amateur writer, a year-round McDonald Forest hiker and runner, and an associate professor in both the Department of Botany and Plant Pathology and the Department of Crop and Soil Science at Oregon State University.

ROBERT and LAURA PECKYNO (Willamette Basin map; Philomath to Bellfountain County Park bike ride; River Valley Loop from Albany bike ride) live in Corvallis, where Laura is an independent web developer and Robert works as a musician, graphic designer, and public information specialist (imaginaurium.com).

IVAN PHILLIPSEN (Kingston Prairie), a biologist who studied several northwestern frog species for his doctoral research at Oregon State University, runs Volcano Lands Nature Tours (volcanolands.com) of Portland, Oregon.

MICHAEL POPE ("Looking Back and Ahead: Protecting the Valley's Natural Treasures") has been the executive director of the Greenbelt Land Trust since 2010 and holds a BS, an MS, and a PhD in wildlife science from Oregon State University.

JERRY ROONEY (Corvallis to the Buena Vista Ferry bike ride) is a nationally certified bike safety instructor (League of American Bicyclists) and teaches bicycle safety classes in Corvallis.

CAROL SAVONEN ("The Fight for Opal Creek"; Paddling the Marys River) is a naturalist, gardener, and conservationist who spent twenty years working for Oregon State University as a science writer.

TINA SCHWEICKERT (Abbey Walk, Mount Angel Abbey; Abiqua Falls) is an independent environmental historian and writer who owns and manages a wildlife sanctuary in the Waldo Hills.

RICHARD SHARP (Shellburg Falls Recreation Area) has a blog at adventurecrow.wordpress.com and, after hiking the length of the Pacific Crest Trail twice, is on a mission to photograph as many waterfalls in Oregon as possible.

LEE ANNA SHERMAN ("Imagining the Marys"), a lifelong resident of the Northwest, is a science writer and editor for *Terra* magazine at Oregon State University and serves on the board of directors of the Marys River Watershed Council.

ESTHER STUTZMAN ("The Beginnings of the Kalapuya People"), an enrolled member of the Confederated Tribes of Siletz, published a book of traditional Coos stories in 1997 and dedicates herself to Indian education and other outreach programs.

WILLIAM SULLIVAN (Fort Hoskins Historic Park; Beazell Memorial Forest) is the author of seventeen books, including *100 Hikes in NW Oregon*, available at oregonhiking.com.

WENDY C. THOMPSON (illustrations of Canada goose, poison oak, native wild rose, rough-skinned newt, banana slug, blue-eyed darner and wild bleeding heart, dragonfly nymph, oak galls and tiger moth, calypso orchid, western pond turtle, Fender's blue butterfly, shaggy parasol mushroom, lungwort, yellow-legged frog, wild ginger, western meadowlark, and trillium) is a self-taught artist who captures Pacific Northwest nature in colored pencil scenes that she self-publishes on cards, calendars, and journals (wendythompsonart.com).

ZACH URNESS (Willamette River Trail, Independence) has been an outdoors writer, photographer, and videographer in Oregon since 2008 and currently works at the *Statesman Journal* in Salem.

DAVID WAGNER (drawings of wild turkey, great blue heron, equisetum, white oak acorns, and North American beaver), a botanist who lives and works in Eugene, writes the "It's About Time" column for the *Eugene Weekly* and created the Willamette Valley Nature Calendar for thirty years, ending in 2013 (fernzenmosses.com).

JOHN WILLIAMS (Tidbits Mountain Trail; McKercher County Park; Santiam Wagon Road; Trout Creek to Rooster Rock; Crabtree Lake Trail) is a native Oregonian who loves to explore Cascadia and writes a blog called Cascade Living (cascadialiving.blogsppot.com/).

TRAVIS WILLIAMS ("Connecting with Your Great Oregon River," Paddling the Mid-Willamette River) has been Riverkeeper and Executive Director of Willamette Riverkeeper since 2000 and authored *The Willamette River Field Guide*.

BARRY WULFF (Marys Peak, East Ridge Trail and Meadow Edge Loop Trail) taught ecology and botany for twenty-two years at Eastern Connecticut State University and is a photographer and avid hiker who leads international hiking and canoeing tours.

JAMIE WYANT ("The North Santiam Microcosm"; Independence to Ankeny National Wildlife Refuge bike ride) worked as an ecosystem scientist in such far-flung places as the oilfields of arctic Alaska, the grasslands of Australia and Asia, and the highlands of tropical Africa before he finally figured out Oregon was meant to be his home.

Credits

The editors thank the following sources for permission to reprint copyrighted material:

John Daniel, "Opal Creek," from *Of Earth: New and Selected Poems* (Lost Horse Press, 2012). Originally published in *The Southern Review*. Copyright © 1994 by John Daniel. Reprinted with the permission of the author.

M. L. Herring, five sketches. Copyright © 2010. Reprinted with the permission of the artist.

Abby Phillips Metzger, "Story Mapping," from *Meander Scars: Reflections on Healing the Willamette River* by Abby Phillips Metzger, copyright © 2013. Reprinted with the permission of Oregon State University Press.

Esther Stutzman, "The Beginnings of the Kalapuya People." Reprinted with her permission as the traditional story-keeper.

William Sullivan, Fort Hoskins and Beazell Memorial Forest descriptions, originally published in *100 Hikes / Travel Guide: Oregon Coast & Coast Range*, third edition. Copyright © 2012 by William L. Sullivan. Reprinted with the permission of the author.

Wendy Thompson, seventeen pieces of art reprinted with the permission of the artist.

Zach Urness, Willamette River Trail, Independence, originally published as "Independence trail features river views, riparian forest" in the *Statesman Journal* on March 27, 2013. Reprinted with the permission of the author.

David Wagner, four sketches originally published in *Eugene Weekly* and/or *Willamette Valley Nature Calendar*. Copyright © 1990–2014 by David Wagner. Reprinted with the permission of the artist. Bald eagle copyright © 2014 by David Wagner, reprinted with permission.

Index

Abbey Walk, Mount Angel Abbey, 268
Abiqua Falls, 270
Achterman, C. A. ("Welcome to Our Valley"), xix
Allen Throop Loop (Fitton Green Natural Area), 50
alter-abled, trail access for, xv
Ankeny National Wildlife Refuge, 215, 233

Bald Hill Natural Area and Bald Hill Farm, 51
 Bald Hill Summit Loop, 54
 Mulkey Creek Trail, 53
Bald Hill Summit Loop (Ball Hill Natural Area), 54
banana slugs, 58
Baskett Slough National Wildlife Refuge, 220
beavers, 181
Beazell Memorial Forest, 108
"The Beginnings of the Kalapuya People" (Esther Stutzman), 84
Benton County Scenic Loop, 77
biking, xvi
 Calapooia watershed, 96
  Brownsville to Peoria Loop via Thompson's Mills, 97
  River Valley Loop from Albany, 96
 Luckiamute watershed, 119
  Corvallis to the Buena Vista Ferry, 119
 Marys watershed, 76
  McDonald Forest, 76
  Philomath to Bellfountain County Park, 77
 Middle Willamette watershed, 233
  Independence to Ankeny National Wildlife Refuge, 233
 North Santiam watershed, 201
  Covered Bridge Loop from Stayton, 201
 Pudding watershed, 277
  Farmland Loop from Silverton, 277

 South Santiam watershed, 159
  Lebanon to Roaring River County Park, 159
 Yamhill watershed, 255
  Farmland Loop from Amity, 255
"Birds of the Mid-Willamette Valley" (Don Boucher and Lisa Millbank), 211
black bears, 112
Blackwell County Park, 242
"The Blessed Truth" (Kathleen Dean Moore), xi
Boucher, Don ("Birds of the Mid-Willamette Valley"), 211
Bowers Rock State Park, 87
Brownsville to Peoria Loop via Thompson's Mills (biking), 97
Brownsville's Pioneer Park, 100
Buck Mountain Loop (Silver Falls State Park), 265
Buena Vista Ferry, 121
Buena Vista Park to Independence Riverview Park (paddling), 32
Build Lebanon Trails, 136
Butte Creek Falls, 273

Calapooia River watershed, 81
Campbell, John R. ("Vision Begins: On Dixon Creek"), 18
Canby Ferry, 275
Cardwell Hill Right-of-Way Trail (Fitton Green Natural Area), 50
Cascadia Cave, 151
Cascadia State Park, 149
Champoeg State Heritage Area, 231
Cheadle Lake Park, 134
Chimney Peak Trail, 154
City of Albany Trails, 86
 Simpson Park Trail, 87
 Talking Water Gardens, 88
 Takena Landing Trail, 89
"Connecting with Your Great Oregon River" (Travis Williams), 25
Corvallis-to-Albany Multiuse Path, 76

Corvallis to the Buena Vista Ferry (biking), 119
Corvallis-to-the-Sea Trail, 48
cougars, 112
Covered Bridge Loop from Stayton (biking), 201
covered bridges, 151, 201
Crabtree Lake Trail, 142
Crabtree Valley, 142

Daniel, John ("Opal Creek"), 175
Dan's Trail to Dimple Hill (McDonald Forest), 59
Deer Creek County Park, 248
Duffy Lake Trail, 198
Dunn Forest, 110

East Ridge Trail (Marys Peak), 47
East Thornton Lake Natural Area, 89
Eckert, David ("Watersheds of the Mid-Willamette Valley"), 3
E. E. Wilson Wildlife Area, 113
Eola Bend County Park, 224
Erratic Rock State Natural Site, 250
ever-changing Willamette River, 207

false brome, 60
Farmland Loop from Amity (biking), 255
Farmland Loop from Silverton (biking), 277
Fender's blue butterfly, 222, 249
"The Fight for Opal Creek" (Carol Savonen), 170
fish passage and habitat, 129
Fishermen's Bend to Mehama (paddling), 204
Fitton Green Natural Area, 49
    Allen Throop Loop, 50
    Cardwell Hill Right-of-Way Trail, 50
flood of December 1861, 207, 224, 229, 231
floodplain in action, 278
"Following the Kalapuya Shadow Trails" (Laura McMasters), 238
Fort Hoskins Historic Park, 106
Fort Yamhill State Heritage Area, 244

Goodrich, Charles ("Reinhabiting the Valley: A Field Guide to Being Here"), 13
Grand Island Access to Rogers Landing (paddling), 35
Grand Ronde Reservation, 244
great horned owls, 55

Henline Falls Trail (Opal Creek Wilderness and Scenic Recreation Area), 188
Hesthavn Nature Center, 56
Homestead Loop (McDonald Forest), 57

Hughes, Henry ("Salmon on the Santiam"), 128

"Imagining the Marys" (Lee Anna Sherman), 39
Independence Riverview Park
    to Keizer Rapids Park (paddling), 32
    Willamette River Trail from, 218
Independence to Ankeny National Wildlife Refuge (biking), 233

Jackson-Frazier Wetland, 66
Joe Dancer Park, 254
John Neal Memorial County Park, 180
Jory soil, 62

Keizer Rapids Park, 226
    to Wheatland Boat Ramp (paddling), 34
Kendall Natural Area, 68
Kincaid's lupine, 222, 249
Kingston Prairie Preserve, 177
Kiwanis Marine Park, 254

Lafayette Locks County Park, 258
Larwood Wayside, 159, 161
lava flows and waterfalls, 264
Leave No Trace camping, 24
Lebanon-Santiam Canal, 135
Lebanon to Roaring River County Park (biking), 159
Little North Santiam Recreation Area, 190
Little North Santiam Trail (Opal Creek Wilderness and Scenic Recreation Area), 189
"Looking Back and Ahead: Protecting the Valley's Natural Treasures" (Michael Pope), 6
Lower Pudding to the Willamette (paddling), 278
Luckiamute Landing State Natural Area, 116
Luckiamute River watershed, 103

Marys Peak, 44
    East Ridge Trail, 47
    Meadow Edge Loop Trail, 46
    North Ridge Trail, 48
Marys River watershed, 37
McCartney Park to Peoria County Park (paddling), 28
McClun County Wayside to McKercher County Park (paddling), 100
McCulloch Peak, 60, 77
McDonald Forest, 56
    biking, 76
    Dan's Trail to Dimple Hill, 59
    Homestead Loop, 57

Old Growth Trail and Quarry Loop, 61
    Section 36 Loop / Powder House Trail,
        62
    Soap Creek Valley to McCulloch Peak
        Loop, 60
McDowell Creek Falls County Park, 140
McKercher County Park, 93
    to Brownsville (biking), 101
McMasters, Laura ("Following the Kalapuya
    Shadow Trails"), 238
Meadow Edge Loop Trail (Marys Peak), 46
Menagerie Wilderness, 152
Metzger, Abby Phillips ("Story Mapping"),
    9
Michael's Landing to Bryant Park
    (paddling), 31
Middle Santiam River, 154
Middle Willamette watershed, 207
Mill Creek county parks, 246
Millbank, Lisa ("Birds of the Mid-
    Willamette Valley"), 211
Miller Woods, 252
Mill Hill Loop (William L. Finley National
    Wildlife Refuge), 71
mining
    in the Little North Santiam watershed,
        189
    on Quartzville Creek, 146
Minto-Brown Island Park, 223
Minto Fish Collection Facility, 203
Molalla River State Park, 275
Moore, Kathleen Dean ("The Blessed
    Truth"), xi
Mount Angel Abbey, 268
Mount Jefferson Wilderness, 198
Mulkey Creek Trail (Bald Hill Natural
    Area), 53

Nelson's checkermallow, 249
Niagara County Park, 192
Niagara Falls, 242
northern spotted owls, 187
North Ridge Trail (Marys Peak), 48
"The North Santiam Microcosm" (Jamie
    Wyant), 166
North Santiam River watershed, 163
North Santiam State Recreation Area, 191
North Santiam Trail System, 164
nurse logs, 273

Ogle Mountain Trail, 188
Old Cascades, 152
old-growth forests, 194
Old Growth Trail and Quarry Loop
    (McDonald Forest), 61
"Opal Creek" (John Daniel), 175

Opal Creek Wilderness and Scenic
    Recreation Area, 185
    Henline Falls Trail, 188
    Little North Santiam Trail, 189
    Opal Pool Loop, 187
Opal Pool Loop (Opal Creek Wilderness and
    Scenic Recreation Area), 187
The Oregon Garden, 266
Oregon's dwindling white oaks, 236
origin of the name Willamette, 26
Over the River and Through the Woods
    Scenic Byway, 93

Pacific lamprey, 43
Packsaddle Park to Fishermen's Bend
    (paddling), 203
paddling, xvi
    Calapooia River, 99
        McClun County Wayside to
            McKercher County Park, 100
        McKercher County Park to
            Brownsville, 101
    Luckiamute River, 121
    Marys River, 79
    Mid-Willamette River, 23
        Buena Vista Park to Independence
            Riverview Park, 32
        Grand Island Access to Rogers
            Landing, 35
        Independence Riverview Park to
            Keizer Rapids Park, 32
        Keizer Rapids Park to Wheatland
            Boat Ramp, 34
        McCartney Park to Peoria County
            Park, 28
        Michael's Landing to Bryant Park, 31
        Peoria County Park to Michael's
            Landing, 30
        Takena Landing to Buena Vista Park,
            31
    North Santiam River, 202
        Packsaddle Park to Fishermen's
            Bend, 203
        Fishermen's Bend to Mehama, 204
    Pudding River, 278
        Lower Pudding to the Willamette,
            278
    South Santiam River, 160
        Sweet Home to Waterloo Park, 161
    Yamhill River, 256
Panther Rock Ridge, 260
Paul M. Dunn Forest, 110
Peoria County Park to Michael's Landing
    (paddling), 30
Pheasant Creek Falls, 242
Philomath to Bellfountain County Park
    (biking), 77
pillow basalts, 115

poison oak, 53
Pope, Michael ("Looking Back and Ahead: Protecting the Valley's Natural Treasures"), 6
Pudding River watershed, 259

Quartzville Scenic Byway, 144

"Reinhabiting the Valley: A Field Guide to Being Here" (Charles Goodrich), 13
Rhododendron Trail, Yellowbottom Recreation Site, 145
River Bend County Park, 147
River Valley Loop from Albany (biking), 96
Roaring River County Park, 159
Rooster Rock, 152

"Salmon on the Santiam" (Henry Hughes), 128
Santiam Wagon Road, Mountain House to House Rock, 157
Santiam Wagon Road trail system, 158
Sarah Helmick State Recreation Site, 121, 122, 123
Savonen, Carol ("The Fight for Opal Creek"), 170
Section 36 Loop / Powder House Trail (McDonald Forest), 62
Scotts Mills County Park, 274
Shellburg Falls Recreation Area, 182
Sherman, Lee Anna ("Imagining the Marys"), 39
Silver Creek Walk, 266
Silver Falls State Park, 262
    Buck Mountain Loop, 265
    Trail of Ten Falls, 262
Silverton, 266, 277
Simpson Park Trail (Albany), 87
Snag Boat Bend Unit, William L. Finley National Wildlife Refuge, 74
Soap Creek Valley to McCulloch Peak Loop (McDonald Forest), 60
South Breitenbush Gorge Trail, 194
South Santiam River watershed, 125
South Yamhill Trail, 254
splash dams, 82
Stahlman Point Trail, 197
"Story Mapping" (Abby Phillips Metzger), 9
Stutzman, Esther "(The Beginnings of the Kalapuya People"), 84
sustainable travel to natural areas, xvii
Sweet Home to Waterloo Park (paddling), 161

Takena Landing to Buena Vista Park (paddling), 31
Takena Landing Trail (Albany), 89

Talking Water Gardens (Albany), 88
Taylor's checkerspot butterfly, 51
Thompson's Mills State Heritage Site, 91
Three Pools Day Use Area, 185
Tidbits Mountain Trail, 94
trail access for the alter-abled, xv
Trail of Ten Falls (Silver Falls State Park), 262
Trout Creek to Rooster Rock, 152

"Vision Begins: On Dixon Creek" (John R. Campbell), 18

wapato, 31
Waterloo County Park, 138
"Watersheds of the Mid-Willamette Valley" (David Eckert), 3
water-treatment wetland, 88
"Welcome to Our Valley" (C. A. Achterman, M.D.), xix
West Cascades National Scenic Byway, 163
western meadowlarks, 179
western pearlshell mussels, 30
western pond turtles, 118
Wheatland Ferry, 230
white oaks, 236
wildfire in wilderness areas, 200
wildflowers of Marys Peak, 46
Willamette Mission State Park, 228
Willamette Park, 68
Willamette River Trail, Independence, 218
Willamette River Water Trail, 27
Willamette Valley ponderosa pine, 225
Willamette Valley Scenic Bikeway, 96
William L. Finley National Wildlife Refuge, 70
    Mill Hill Loop, 71
    Snag Boat Bend Unit, 74
    Woodpecker Loop, 72
Williams, Travis ("Connecting with Your Great Oregon River"), 25
winter steelhead, 270
wolf trees, 64
Woodpecker Loop (William L. Finley National Wildlife Refuge), 72
Wyant, Jamie ("The North Santiam Microcosm"), 166

Yamhill Oaks Preserve, 249
Yamhill River watershed, 235
yampah, 232
Yellowbottom Recreation Site, 145
yellow-legged frogs, 148